The
Reference Shelf®

Social Networking

Edited by

Kenneth Partridge

The Reference Shelf
Volume 83 • Number 1
The H.W. Wilson Company
New York • Dublin
2011

3/11

The Reference Shelf

The books in this series contain reprints of articles, excerpts from books, addresses on current issues, and studies of social trends in the United States and other countries. There are six separately bound numbers in each volume, all of which are usually published in the same calendar year. Numbers one through five are each devoted to a single subject, providing background information and discussion from various points of view and concluding with a subject index and comprehensive bibliography that lists books, pamphlets, and abstracts of additional articles on the subject. The final number of each volume is a collection of recent speeches, and it contains a cumulative speaker index. Books in the series may be purchased individually or on subscription.

Library of Congress has cataloged this serial title as follows:

Social networking / edited by Kenneth Partridge.
    p. cm. -- (Reference shelf ; v. 83, no. 1)
Includes bibliographical references and index.
ISBN 978-0-8242-1110-3 (alk. paper)
1. Online social networks. 2. Social media. I. Partridge, Kenneth, 1980-
  HM742.S629 2011
  302.30285--dc22

         2010051638

Cover: Facebook founder and CEO Mark Zuckerberg speaks during a news conference at Facebook headquarters August 18, 2010 in Palo Alto, California. Zuckerberg announced the launch of Facebook Places, a new application that allows Facebook users to document places they have visited. (Photo by Justin Sullivan/Getty Images).

Visit H.W. Wilson's Web site: www.hwwilson.com

Printed in the United States of America

Contents

Preface   vii

**I   From Bulletin Boards to Facebook: Social Networking
       Comes of Age**

Editor's Introduction   3
1. The Complete History of Social Networking—CBBS to Twitter.
       Michael Simon. MacLife.com.   5
2. What the Past Can Tell Us About the Future of Social Networking.
       Mark Suster. TechCrunch.   11
3. Facebook Boosts Smaller Groups. Benny Evangelista.
       The San Francisco Chronicle.   22
4. Is Foursquare the New Facebook? Helen A.S. Popkin. MSNBC.com.   25
5. The Life and Death of Online Communities. Phoebe Connelly.
       American Prospect.   28
6. Losing Its Cool. Mark Lacter. *Los Angeles Magazine.*   32
7. Will Social Networks Ever Make Money? Andrew Saunders.
       Management Today.   36

II   "Does Social Sell?" Doing Business in the Digital World

Editor's Introduction   45
1. Reaping Social Media Rewards. Lyndsie Bourgon. *Canadian Business.*   47
2. 7 Questions Key to Social Networking Success. John Soat.
       Information Week.   49
3. Deleted, De-Friended: Social Media Great for B2B Until You
       Misuse It. Brian Shappell. *Business Credit.*   55
4. The Tweet Life of CMOs. Barbara Lippert. *Mediaweek.*   59
5. Can You Measure the ROI of Your Social Media Marketing? Donna L.
       Hoffman and Marek Fodor. *MIT Sloan Management Review.*   62
6. Does Social Sell? Brian Morrissey. *Adweek.*   75

III   Tweeting for a Cause: Social Media Meets Politics and Activism

Editor's Introduction   83
1. Social Media Paves Obama's Way to White House.
       Michael Learmonth. *Advertising Age.*   85
2. Can the Mama Grizzlies Pull Off a Twitter Revolution?
       Noreen Malone. *Slate Magazine.*   88
3. Facebook Politicians Are Not Your Friends. Frank Rich.
       The New York Times.   91
4. In Social Media Election, the GOP Capitalizes. Jake Coyle.
       The Associated Press.   95
5. What You Need to Know About Social Networking.
       Pam Greenberg and Meagan Dorsch. *State Legislatures.*   98

6. Road Kill Social Media. Mark Hrywna. *The Non-Profit Times.*   103

IV   Tweeting is Fundamental: Social Media in the Schools
Editor's Introduction   109
1. Social Networking Goes to School. Michelle R. Davis.
   Education Week.   111
2. Social Media in the Classroom—For Kindergartners(!) Through
   High Schoolers. Renee Ramig. *MultiMedia & Internet @ Schools.*   117
3. Schools Get on Web 2.0 Bandwagon. Denise Smith Amos.
   The Cincinnati Enquirer.   121

V   Bullied, Spied On, Fired, Never Hired:
  The Dangers of Social Media
Editor's Introduction   127
1. Why We'll Never Escape Facebook. James Cowan. *Canadian Business.*   129
2. Social Media. Eileen Morgan Johnson.
   New York Public Personnel Law.   137
3. Addicted to Facebook. Scott Kerbs. *The Spectrum* (St. George, Utah).   147
4. Cyberbullies Ramp Up the Taunting—Anonymously.
   Roger Neumann. *Star-Gazette* (Elmira, N.Y.).   151

VI   The Social-Networking Phenomenon: What It Says About Us,
  How It Affects Our Lives
Editor's Introduction   157
1. With Friends Like These. Jeremy McCarter. *Newsweek.*   159
2. A Cyber-House Divided. *The Economist.*   163
3. Do You Own Facebook? Vanessa Grigoriadis. *New York Magazine.*   166
4. Curb Your Urge to Overshare. Fernanda Moore. *Women's Health.*   178
5. We Are Not Alone. Garvan Grant.
   Sunday Business Post (Dublin, Ireland).   182
6. The Web Means the End of Forgetting. Jeffrey Rosen.
   The New York Times.   184

Bibliography
Books   201
Web Sites   203
Additional Periodical Articles with Abstracts   205

Index   213

Preface

With the release of director David Fincher's 2010 film *The Social Network*, Facebook fans around the world met the man—or at least a fictionalized version of the man—behind their favorite pastime. His name is Mark Zuckerberg, and in 2004, while a student at Harvard University, he launched a Web site that, as of this printing, has attracted more than a half-billion members. Facebook is more streamlined and user-friendly than once-popular predecessors Friendster and MySpace, but it basically functions the same way, allowing users to "friend," or formally establish on-line relationships with, people with whom they share some connection. A typical Facebook user's friend list might include grade school pals, high school buddies, college roommates, passing acquaintances, coworkers, aunts and uncles, second cousins, and even computer-savvy parents.

Indeed, in 2011, it's no great exaggeration to say everyone and their mother is on Facebook.

When not sending friend requests and growing their lists of digital contacts, Facebook users spend their time playing games, responding to personal questionnaires, "tagging" each other in photos, posting links to articles of interest, and writing "status updates," or quick descriptions of what they're up to at any given moment. The subjects of people's status updates range from the mundane ("just ate cereal") to the monumental ("JUST GOT ENGAGED!!!"), and through such digital exchanges, Zuckerberg has said he aims to promote "openness" and help his generation satisfy its urge to share.

If *The Social Network* is at all accurate, Zuckerberg's claims are more than a little ironic. Much of the film details the programmer's legal battles with a disgruntled Facebook co-founder and a pair of twin brothers who claim Zuckerberg stole their idea. As played by actor Jesse Eisenberg, Zuckerberg is cool, aloof, and unreadable. Since he's not driven by money, his motives for making Facebook the most popular social-networking Web site of all time remain somewhat unclear. Does he want fame, respect, or simply the satisfaction of being the smartest person in the room? Whatever he's after, Fincher's film suggests, it's not friendship. Eisenberg's Zuckerberg spends the movie sulking around in flip-flips and hooded sweatshirts, talking down to anyone he deems intellectually inferior. (This, it turns out, is just about everyone.) All the while, millions of people use his software to connect with others and foster feelings of community and belonging.

The articles in this volume of The Reference Shelf take a broad look at the social-networking phenomenon, tracing its history, weighing its pros and cons, and raising some of the key questions Fincher's film asks us to consider. Among them: What do Facebook, its former competitor MySpace, the popular micro-blog platform Twitter, and other such sites say about society? Do they really encourage friendship, or have they cheapened the word?

The book opens with "From Bulletin Boards to Facebook: Social Networking Comes of Age," a primer course on social media past and present. Articles included in this chapter explain how the text-only message boards of the 1970s and gaudy, graphics-heavy GeoCities pages of the 1990s led to modern heavyweights Facebook and Twitter. In the piece "Will Social Networks Ever Make Money?" Andrew Saunders looks at how these and other leading sites are struggling to generate profits worthy of their enormous member bases.

Entries in the second chapter, " 'Does Social Sell?' Doing Business in the Digital World," explore how companies are using social-networking sites to promote their products. While the general consensus among marketing experts is that forward-thinking businesses need to establish themselves on-line, the costs can be high, and the benefits can be difficult to measure. A CEO's daily Facebook status updates or Twitter posts—called "Tweets"—might not lead directly to higher sales, but by refusing to enter the digital world, Luddite companies risk losing touch with the next generation of consumers.

For proof social media can be an effective means of swaying public opinion, marketers might look at how the Internet has transformed the political process. Selections in the third chapter, "Tweeting for a Cause: Social Media Meets Politics and Activism," look at how activists, nonprofit organizations (NPOs), and candidates for offices big and small are taking their messages on-line.

In "Tweeting is Fundamental: Social Media in the Schools," the collected articles explore the educational benefits of social networking. With proper safety precautions, some educators insist, social media can be used to broaden students' worldviews and encourage teachers to share ideas and craft innovative lesson plans. Not all districts are onboard, however, and following highly publicized cases of "cyberbullying"—one of the dangers referenced in the next section—and inappropriate student-teacher relations, some continue to block social-media sites.

Entries in the fifth chapter, "Bullied, Spied On, Fired, Never Hired: The Dangers of Social Media," outline the kinds of personal troubles that can result from joining an on-line network. As several of the articles point out, many employers now use Facebook to vet potential hires, and young people entering the workforce need to be mindful of maintaining clean digital footprints. One incriminating photo taken at a college kegger could mean the difference between a job offer and a missed opportunity.

The book ends with "The Social-Networking Phenomenon: What It Says About Us, How it Affects Our Lives," a look at how social media has shaped and been shaped by society. Authors of the included articles offer both positive and negative criticisms of on-line networks, alternately praising them as revolutionary communication tools and dismissing them as colossal wastes of time.

Having now edited five volumes of The Reference Shelf, I know these books are only as good as the articles they contain. With that in mind, I would like to extend my sincerest gratitude to the many authors and publishers who granted permission to reprint the material that follows. I would also like to thank my H.W. Wilson colleagues Paul McCaffrey and Richard Stein—editors I'm proud to consider friends in the old-fashioned, pre-Zuckerberg sense—and my wife, Lindsey, even if she's sometimes too entranced by Facebook to hear what I'm saying.

Kenneth Partridge
February 2011

1

From Bulletin Boards to Facebook:
Social Networking Comes of Age

Editor's Introduction

In economics, the term "network effect" explains why some goods grow increasingly valuable the more popular they become. The classic example is the telephone. After the first was built, it was imperative inventors add a second—otherwise, there would have been no one to call, and the device would have been useless. As more and more people acquired telephones, the prospect of owning one became all the more attractive, and soon they were ubiquitous in households around the world.

The same principle applies to social networking, the history of which we explore in this chapter. Such leading sites as Facebook and Twitter boast millions of members, and it's partially because they're so popular that they continue to expand. When signing up means being able to converse with coworkers, old high-school crushes, distant relations, and that charming barista you met last week, even the technophobic have reason to do so.

Social networking hasn't always been so popular and user-friendly. In "The Complete History of Social Networking—CBBS to Twitter," the piece that opens the chapter, Michael Simon traces the phenomenon back to a snowy January day in 1978, when a pair of Chicago computer enthusiasts hunkered down and wrote the code for the CBBS, or computerized bulletin board system. The CBBS was little more than a digital corkboard, allowing members of the Chicago Area Computer Hobbyists Exchange to announce meetings and plan group chip-buying outings, but as Simon explains, that idea started the movement that would eventually render "friend" a verb and vault the word "Tweet" into the popular lexicon.

The history lesson continues with "What the Past Can Tell Us About the Future of Social Networking," originally a series of blog posts by Internet entrepreneur and venture capitalist Mark Suster. While Suster praises Facebook for allowing third-party developers to create and make money on the apps and innovations that keep the site fresh, he looks ahead to a time when users can transport their social graphs—contact information for friends, essentially—to other platforms. In the future, he predicts, people will join smaller, more topic-specific social networks, perhaps bringing an end to Facebook's dominance.

In "Facebook Boasts Smaller Groups," the next selection, Benny Evangelista looks at how the world's largest social-networking platform is attempting to tweak its design and create an experience that more closely resembles the way people interact in the real world. With the creation of its "Groups" feature, Facebook has enabled users to organize "friends"—the catchall term for all on-line contacts—according to subcategories, such as coworkers, family members, softball teammates, etc. It's now possible to post messages and photos that will only be seen by certain people—a useful feature, since as analyst Ray Valdes tells Evangelista, "We all have multiple independent sets of friends. But you don't necessarily want them all to co-mingle."

Of course, Facebook's motives aren't purely altruistic. The company ultimately wants to make money, as does the rival platform Helen A.S. Popkin discusses in this chapter's next article, "Is Foursquare the New Facebook?" Foursquare is a location-based social-networking site that encourages users to "check in," or broadcast their whereabouts, from stores, restaurants, and other such locations. It's a way for people to share dining and travel tips and keep track of their own comings and goings, but it's also a chance for Foursquare to sell advertising. As Popkin puts it, "All these new-fangled social networks that play to our narcissism and our need to belong are tools for capitalism."

Among the early sites Simon mentions in his social-networking history is Geo-Cities, the subject of Phoebe Connelly's "The Life and Death of Online Communities," the next selection in this chapter. Launched in 1994, GeoCities helped the Internet's first wave of self-publishers create their own homepages. By October 1997, GeoCities had attracted more than a million users, or "homesteaders," many of whom built elaborate pages dedicated to hobbies and pop-cultural interests and decorated with animated GIF (graphics interchange format) files—moving pictures now seen as humorously anachronistic. While GeoCities was ultimately done in by bad business decisions and the rise of blogs and other, more sophisticated competitors, the site remains a point of interest for the digital historians working to archive the millions of homepages that tell the tale of the Internet's awkward formative years.

In the competitive world of social media, the network effect isn't the only thing that causes some sites to flourish and others to flounder. In "Losing Its Cool," the subsequent article, Mark Lacter looks at how the once-mighty MySpace has lost its all-important hip factor and fallen out of favor with taste-making young people. Since 2005, when media mogul Rupert Murdoch's News Corp. purchased the company for $580 million, MySpace has lost users to the more streamlined, less youth-oriented Facebook. In order to survive, Lacter writes, MySpace should target younger users and focus on streaming music and videos.

While such major sites as MySpace, Facebook, and Twitter have proven capable of signing up millions of members, they've struggled to turn those numbers into major profits. As Andrew Saunders explains in "Will Social Networks Ever Make Money?" the final piece in this chapter, the top social-networking sites are in the midst of figuring out how to transition from growing their user bases to making money. Advertisements provide some revenue, but down the line, Saunders writes, sites will need to open up new streams. The answer may lie in "analytics"—consumer data that can be culled from users and sold to companies.

The Complete History of Social Networking—CBBS to Twitter[*]

By Michael Simon
MacLife.com, December 14, 2009

It was Jan. 16, 1978, and the world was in transition. The Sex Pistols were on the verge of disbanding. Future Macintosh architect Jef Raskin was settling into his new job at Apple Computer Inc. And it was snowing in Chicago. A lot.

But while Ward Christensen and Randy Suess, two members of the Chicago Area Computer Hobbyists Exchange, were holed up during the not-so-great blizzard of '78, they weren't wasting their time playing Uno or watching "Logan's Run." They were making history.

Just two weeks after that fateful snowstorm (though the pair waited another two weeks to unveil their creation, since "no one believed it could be written in two weeks of spare time"), the world's first online social network was born.

ALL POINTS BULLETIN BOARD

It all started with former IBM employee Christensen's simple concept.

> At our club meetings, we had a cork board and push-pin bulletin board, with 3x5 cards with things like Need ride to next meeting, Let's get together for a group-purchase of memory chips, Anyone else have a KIM-1? etc. So, I came up with the idea of computerizing that.

Dubbed CBBS (Computerized Bulletin Board System), Christensen and Suess developed a virtual system where users could post public messages akin to an office cork board. Built to utilize Wards own MODEM (later XMODEM) file transfer protocol, CBBS was created to fill a specific need—informing the groups other members of their group about meetings and important announcements without placing dozens of phone calls—but as more members began to dial in to talk and share information through individual postings, the early makings of a small virtual community began to emerge.

The original CBBS ran off a S-100 motherboard kit that Suess had purchased at "some fleamarket" and was limited by its inability to allow simultaneous users. But that's not to say Suess' brainchild wasn't impressive:

> (The S-100) was mounted on a BUD chassis with a single density 8 inch floppy drive. On the motherboard was some 8080 cpu (upgraded to a Z80) a Hayes 300 baud modem card, a 3P+S board with the parallel port used for control signals, a Processor Technology VDM video display card, and an 8k memory board. There was also a card with 8 1702 EEPROMS that held the CP/M BIOS, video display drivers, and debug code, all written by Ward. I had a EPROM burner, and Ward made sure all the BIOS variables and experimentor stuff ended up in the last 1702. Musta re-programmed that sucker 10 times a week for a few months.

All that reprogramming paid off. While CBBS didn't exactly set the world on fire—after all, only a select few could take advantage of it—other ASCII bulletin boards followed its lead and began to pop up across a variety of platforms (including AppleNet and GBBS for the Apple II), each with a specific purpose. In the early 1980s, Bulletin Board Systems slowly began to become more streamlined as the Microsoft Disk Operating System brought a measure of standardization to the industry; not long after, MS-DOS BBS programs—pioneered by RBBS-PC and Fido—sprouted up as modem speed improved and boards attracted more members.

As bulletin boards expanded, so did their scope, and soon members began to actually converse with each other, replying and responding to posts as multi-user capability became available. One of the first of these types of communities, the Whole Earth 'Lectronic Link (WELL), was conceived in 1985 as a place for Stewart Brand's Whole Earth Review readers and contributors to voice their opinions and bounce ideas off one other and grew into one of the oldest, most respected boards around.

But it wasnt until the rise of commercial Internet service providers—first Compuserve, followed by AOL, Prodigy, EarthLink and others—when social networking truly began to take shape.

CONNECT THE DOT-COMS

As ISPs opened the Internet to anyone with a phone line, once-exclusive clubs became overrun with members, and the desire for individuality quickly took root. Bulletin boards certainly had their place in the fledgling World Wide Web, but a few sites began to offer users more variety and personality with a focus on establishing unique online identities.

One of the earliest and most successful of these virtual metropolises was BHI (Beverly Hills Internet), which turned the BBS concept on its head. Instead of scanning a giant board to find a topic worth discussing, BHI users (dubbed Homesteaders) chose one of several specialized neighborhoods to call their home. Inside, community members were introduced to a brave new world of HTML that most of them used to create god-awful representations of themselves. As more users began to crowd BHIs chat rooms, galleries, member pages and, of course, message boards—to the tune of six million page views a month—a more suitable name was slapped on the site in late 1995.

Now known as GeoCities, the community flourished in the face of stiff competition from Tripod, Xoom and Angelfire, and by 1997 boasted a Homesteader population of more than a million members.

Around the same time, a pair of Cornell students were launching a boom town of their own called theglobe.com. Built much like GeoCities—but without the Hollywood gloss—the network gave users the freedom to personalize their on-line experiences by publishing their own content and interacting with others with similar interests. Ultimately doomed by its own inventiveness, theglobe became the poster boy for the dot-com bubble, posting a record IPO that fell from $850 million to barely $4 million in less than three years.

But while theglobe may have faded more quickly than its peers, its impact on the social networking world cannot be denied. Founders Todd Krizelman and Stephan Paternot saw in the Internet a way to shrink the world by linking people's common likes and dislikes, a concept even Apple tried to tap into with the launch of its eWorld online service on June 20, 1994. Built around a Community Center where ePeople would gather to meet and mingle, the high-priced eWorld experiment struggled to attract members, lasted less than two years and barely registered on the social-networking radar.

But while GeoCities and theglobe.com struggled to squeeze money out of their significant membership rolls, one specialized service hit on on idea that immediately paid dividends. Founded in 1995 by ex-Boeing exec Randal Conrads, Classmates.com promptly filled a need no one realized they had. Born out of a basic desire to help people rekindle their youth, Conrads archetypal site ignited a torrent of grads eager to hook up with old flames, football buddies, lab partners and crushes.

Registration, as expected, was initially free, but as more and more matches were made, Classmates.com eventually adopted a subscription format that set it apart from its contemporaries. Tens of millions of users signed up to track down their school chums—to varying success; reports of spam, overcharging and cancellation issues plagued the site for years—and its self-contained business model (all communication was routed through Classmates.com's servers) became a paradigm for future networks. An equally successful subscription site, Reunion.com (later MyLife.com), started in 2002 and expanded Classmate.com's objective well beyond the classroom.

(As social networking was still finding its legs, a new method of communication called instant messaging was sweeping the globe, propelled by the 1997 release of AOL Instant Messenger. Though mostly limited to friends you actually knew, IM's system of short, rapid correspondences had no small impact on the proliferation of online communities.)

A bona fide precursor to the modern social networking sites, the short-lived SixDegrees.com (1997–2001) didn't attach any strings or conditions to its match-making. After setting up an account, users with similar likes and dislikes logically began to fill each others rings based on the strength of their connection (closest friends occupied the fifth degree and so on) to create—quite literally—a circle of friends. Inventive and popular, but saddled by an unprofitable, ad-supported system, SixDegrees was sold in 2000 and jettisoned shortly thereafter.

Its focus on indirect relationships, however, didn't go unnoticed. In March 2003, programmer Jonathan Abrams launched the first site that got everything right. Melding many of its predecessors finer points, Friendster was an immediate hit, attracting some three million registrants inside of its first six months. On a path to make "friend" a verb long before Facebook hit the scene and took over a niche it basically created, Friendster should've become a household word. Instead it fell victim to its own success.

As Friendsters logs grew, the site's servers struggled to handle the traffic and performance slowed to a virtual crawl—it's still slower than 85 percent of sites, according to Alexa Internet—but Abrams was too focused on the future to worry about the nagging problems of the present. In November 2003, the free-wheeling CEO spurned a Google buyout offer of $30 million with dreams of turning Friendster into a multi-billion dollar enterprise. Turns out he could have used the muscle.

MYSPACE INVADERS

A few months before the Google offer, a small group of L.A.-based eUniverse employees (and Friendster members) trained their sights on knocking the social network site off its lofty perch. Using the full lot of their company's resources—including all 250 colleagues, who were tasked with joining and signing up at least 10 buddies—MySpace hit the ground running and never really slowed down.

Armed with deep pockets and a vast database, co-founders Chris DeWolf and Tom Anderson utilized eUniverse's marketing savvy to quickly set itself apart from Friendster. By giving users total control over content and peddling their site as a true virtual self-expression, musicians, celebrities, movies, TV shows, start-ups, presidential candidates and every adolescent with access to a computer soon flocked to MySpace to establish online identities.

While DeWolf reportedly toyed with the notion of a monthly MySpace subscription fee, the site's founders ultimately decided on an ad-generation system that attached semi-obtrusive banners to individual sites; a later platform, dubbed HyperTargeting, sharpened this model by routing advertisers to sites based on users specific interests. After it was sold to Rupert Murdoch's News Corp. in July 2005—barely two years after its founding—MySpace aggressively expanded its role as a social networker with MySpaceIM (instant messaging), MySpaceTV (video sharing), MySpace Classified (personal ads) and MySpace Mobile in an attempt to keep pace with the new kid on the block who was making a lot of noise.

As our social actions become both public and location specific it opens up all types of future potential use cases. One obvious one is dating where players like Skout are trying to cash in on. When you think about it, young and single people go out to bars and clubs in hopes of meeting people to "hook up" with. In a perfect world you'd like that person to be compatible with you in additional to being attracted to them, yet as a society we go into bars and have no idea what is behind any of the people we see other than the immediacy of their looks and whether we can get enough liquid courage into ourselves to talk with them and learn more.

It's obvious to me that the future of dating will involve mobile, social networks that tell us more about the compatibility of the people around us. It doesn't take a rocket scientist to see how big people like Match.com and eHarmony became on the trend of helping us find our dating partners and why this would be improved by mobile, social networks. How long this trend takes is unclear—but in 10 years I feel confident we'll look back and say, "duh."

FourSquare obviously brings up a lot of interesting commercial opportunities. For years I saw companies pitching themselves as "mobile coupon companies" and I never believed this would be a big idea. I'm not a big believer that people walk around with their mobile devices and say, "let me now pull out my device and see whether there are any coupons around me." I always said that if an application could engage the user in some other way—like a game—it would earn the right to serve up coupons as a by-product. I think that is what FourSquare has done well.

In the future I don't believe that FourSquare's "check-in" game with badges will be enough to hold users' interests but for now it's working well. I've always said that if FourSquare has a "second act" coming it could be a really big company. In the long-run I believe that check-ins will be more seamless—something handled by infrastructure in the background. So I expect more and new games from Four-Square in the future. One awesome feature of today's FourSquare that often isn't talked about is the ability to graph your friends on a real-time map and see where everybody is. This is a killer feature for the 20 and 30 something crowds for sure. Me? When I go out I mostly prefer to eat in peace with my wife and friends without people knowing where we are—I guess we all get old.

In the first post we talked about the history of social networking from 1985–2002 dominated by CompuServe, AOL and Yahoo! In the second post we talked about the current era which covers Web 2.0 (blogs, YouTube, MySpace, Facebook), Real-Time (Twitter) and mobile (FourSquare).

Is the game over? Have Facebook and Twitter won or is there another act? No prizes for guessing . . . there's ALWAYS a second act in technology.

THE FUTURE: WHERE IS SOCIAL NETWORKING HEADED NEXT?

1. The Social Graph Will Become Portable

Right now our social graph (whom we are connected to and their key information like email addresses) is mostly held captive by Facebook. There is growing

---

FACE TO FACEBOOK

It all started with Harvard computer science major Mark Zuckerberg's juvenile concept.

In October 2003, an inebriated Zuckerberg hacked into some of his compatriots' "face books" and set up his own site, Facemash, to compare their less-pleasing attributes in a split-screen comparison. It lasted just a few days before school administrators shut it down, but the seed was planted.

The following semester Zuckerberg gathered three of his roommates—Chris Hughes, Dustin Moskovitz and Eduardo Saverin—and set to work on creating a universal face book for Harvard students. Wildly popular on campus, Zuckerberg quickly opened up thefacebook.com to other universities (Stanford, Columbia and Yale joined first in March) and by June, the whole operation had moved to California.

Not to be contained to higher education, Facebook (which dropped its "the" and capitalized the "F" in August 2005) expanded to add high school networks later in 2005 and opened its doors to the rest of the world in September 2006. With a healthy buzz already brewing, a cadre of MySpacers confined by their cluttered, ad-laden pages swiftly jumped ship, and by year's end some 12 million registered users were already intermingling.

Light on customization but just as heavy on content, Facebook's clean, uniform pages, instant status updates and orderly Wall of messages forever altered the landscape, and Zuckerberg's vision of a mature, sophisticated system of correspondence may have saved social networking from eventually succumbing to the next hip, young fad.

MEMBERS ONLY

While Facebook and MySpace were dueling for supremacy, other sites eager for a piece of the expanding pie were left to fight over the scraps with an array of professional alliances, specialized clubs, cultural leagues and plain old copycats.

In 2004, Ezer Ratchaga launched his holistic personal networked called Friend-Circles as a place to organize around hobbies, interests or career goals; and a few months later, Tagged.com opened a site targeted to teens. By 2005, webcam junkies had Stickam and news hounds were flocking to Buzznet to share Hurricane Katrina survival stories—everyone from nightclubbers to artists were given a social niche on the Web.

One notable exception to the field of wannabes was Bebo, a personalized blogging site launched in early 2005. An acronym for Blog Early, Blog Often, Bebo founder Michael Birch, found far greater enthusiasm for his site in his homeland of England than the United States. With an assertive overseas push (Bebo was originally based in San Francisco where his wife and Bebo co-founder, Xochi, grew up),

born under the idea that most of the information shared there was open and viewable by anybody. This was revolutionary in thinking and worked because as a user you understood this bargain when you started. Twitter is not the place to share pictures of your kids with your family.

Another Twitter's innovation was "asymmetry" because you didn't have to have a two-way following relationship to be connected. You could follow people who didn't necessarily follow you back. This allowed followers to be able to "curate" their newsfeed with people that they found interesting. Twitter restricts each post to 140 characters so users often share links with other people—one of the most important features of Twitter. So this combination of following people you found interesting who share links drove a sort of "news exchange" that mimicked many of the features of RSS readers except that it was curated by other people!

Twitter is much more. I've written extensively on the topic, but in a nutshell it is: an RSS reader, a chat room, instant messaging, a marketing channel, a customer service department and increasingly a data mine.

But what is magic about Twitter is that it is real time. In most instances news is now breaking on Twitter and then being picked up by news organizations.

The one major thing that Twitter doesn't seem to have figured out quite yet is that platform thing or at least how to encourage a bunch of 3rd-party developers to build meaningful add-on products. Twitter seems to have become a bit allergic to third-party developers (or maybe vice-versa). 18 months ago 25% of all pitches to me were ideas for how to build products around Twitter's API. Now I don't get any. Not one. Yet the number of businesses looking to build on the Facebook platform seems to have increased.

Given I'm a passionate user of Twitter, I sure hope somebody there will re-read the MySpace vs. Facebook section above. Lesson learned (to me at least)—let people get stinking rich off your platform and tax 'em later. That way other companies innovate on their own shekels (or at least a VC's) and let the best man win. Close shop to try and control monetization and you can only rely on your own internal innovation machine and capital. Seems kinda obvious or am I missing something? Rupert?

SOCIAL NETWORKING IS BECOMING MOBILE: FOURSQUARE AND SKOUT

The trend that is unfolding before our eyes is that Social Networking is now becoming mobile and that adds new dimensions to how we use social networks. The most obvious change is that now social networks become "location aware." The highest profile brand in this space is FourSquare. Pundits are mixed on whether FourSquare represents a major technology trend or a fad but undoubtedly it has captured the zeitgeist of the technology elite at this moment in time. At a minimum it has been a trailblazer of innovation that a generation of companies is trying to copy.

pressure on Facebook to make this portable and they have made some progress on this front. Ultimately I don't believe users or society as a whole will accept a single company "locking in" our vital information.

Facebook will succumb to pressure and over time make this available to us to allow us more choice in being part of several social networks without having to spam all of our friends again. I know in 2010 this doesn't seem obvious to everybody but it's my judgment. Either they make our social graph portable or we'll find other networks to join. I predict this will come before the end of 2012.

2. We Will Form Around "True" Social Networks: Quora, HackerNews, Namesake, StockTwits

Since 2006 I have been lamenting what I see as "the Facebook problem"—they are trying to lump me into one big social network. Nobody exists in one social network. I have the one with my friends where I want to talk about how wasted we were at the party last weekend that I don't want to share with my family network where I share pictures of the kids with my parents and siblings.

I don't want either of these mixed with the business social network in which I want to maintain the appearance that I'm "all business" and certainly don't want to see college pictures of me in Mexico floating around. I don't want to mix my "public network" with my "private networks." Facebook has jumbled these all together and then tried to bandage it by making groups available. I don't think this really solves the problem.

And young people aren't stupid—they certainly aren't as digitally naïve as their elders like to think. To get around all of this jumbling of social graphs they simply create multiple Facebook accounts under pseudonyms or "nom du guerre" for their real discussions and more pristine Facebook accounts for their real names. I wonder how many of Facebook's 500 million users are created for this purpose? I've confirmed this trend with several young people.

I believe that people already form topical social networks as evidenced in places like HackerNews or Quora. We are also seeing the growth of social networks around topics of interest like StockTwits for people interested in investing in the stock market. There are new networks forming to try and address the needs of specific social networks such as Namesake that is in its experimental stage but sees a world in which people want to network outside of Facebook.

3. Privacy Issues Will Continue to Cause Problems: Diaspora

Facebook made a deal with us that our social network was private. When they jealously watched the rise of Twitter they decided that it should be made more public, but that wasn't the bargain we made when we signed up in the first place. If I were Facebook I would have simply created two places where you could network, Facebook "private" and Facebook "open." The latter product could have competed directly with Twitter and could have had an asymmetric follow model.

Sure, we would have had to choose which followers to have in that separate timeline and they wouldn't have gotten all the synergies that they have by just lumping them together. But if they would have done it this way they never would have crossed the ethical lines that they did and we could all just love Facebook instead of our love-hate relationships. I'm still there daily to see pictures of my nieces and nephews—but I never connect more broadly with anybody in the business community. So 95% of my social networking time goes to Twitter.

I know most people aren't troubled by the loosening of their information—but I believe that's because most people don't understand it.

What I realized in working with so many startup technology firms is that even if you don't give permission to third-party apps to access your information much of it is available anyways as long as somebody you're connected to is more promiscuous with third-party apps. Also, all of those "Facebook Connect" buttons on websites are awesome for quickly logging in, but each gives those websites unprecedented access to your personal information.

I believe that privacy leaks will cause a longer-term backlash against misusing our information but in the short-term not enough people understand the consequences to be alarmed. Diaspora was created in direct response to the growing concerns about Facebook privacy and lock-in. Whether or not Diaspora will take off is anybody's guess. But a lot of people would love to see them or similar players emerge.

4. Social Networking Will Become Pervasive: Facebook Connect Meets Pandora, NYTimes

As our social graph becomes more portable I believe that social networking will become a feature in everything we do. You can already see it slipping into services like Pandora where my social graph instantly appears and my friends' musical tastes are displayed without my knowing this would happen. On NY Times I'm getting recommended articles by friends and I didn't explicitly turn this feature on. This trend of social pervasiveness will continue.

5. Third-Party Tools Will Embed Social Features in Websites: Meebo

One thing that is obvious to me is that while many websites want to have Facebook Connect log-ins to know more about you, they don't really know what to do with you once they have that information. They're mostly now thinking about serving demographically targeted ads to you, but that's not very interesting. Third-party software companies will start to offer features to websites to actually drive social features. This will take a few years but players such as Meebo are already innovating in this category though their toolbar.

6. Social Networking (like the web) Will Split Into Layers: SimpleGeo, PlaceIQ

One of the most interesting trends in the last few years has been watching the Internet split into layers. At the bottom end of the stack is storage (S3) and processing (EC2). At the top end is the business logic created by startups and established technology companies. I'm going to write a whole post on BothSid.es in the next few weeks on the layering of the Internet and the most important layer that will emerge in the next few years. We know that the layering of the PC era led to huge innovation at each layer in the stack and I expect the same to continue to emerge on the Internet. But for now suffice it to say that we're already seeing this happen in social networks.

One interesting layer is the "mapping layer" that is emerging in mobile social networks. If every startup had to figure out the locations of every business, what type of business they were and where they were located on a map we'd have very few startups. SimpleGeo is designed with the idea that startups can create new mobile products without having to each build their own mapping functionality. This is an awesome trend and will further lower the cost of startup development. I predict that SimpleGeo will do well in the mapping layer but I see more innovative companies emerging at the data layer.

And there are other companies racing to create horizontal platforms. One I saw recently was PlaceIQ. Their goal is to create a horizontal platform that allows marketers or developers to know a lot more about the geo-locations and not just the specific businesses/points-of-interest. They're capturing information about the demographics of map tiles, levels of LBS activity, what certain zones are known for (i.e. romantic spot, financial district) and want to make this available to others.

7. Social Chaos Will Create New Business Opportunities: Sprout Social, CoTweet, awe.sm, LocalResponse

We know that Twitter is leading to customer service opportunities for businesses but the opposite is also true. If you don't manage what is said about you in social networks it could be detrimental. Products such as Sprout Social and CoTweet are emerging to help businesses better track and communicate with their customers and leads. Products like awe.sm (I'm an investor) will help you manage the efficacy of your social media marketing campaigns.

And one of the cooler new products that will emerge in 2011 is called LocalResponse and is being created by Nihal Mehta, who has pivoted from his previous company Buzzd, but I'm sworn to secrecy on what he's up to until he releases it publicly. I saw the product recently in New York and loved it. It will address the world of what happens to businesses when consumers are increasingly mobile and social.

8. Data Will Reign Supreme: Bit.ly, Datasift and Klout

One thing has become clear in the era of "participation" is that as more people create content the more important the ability to sift through data, organize it, share it, analyze it and present meta-data/trends will become. I think this is already becoming obvious. If you look at the power of Bit.ly it's not because you can create short links but because of the analytics that bit.ly provides you. For this reason one of the most important companies for me at TC Disrupt was Datasift. They're based in London. My view is if they were based in Silicon Valley they would be hot, hot, hot.

The explosion of data is creating opportunities just in the management of the data in and of itself. Once we're uber connected and getting information online from people we've only met online we need to know more about the "authority" of the people we're following. Enter Klout, a service that tracks the influence of individuals in social networks. It can be imported into other products (e.g. StockTwits) where you really want to know more about the person giving you advice.

9. Facebook Will Not be the Only Dominant Player

I know that in 2010 it seems ridiculous to say anything other than "Facebook has won—the war is over" and I know that it feels that way right now. Facebook is so dominant it is astounding. In a complete return to where we all began with AOL—the world is "closed" again as Facebook has become this generation's walled garden. When you're on Facebook you're not on the Internet—you're on the InterNOT. It is an amazing service and I use it regularly myself (although much less than I use Twitter). But it makes me laugh to now see so many brands advertising their "fan pages" as they did their AOL Keywords back in the day. Plus ça change . . .

Well, here's a quick history primer that may change your mind:

1. In 1998 the Department of Justice launched an anti-trust case against Microsoft. People feared they were going to have a monopoly over the Internet due to "bundling" Internet Explorer with their operating system. A bit laughable in 2010, just 12 years later. These days people would sooner fear Apple than Microsoft, proving that reality is stranger than fiction.

2. In April of 2000 there were fears that the AOL/Time Warner merger would create a monopoly on the Internet. As you know, Time Warner eventually spun off AOL for peanuts. AOL is in the process of rebuilding itself and emulating a little-known LA-based startup called Demand Media. AOL seems to be doing great things to reinvent itself under the leadership of Tim Armstrong, but monopoly? Never.

3. In May 2007 there were fears that Google was becoming a monopoly. It controlled two-thirds of all Internet searches in the US and as we all knew—search was inevitably going to be the portal to finding information on the Internet. Or was it? We now know that social networking is having a profound impact on how we discover and share content online.

4. So . . . November 2010 and Facebook has 500 million users. They have more page views than even Google. More than 10% of all time on the web is now Facebook. They have become a juggernaut in online advertising, pictures, video and online games. And now they want to revolutionize email. It is no doubt that the next decade belongs to Facebook. But the coincidence is that 10 years out will be 2020 and it's when we look back from that date I'm certain that people will find a Facebook monopoly a bit laughable.

Facebook Boosts Smaller Groups[*]

By Benny Evangelista
The San Francisco Chronicle, October 9, 2010

Most Facebook members seemed to be content having one big circle of friends, with photos, status updates, news items and other "likes" visible to anyone inside the circle whether they cared or not.

But Facebook, which never seems to be content with leaving well enough alone, now wants to push its more than 500 million members into dividing their big circles into smaller circles based on why they are connected with each friend in the first place.

With Groups, the new feature that Facebook began rolling out this week, family members won't be inundated with status updates on topics that only co-workers would understand.

Or a Facebook member can group high school buddies to openly discuss topics that would shock his or her church friends.

With Groups, Facebook is hoping to solve what CEO Mark Zuckerberg called "the biggest problem in social networking," finding a way to replicate online how people organize themselves socially in the real world.

"No one has just one single group of friends who are all alike and homogeneous," said analyst Ray Valdes of Gartner Research. "We all have multiple independent sets of friends. But you don't necessarily want them to all co-mingle."

There have already been complaints that Groups can unleash a deluge of e-mail notifications and potentially opens the way for more spam. And critics note that friends can easily add to a group a user who may not want to join.

Tech blogger and entrepreneur Jason Calacanis, for example, complained directly to Zuckerberg in an e-mail, saying he was "force-joined" without his consent to a group named "NAMBLA," which apparently had nothing to do with a controversial organization of the same name. Zuckerberg was also added to the group.

[*] Article by Benny Evangelista from *The San Francisco Chronicle* October 9, 2010. Copyright © *The San Francisco Chronicle*. Reprinted with permission.

The company, however, says that members can only be added to a group by a recognized friend. The member can choose to leave the group, which blocks them from being reinstated unless they request it.

CHANCE FOR CONTROL

And Kurt Opsahl, senior staff attorney for the Electronic Frontier Foundation, said in a blog post that, if widely adopted, Groups "goes a long way to providing users even more control over their contextual privacy."

"To get the most out of social networking without unduly sacrificing privacy, it is critical that users be able to easily share information with subsets of one's Facebook friends," he said.

Why is Facebook Inc. adding Groups, one of several upgrades introduced in recent weeks? Valdes said Facebook wants to take pre-emptive strikes against potential competition, especially Google Inc.

"Using a sports metaphor, it's both offense and defense," Valdes said. "It's offense in that it really moves the ball forward in terms of fleshing out the overall Facebook experience. It's defense in that it's a blocking maneuver from this potential threat from Google or any other company that wants to be a major player in the social sector, whether it's Yahoo or Microsoft or Twitter."

Valdes noted that three months ago, Google researcher Paul Adams published an online slide presentation that highlighted how Facebook's big social circle design did not reflect how people organize themselves in real life.

Adams illustrated the point with a San Diego woman who teaches swimming to children, yet loved to comment about friends who posted about their wild nights in a Los Angeles bar.

'LOCKDOWN' STRATEGY

Not so coincidentally, Valdes said, Zuckerberg soon had his engineers hunkered down in a 60-day "lockdown," working long hours seven days a week in Facebook's Palo Alto headquarters to find solutions to problems. Groups is one of the innovations that came out of that lockdown.

During a news conference, Zuckerberg stressed that others have tried solving this problem with computer algorithms, a veiled reference to Google's much-derided Buzz social-networking service.

Instead, Groups uses what Valdes calls a "friend-sourcing" model, getting Facebook members to do the work of deciding which groups to form and who should be included.

Facebook has long let members organize friends by different lists, such as co-workers and families. But only 5 percent—which still equals more than 25 million people—took the time to create lists.

"It felt too much like work," Valdes said.

By default, Groups are "closed," which means only those already admitted can view the content and discussions, although the subject and membership list is public. Groups can also be set to "open," where the content is public, and "secret," which keeps the membership list and content blocked from public view.

GROUP CHATS

Within a group, members can post discussion topics and initiate a live group chat. They can also create a special group e-mail address and edit shared documents.

Zuckerberg said that even if a small percentage of members go to the trouble of forming a group, the idea will spread virally as members invite others to participate, eventually spreading to cover about 80 percent of Facebook members.

Indeed, membership in a group of noted tech reporters and bloggers that formed even before the news conference ended grew overnight to more than 100.

Michael Murdock, who heads a website consulting firm in Arizona, complained that Facebook needs to make it easier for members to avoid getting deluged by notifications.

"What Facebook should do is group the group who created this nightmare and toss them into the parking lot and make them 'dance for their lives,'" Murdock said in an e-mail to *The Chronicle*.

"What they fail yet again to tell people is that when you sign up for this or get added to a group that you will be barraged with e-mails for every action that takes place from that signup."

Facebook does allow each person in a group to set which types of notifications he or she will receive, if any.

The site introduced two other features the same day:

Download: Members will be able to download a copy of their Facebook profiles into a compressed file. This includes friends lists, any photos albums or video uploaded to the site, inbox messages and notes.

The feature could be used, for example, to retrieve photos in the event of a home computer failure. Or it could be used to archive information or move to a new social-networking site.

Applications Settings Dashboard: Starting next week, the company will roll out a tool that shows what kind of information from a member's profile have been accessed by third-party applications like games or websites. The dashboard is supposed to make it easier to edit permissions granted to the applications or delete them altogether.

Is Foursquare the New Facebook?[*]

By Helen A.S. Popkin
MSNBC.com, March 17, 2010

The battle for my gentleman friend's attention used to be between me and his cell phone. Now it's between me and Foursquare, and kids . . . it ain't lookin' good for me.

Saturday nights were punctuated by the constant ring of his phone, each call a "possible emergency" . . . you never know. Now it's a single application on my gentleman friend's iPhone that needs regular tending, for each location in our travels must be immediately checked on Foursquare. And as long as the app is open, why not check for tips from friends who have been at this bar or gallery before, and have a look to see what his Foursquare friends are up to?

Sigh.

Foursquare, if you don't know yet, is a hipster-habituated, location-based social networking Web site in which you earn virtual merit badges by punching your coordinates into your iPhone (or whatever) whenever you hit a bar, brunchery, gallery—or hook up with other Foursquare friends.

(Hitting four spots in one night earns you the "Crunked" badge. Checking in with three members of the opposite sex gets you the "Player Please!" badge. Meanwhile, check in at one place enough times and you may earn the "Mayor" title. You get the idea.)

If you haven't heard of Foursquare—let alone "location-based social networking"—it's probably because you don't live in a major metropolitan area and/or aren't a social media nerd.

Here in New York City, a major metropolitan area lousy with social media nerds, I can't swing a dead cat without hitting a friend or acquaintance in the act of notifying Foursquare pals about what groovy establishment he or she is chilling at right that very moment. (Not that I would swing a dead cat. That's wrong.) Soon enough—just like that Facebook you said you'd never use and the Twitter you just didn't get—that may very well be you.

Recently, Foursquare, which has approximately 500,000 users, made a big splash at the interactive portion of the South by Southwest festival in Austin, Texas. SXSW is like Burning Man for social media nerds . . . unless Burning Man is Burning Man for social media nerds. Hmmm.

Well, anyway, SXSW is a big nerd conference where lots of nerd leaders make keynote speeches, the highlights of which are tweeted by their nerd minions. Also, a bunch of startups and whatnot host booths and give away lots of swag in an attempt to convince industry-types that they're the next big thing. (If I sound bitter, it's because I never get to go.)

Foursquare was the belle of the ball when it premiered at SXSW last year, and this year it's touted as the social network to beat at the center of what the technorati are calling the "location war." The guys behind Foursquare are also the guys behind Dodgeball, a similar location-based social network that was acquired, then killed, by Google.

Back in the Dodgeball days, GPS-enabled smart phones weren't as prevalent or effective as they are today. Now everyone wants a piece of the location-based mobile advertising dollar. Gowalla, which is a lot harder to cheat (log into places you didn't go) because it requires GPS coordinates, is coming up fast. Facebook and Twitter—both developing location-based features—are snapping at Foursquare's heels.

None of the other location-based social networks have merit badges, however. Foursquare has loads—each more entertaining than the next. These charming virtual prizes are compelling to earn and may be just the bit of creative genius that keeps Foursquare ahead of the pack.

(And now, you can even buy corporeal versions of the merit badges at the Nerd Merit Badges Web site.)

Earning the merit badges on Foursquare isn't as easy as you might think—the exact behavior algorithm is sort of a secret, so it's tough to know what activities will get you one.

Holding the title of "Mayor" at 16 or 17 locations earned Internet-famous art blogger/Foursquare friend Paddy Johnson the coveted "Super Mayor" badge. She's even "Mayor" of the Detroit airport, because she's checked in there twice. (She will, of course, lose that title once another Foursquare member checks in three times.)

"I wouldn't say I use it because of the (merit badges) but I do feel disappointed when I see I've lost a mayorialship," Paddy says. She also boasts the "Warhol" badge (for many, many art gallery check ins) and the "Far and Away" badge (for traveling to the scary netherworld above 57th Street in Manhattan).

Despite Paddy's merit badge treasures, "I'm still disappointed that I haven't got the 'D***ebag' badge," which one achieves by frequenting bars frequented by . . . well . . . you know.

Mostly, however Paddy says she uses Foursquare as sort of a digital Day Runner to keep track of all the places she's been and the things she's done. "I do a lot,"she says. "I want a record of it." As the early badges imply, Foursquare was launched, and is most useful, for those with an active nightlife. But not so much Paddy's kind of nightlife.

"I hate the art world!" Paddy says. But really, Paddy doesn't hate the art world. If she did, blogging about art would be just weird. She's frustrated that more of the art world isn't on Foursquare, where it would do her some good during gallery openings and art fairs.

"Galleries have these analog versions of Foursquare," she says, referring to the guest books often posted at the desk. Those people use to both sign in and see who else stopped by. But you can't tell if those people are still in the area.

During the New York City art openings in September, "I had 30 friends I wanted to meet up with, and I couldn't really text them all at the same time," Paddy says. Foursquare would've really come in handy. "There aren't enough people in the art world or other professions yet to make Foursquare really effective," she says.

Maybe you've read this far into the article and you're still all, "No way! Foursquare (and by association, any other location-based social network) is something I will never do." And if you're me, with my formidable history of stalkers, you probably won't. Otherwise, you probably will. Just like you joined Facebook.

Anyway, it's not about you. Neither is Facebook, Twitter, MySpace and Friendster before that. (Hey, remember Friendster?)

All these new-fangled social networks that play to our narcissism and our need to belong are tools for capitalism. You know, ways to sell you crap. How can Foursquare and other such networks sell advertising, which in turn will attempt to sell you crap? Take Foursquare friend André Sala.

The other night André's sitting on the couch, watching TV and poking around on Foursquare. He notices that a lot of people are checking in at the Mercury Lounge, a music venue a few blocks from where he lives.

Digital guy that he is, André heads over to Twitter search, plugs in "Mercury Lounge," and learns that his most favoritest band MGMT is having some sort of super-secret record release party via a bunch of tweets that pretty much read like this: "holy [smokes], MGMT coming on stage, performing their new album, and mercury lounge is half empty."

This is exactly how location-based social media is supposed to work. Well, this is exactly how location-based social media is supposed to work if André bolted off the couch and over to the Mercury Lounge, thus benefitting the venue and any surrounding businesses Foursquare might recommend once André "checked in."

"Sadly, I'm a lazy old man and didn't actually get dressed and head out," the . . . ahem . . . 29-year-old says—not that he didn't appreciate the social network synergy. "I thought it was pretty magic," he says.

Of course, this is only magic for Foursquare if, unlike André, most people get off the couch.

The Life and Death of Online Communities[*]

By Phoebe Connelly
American Prospect, September 2009

When Yahoo announced earlier this year that it was shuttering GeoCities, an online community of user-created Web pages from the early days of the Internet, the response was more mocking than mournful. "So Long GeoCities: We Forgot You Still Existed" read one *PC World* headline. When it's remembered at all these days, GeoCities is an Internet punch line, with its amateur code and garish color schemes (one programmer friend termed it "an animated-gif-athon"). But it was a hot startup in the mid-1990s. With its user profiles and pages organized by topic, the service was a precursor to online networks like Facebook, MySpace, and accessible blogging platforms like Blogger and WordPress. And, much like those sites, it is owned by a private corporation that has ultimate say over what happens to information, photographs, conversations, and interaction that occurred within that space.

GeoCities began in 1994 as Beverly Hills Internet (BHI), a California company that offered free Web hosting and development tools. Users could claim space for their Web pages in a variety of thematically organized "neighborhoods," (including "Sunset Strip" for rock and punk music, "Wall Street" for personal finance and investing, and "Area 51" for science fiction). These neighborhoods were run by volunteers known as community leaders who helped patrol for inappropriate content and, according to a 1999 *CNET* article, offered new users "suggestions to jazz up their pages." BHI renamed itself GeoCities in 1995 and sold the idea that when you joined the service, you weren't just getting a Web page; you were joining a community of users.

The geographic nomenclature of GeoCities gave those new to the Internet a familiar shorthand for how social interaction could unfold. Sure, the tools might be different, but the concept of neighbors and like-minded groups of people, would, GeoCities promised, operate the same online as in the real world. Our desire for community is an insight key to many successful online ventures that have come after. Facebook lets users "become a fan" of bands, magazines, and businesses, join groups that petition for health-care reform, and organize high school reunions. Blogs organize themselves into like-minded groups known as rings, even holding "carnivals" where all bloggers involved publish entries on a set theme.

The demise of GeoCities is not just the disappearance of a gif-riddled online ghost town—it's the death of a pioneering online community. And it's a reminder that we should think critically about who owns online spaces, how they are managed, and what happens when they are razed.

GeoCities pages were proto-blogs. "People updated them very frequently," says Alice Marwick, a doctoral candidate at New York University who studies social media. "I think you'll find that personal homepagers of yesteryear are bloggers now." GeoCities was packaged for inexperienced Internet users, and by 1998 it was the third most-visited site on the Web. Jason Scott, who along with a group of around 15 volunteers called the Archive Team is working to archive GeoCities, says the selling point was ease of use: "Users were offered a worldwide audience, and the ability to say things any way they wanted to."

Other online platforms began to spring up, and soon GeoCities became a fond memory for most users. Blogger was introduced in 1999 (and purchased by Google in 2003), making it easy for anyone to start a blog. MetaFilter, a community blog, was launched in 1999. The social networking site MySpace was founded in 2003. These services also marked the entrance of a very public form of socializing— where, unlike email or listservs, the conversation, and content, was accessible to those not part of the conversation. In offering a platform for creating online identities, GeoCities started a trend that has been replicated by companies ever since.

But once those online identities are created, are they the property of the users or the corporations that host them? David Bollier, author of *Viral Spiral: How the Commoners Built a Digital Republic of Their Own*, calls corporate-controlled spaces like GeoCities and Facebook, "faux commons." For him, true online community spaces are defined by users having control over the terms of their interaction and owning the software or infrastructure. Corporate spaces come with "terms of service" agreements that lay out the rules users must abide by and what control they agree to surrender in exchange for using the product. "Oftentimes corporate-controlled communities are benign, functional, and perfectly OK," Bollier says. "It's just that the terms of services those companies have or the competitive pressures of business may compel them to take steps that are not in the interest of the community."

Consider the case of Peter Ludlow, a philosophy professor at Northwestern University. Ludlow ran a newspaper for the virtual community The Sims Online and was kicked out of the community by the owner, Electronic Arts, for publishing accounts of theft, prostitution, and money laundering that (virtually) occurred there. Because it happened in a corporate-controlled online space, his speech wasn't protected. As Ludlow told an interviewer, "The platform owners have responsibilities to care for those communities and see that they are not harmed."

Bollier agrees. "At the point where the business model becomes tethered to a happy community, you have to reach an agreement about how you are going to interact. If you piss people off too much, they are just going to flee the site." When GeoCities was purchased by Yahoo in January 1999, the new corporate overlord immediately began to clash with users. That June, Yahoo changed the terms of service for the site, claiming the right to full ownership of anything users posted to their pages. By December, Yahoo announced it would disband the popular community-leader program. The changes should sound familiar to anyone who has followed recent tempests over privately controlled social-networking sites. Facebook made a similar change to its terms of service this past February, causing uproar among users already annoyed with a redesign and a short-lived feature that broadcast users' purchasing habits. Under pressure, Facebook reversed the decision within weeks.

The decay of an online social space cannot always be pinned on corporate ownership. Online communities tend to mirror the shortcomings of the real world— racism, exclusivity, and class privilege. In a presentation at this year's Personal Democracy Forum conference, social media researcher danah boyd asked what really separated users of the older MySpace from the newer Facebook. MySpace, started by the advertising company eUniverse as a rival to Friendster, has always had a low bar for entry, allows users to remain anonymous, and enables more customization of profile pages. Facebook, by contrast, was born at Harvard as an online version of freshman-orientation "facebooks." It slowly opened admission to other Ivy League universities, then most colleges, and finally to the public at large. While both sites enjoy about 70 million unique visitors, in recent years wealthier, more educated users "were more likely to leave [MySpace] or choose Facebook," boyd said. "Those who deserted MySpace did so by 'choice' but their decision to do so was wrapped up in their connections to others, in their belief that a more peaceful, quiet, less-public space would be more idyllic." She continued, "What happened was modern day 'white flight.'"

In other words, despite some declarations that MySpace has gone the way of GeoCities, it isn't really dead. Not yet, anyway. But because MySpace, like the vast majority of social-networking sites and blogs, exists in corporate-owned space, it is vulnerable to being shut down if it is perceived as no longer having a profitable or attractive user base. Given that we are stuck with much of our digital commons existing on corporate-controlled sites, what then happens when the corporation decides to close its doors? If these are our new commons, what does it say that we abandon spaces once they are clearly marked as unsophisticated?

Scott says the Archive Team's efforts have proved to him the worth of Geo-Cities. "A lot of people see GeoCities as this sea of amateurish, poorly written Web sites. I understand that thinking; I certainly don't want people to think that I'm saying GeoCities is an example of the best the Web could be, but I do think it's an example of what the Web was." Scott says while he's pulled up plenty of pop-culture fan sites, he's also found meticulously detailed outlines of Roma history and documentation for products and software manufactured during the late

1980s and early 1990s. The better-known Internet Archive has announced it, too, is working to archive GeoCities. (Yahoo got in touch with it about preserving the pages.) Still, it's a stark reminder that just because some-thing is published on the Internet doesn't mean it will last forever.

Yahoo has now set an official date for the closing of GeoCities—October 26, 2009—but the question of how we protect and archive the history of our inter-action in the digital commons is still unanswered. As the Internet continues to evolve, we will be forced to decide which left-behind digital communities to pre-serve. "There is a very real chance of this digital culture just disappearing from our lives, and there's not really any formal mechanisms in place to store or aggregate this knowledge, which is really a shame," says Marwick. "There need to be more public efforts to store and archive."

In a keynote address at a 2001 conference on preserving digital media, science-fiction writer Bruce Sterling observed, "Bits have no archival medium. We haven't invented one yet. If you print something on acid-free paper with stable ink, and you put it in a dry, dark closet, you can read it in 200 years. We have no way to archive bits that we know will be readable in even 50 years."

He added, "Tape demagnetizes. CDs delaminate. Networks go down."

Losing Its Cool*

By Mark Lacter
Los Angeles Magazine, October 2009

Perhaps you remember MySpace? Two years ago it was the kingpin of social networking, the first site for millions of people to create their own Web pages, pore over mindless blogs, listen to bootlegged music, post pirated photos, and most of all connect with hundreds or sometimes thousands of other MySpacers. Companies felt obliged to set up pages, too. So did countless bands. Rupert Murdoch's News Corp. purchased the parent company in July 2005 for $580 million (much to the chagrin of another media mogul, Sumner Redstone, who had also gone after the site). Later came a three-year $900 million advertising deal with Google—a transaction that at the time was unheard of in social media.

MySpace continues to bring in millions of visitors each month, but the numbers are trending downward. June marked the first time that more visitors were on Facebook—77 million to MySpace's 68.4 million. Fewer visitors means less advertising, and the Google deal expires next year. Though still a relative sliver of News Corp.'s $30 billion business, MySpace was largely responsible for the media conglomerate's $203 million loss covering the three months ending on June 30.

But never mind the numbers. What MySpace has really lost is its coolness, the main thing that got it going (a recent survey found six out of ten users visit less often). Last spring News Corp. fired cofounder Chris DeWolfe and brought in new management, including a former executive at archrival Facebook, to resurrect the division. First order of business: laying off 30 percent of the ballooning workforce and canceling a planned move from its Beverly Hills headquarters to the South Bay.

Cost cutting is always the easy part. Now comes figuring out how MySpace fits into an expanding social media world that is made up of Facebook, Twitter, Linkedin, and thousands of smaller online communities. Everybody wants in. "You must focus on only a few things. You can't do everything, even though you want to play catch-up," says Jonathan Miller, the former head of AOL whom Murdoch hired last spring to handle News Corp.'s digital operations.

Oh, and there's the matter of making money: how to persuade companies to place their ads alongside the assorted scribblings and videos of average folks. So far, users of social networking sites aren't tuned into ads, which is why the click-through rate has been so low. "Television advertising is mass to mass," says Chris Anderson, editor-in-chief of *Wired* magazine. "Coke ad against *American Idol*. OK, but what do you put against a cat video? What do you put next to your favorite soldering video?"

In talking to a bunch of experts in the social media world—smart, ambitious entrepreneurs who deal with those kinds of questions all the time—I kept hearing the same three letters: TBD. I'm not a big fan of "to be determined" strategies; they're an unsettling throwback to the tech boom of the late 1990s, when other smart, ambitious entrepreneurs insisted that it was all right not to have a business model and to lose gobs of money because in due course profits would keep pace with concepts.

Facebook isn't losing gobs of money—the company expects to be cash-flow positive sometime next year—but annual ad revenues reportedly run a paltry $230 million, which is less than half of what MySpace continues to bring in. (I say "reportedly" because none of these sites provides exact financials, and the numbers bounce around a lot.) Facebook chief executive Mark Zuckerberg has turned down several buyout offers, choosing instead to take the company public in the next few years. Waiting it out has been made easier by several hundred million dollars in venture capital dollars (not to mention the massive valuation it is receiving). Yet Facebook and other successful Web sites cannot keep relying on the kindness of deep-pocket investors. They have to become real, functioning businesses.

The guys who started MySpace couldn't have anticipated any of this. Back in 2003, De-Wolfe and cofounder Tom Anderson were with a Santa Monica Internet company called eUniverse (later renamed Intermix) when they had this wild idea: Why not construct a spiffier version of Friendster.com, which itself was a step above the typical on-line-dating service? Each MySpace user would be provided a page for a profile, pictures, Hogging, and other odds and ends. Working out of a small office near LAX, DeWolfe and Anderson built the site on a shoestring budget, using two Dell computers and a single database (they chose not to start their own company because it would have meant losing promised payouts from eUniverse).

Their timing was impeccable, what with a sharp increase in the use of high-speed broadband. The higher speed greatly reduced the wait for uploading photos, graphics, and music Among the earliest adopters were teenage girls eager to socialize and drawn to the possibilities of nonstop exchanges—for free. But MySpace launched with so little planning that it was bound to run into trouble. An early mistake was enabling users to build those ghastly wallpapered pages (think paisley on paisley). That badly overloaded the MySpace servers; technicians who should have been working on updated versions were too busy trying to keep the site going.

Some miscues were just dumb, such as letting people use phony identities that were hard to trace (e-mail addresses were never verified). Beyond understandable concerns about sexual predators, the anonymous users created a creepy atmosphere, not unlike what you would find in an adult bookstore. "In a place where 'U are soooooooo hot!' passes for wit, MySpace isn't doing much to elevate the level of social discourse," concluded *PC World* magazine several years ago in naming it the worst site on the Internet

News Corp. quickly recognized that it had problems—that DeWolfe and Anderson were resistant to change (they even balked at a move from Santa Monica to Beverly Hills), and third-party programmers who developed widgets for MySpace were not given nearly the same financial opportunities as at Facebook. The place was practically held together with duct tape, and the limited system upgrading led to, among other problems, huge vulnerability to hacking. "It seemed as if they didn't iterate their technology and features quickly enough," says Jason Nazar, cofounder and chief executive of the LA. Internet company Docstoc.com.

Facebook, meanwhile, was easier to use, had better features (especially the photo-sharing function), and discouraged fake identities. Where MySpace had a freewheeling, renegade quality, Facebook came across as accessible and friendly. Older people felt comfortable showing off pictures of their family vacations. "That's the difference between a Los Angeles company and a Silicon Valley company," Zuckerberg was once quoted as saying (Facebook is based in Palo Alto). "We built this to last, and these guys [at MySpace] don't have a clue."

Reid Hoffman, an early investor in Facebook, believes that social media is in its early stages and that users and companies are only getting their feet wet. But he knows from experience that the industry cannot amble on forever. Hoffman is founder and chief executive of LinkedIn, the social networking site that's aimed at business people and is among the few sites that is making a profit. It has a potential competitor, though, in *The Wall Street Journal* (owned by News Corp., too), which wants to replace its own fledgling social networking site, WSJ Community, with one called WSJ Connect Insiders have dubbed it the "LinkedIn Killer."

"When people ask me about the future, I say it's sooner and stranger than you think," Hoffman told me at a technology conference in Pasadena, pointing out that no one would have expected Twitter to be such a phenomenon 12 months ago. "The same way you can have millions of people creating new kinds of social media," he said, "I think you'll have interesting new ways of creating and participating in advertising. The question is how we figure it out."

Actually, Hoffman might be creating an industry model at LinkedIn. Rather than relying solely on broad cast-type advertising from Fortune 500 companies, the site has been generating revenue through subscriptions charged for premium services (say, access to special features or information), paid job postings aimed at target audiences, and the licensing of its recruiting software to human resource departments. Not everything will work on each social networking site, but the point is to find multiple ways of selling the product. A music label, for instance, could give away a thousand DVDs to MySpace members on the bet that word of mouth might prove more valuable than a traditional ad.

Along with a revamped ad strategy, MySpace must forget about trying to appeal to everyone. It's not going to happen. Better to concentrate on the people who have stayed with the site—generally younger, single, and more interested in music—and then build on that base by adding features like videogames. Murdoch says the idea is to become more of an entertainment portal (it's dropped the tag line "a place for friends"). Already the free streaming site MySpace Music has seen a huge spike in traffic and is beating out such competitors as MTV, Pandora, and Rhapsody. You can see where this is heading: MySpace, given up for dead only a few months ago, could become cool again. Whether it can become a moneymaker as well is the big TBD.

Will Social Networks Ever Make Money?[*]

By Andrew Saunders
Management Today, October 2009

To some, they are the undisputed darlings of web 2.0, spearheading a virtual revolution that will replace the net as we know it with a connected world where status, street cred and even employability are determined not by the old credos of class, geography and education but by the number and quality of nodes on your personal global network. To others, social networks such as Facebook and Twitter are the last word in navel-gazing-online platforms for the swapping of trivial opinions by the terminally self-obsessed.

Whichever side of the fence you prefer to be on, if the grand vision promised by the boosters is to stand a chance of coming even halfway true, the big social networks will have to start doing something that they have so far singularly failed to do—making decent, sustainable profits. The question being asked with growing urgency out in the real world, where the wheels of commerce have yet to become frictionless and still need greasing with plenty of moolah, is: can they ever do so?

Some veterans of the dot.com bubble of the late '90s have their doubts. Michael Wolff, American author of Burn Rate, the most compelling first-hand account of life in Silicon Valley in that frenzied period of boom and bust, is one. 'Social media is based on the internet model, and we are right to be alarmed by that model. It creates moments of intense enthusiasm, but they do not—cannot—last.'

Enthusiasm is the word. Facebook has signed up a mindboggling 300 million users in just three years. That's a fifth as many followers as the world's largest religion, Christianity, has accrued over two millennia, and it's still growing fast—five million new users a week.

Founder Mark Zuckerberg's ambition is also of biblical proportions. He wants to get to a billion users in a year or two, and—having turned down at least one billion-dollar offer, from Yahoo!—shows no inclination to sell out. Facebook has attracted a zealous following from the investment community—the purchase of a 5% stake by Microsoft in 2007 valued the company at $15bn, although more recent share sales suggest $5bn is closer.

And yet in its more established territories, Facebook is already old hat. How long can it find new markets where punters still think it is cool, to make up for those where it has passed into the ranks of the web establishment?

Blake Chandlee, commercial director EMEA for Facebook, is ex-Yahoo! and was Facebook's first international employee, way back in 2007. He is confident the firm has what it takes to stay at the top for a while yet. 'How do you avoid being blindsided by the next big thing? I asked Mark [Zuckerberg] exactly the same question when I went for the job,' he says. 'He really wants to connect users, to make Facebook more of a utility than a content-driven thing, like some other social sites.

'Facebook is about nodes and edges—it enables you to keep in touch much more effectively with people at the edges of your network, people you might know only superficially, than you can in any other way. That has real global appeal, more so than content plays.'

At least Facebook has viable revenue streams—it makes money from advertising on the site, and is exploring other sources of income, such as stored credit, which users can spend on the site, and a new VOIP telephony service to compete with Google and Skype.

Last month, Zuckerberg announced that Facebook will be cashflow-positive this year, which means that it will earn more in revenues than it spends on capex—a vital turning-point for any start-up.

But it's very cagey on exact figures. Even mundane facts such as employee numbers are not 'officially' public (it's around 1,000 people, by the way) and revenues and expenditure details are closely guarded secrets. 'Leaked' estimates suggest annual revenues of around $500m and climbing fast, prompting sceptics to wonder why getting cashflow-positive has taken Facebook so long, and whether it can sustain such a frenetic pace of growth and technological diversification without burning out.

Twitter, meanwhile, the über-fashionable new kid on the block, has much less in the way of visible means of support. The microblogging site was founded in 2006 but didn't really get going until last year. It now has 45 million users, of which nearly three-quarters joined in the first five months of this year, according to data from Twitter research specialist (yes, such firms do exist) Sysomos.

Endorsed by celebs such as Stephen Fry and 'Mr Demi Moore' Ashton Kutcher, it has attracted more than $100m of funding. That includes $35m raised at a valuation of $250m earlier this year, and $50m or so raised last month at an eyewatering $1bn valuation. All for a company with no clear source of income.

The unprecedented—and to some inexplicable—mass appeal of posting short (140 character) messages on any subject at all in real time on the Twitter site seems to have taken even founders Jack Dorsey, Biz Stone and Ev Williams by surprise. They neglected to work out a business model before they got started—a source of embarrassment now that they've hit the big time. Having maintained since very early days that it would never look to advertising on the site to make money, Twitter recently changed its terms and conditions to allow it to do so—in theory, at least.

In July, it was reported that Twitter had spent $15m getting to 30 million users, so, compared with those profligate '90s dot.coms, it is prudently managed and should have plenty in the kitty. So why the need for this latest round of funding? Sceptics suggest that the founders are keen to extract as much cash from the VCs as possible before the true scale of Twitter's 'monetisation problem' becomes a deal-breaker.

The question of whether to go for growth or profit is a classic social-media dilemma, says Nic Brisbourne, partner in venture capital firm DFJ Esprit. 'Does profit matter? Yes, in the long run it matters tremendously. Any business is only worth the sum of its future net cashflow, and without profit you haven't got any of that. But the key phrase is "in the long run". The revenue potential of a business like Twitter or Facebook is theoretically proportional to its user base, so providing you have the capital to cover your losses, it make sense to grow the user base. That's adding more value. But you have to transition to thinking about profit.'

He believes that Facebook has passed this financial rubicon, but that Twitter is not yet in a position to. 'Facebook is clearly in revenue mode—there's definitely a viable business there. The question is: will it be a Google, or will it be an AOL? But Twitter is right at the beginning of the cycle—it doesn't have the revenue to go for profit, even if it wanted to.'

The question bothering investors in social media must be: how long will it last? It is the pace with which these bursts of fame and fandom succeed one another, says Wolff, that makes the social networking business model suspect. Dominant players can rise and fall so quickly that they never have time to earn investors their money back.

Look at what happened to MySpace, the first social network to make it really big, he says. 'There's a company that pretty much created the market, had a potential valuation of some $20bn at one point; now it's the sick man of social media.'

MySpace collected 50 million users in two years, a number that looks less impressive today than it did then only because of the extraordinary numbers subsequently posted by Facebook. But it rapidly lost its mojo in the face of its sharp-elbowed new rival. It has now made 30% of its workforce redundant and is bleeding ad revenue at the rate of 15% per annum. Being acquired by Rupert Murdoch's News Corp—whose lamentable record in the online arena is well known—didn't help.

Even Zuckerberg and his all-conquering chums may not get much more than an hour or two in the sun. Peter Cook once said of archrival David Frost that he 'has risen without trace'. The same could be said of Twitter, which, revenue or no, is now clearly way cooler than dreary old Facebook, at least for the opinion-formers of the online community.

In such a world, where both technology and user behaviour are transient, little can be taken for granted. 'It's a Facebook game now, but what happens next?' asks Wolff. 'Will Twitter upend Facebook? Will Facebook acquire Twitter? Suddenly, we're talking about a strategic defence of a business that hasn't even defined what it is. What are they preparing to defend exactly? We don't know.'

The UK has its own, smaller, cautionary tale in Friends Reunited. Bought by ITV for £120m in 2005, when it had 15 million members and solid revenues from advertising and paid subscriptions, its model was undermined by the arrival of Facebook—yes, them again—which offered better functionality for free, as well as a much bigger hype machine. Although profitable in 2007, it rapidly went into reverse, and when ITV disposed of what remained of Friends Reunited earlier this year for a paltry £25m, it made a thumping loss of £95m.

But it's easy—and often unproductive—to knock new ideas before they've had a chance to prove themselves. Let's retreat from all this naysaying and take a rational look at what is going on. Are social networks really inherently hard to monetise, or is the conspicuous lack of profit from some players simply a natural part of early-stage business life?

It's the latter, argues Facebook's Chandlee. 'Where we are at is consistent with business trends for the last 100 years. It amazes me that people so often say we are not monetising; I think we're doing a pretty good job. The pace of change here is like nothing I have ever seen. We're clearly building a robust and commercially viable business.'

Furthermore, it's simply not true that social networks can't turn a profit. Many do, typically the niche players whose backers don't have quite such deep pockets and whose businesses were built from the start with ROI in mind—firms such as LinkedIn, a network for professionals which has inevitably attracted the moniker 'The Facebook of business'. Since it declared itself profitable in 2007, it's arguably more successful than its bigger and better-known rival. But, like Facebook, it also plays its financial cards close to its chest: revenue and profit figures are not revealed.

The quantity of its membership may not be in the premier league—43 million—but their quality is outstanding, says Christina Hoole, marketing director for Europe. 'Eighty-one per cent are university-educated, the average age is 41 and the average income is £75,000.'

Those are the kind of numbers to make any advertiser drool. And, in a sector where the pedestrian reality of making money can often look like an afterthought, its business model is copper-bottomed. 'Our revenue model is mixed—roughly one-third each advertising, subscriptions and corporate solutions,' says Hoole.

Ironically, sales to corporates have been particularly strong during the downturn, because using LinkedIn as a recruitment tool helps clients to do their own headhunting—at a fraction of the price charged by specialist recruitment firms. 'You can seek out both active candidates—those looking for a new job—and passive ones. These are the people who aren't looking but might move for the right offer.'

Adds Hoole: 'We're in a privileged position, because people's professional networks last for life; they take them from job to job.'

It's also easy to forget that social networking is a young sector, and that people are still feeling their way in it. There's a lot more value to come, says Peter Ward, co-founder of another niche player, UK-based social network for travellers Wayn. com. Wayn may have 'only' 15 million members, but it has been profitable almost from the start, he says. 'There's this idea that all social networks are the same. They are not. We can do more specialist, focused things on Wayn that they couldn't do on Facebook.

'Social media has plenty of untapped value, but a lot of people who claim to understand social media don't. Success depends on using the power of the medium and understanding the psychology of your users.'

Twitter's lack of obvious revenue streams has led to speculation that the firm's best hope for the future is to get up the noses of bigger rivals in order to encourage them to buy it out—something it has managed with considerable aplomb. Rumour has it that at least one such approach has been rebuffed by Twitter's top team. Did they not want to sell, or was the price too low? Only time will tell.

Internet veteran Brent Hoberman, the co-founder of Lastminute.com who now heads up the PROfounders investment fund, thinks a sale could be on the cards for Twitter. It certainly worked well for his investment partner Michael Birch, who sold the social network he founded, Bebo, to AOL for $850m last year.

'Microsoft, Google, Facebook—they'd all like to buy it,' he says. 'The question is, would a sale kill it?' In other words, how many users would desert a corporate-owned Twitter on a point of principle? Hoberman doesn't think it would amount to many. 'Maybe the techies who were on there first would stop, but in the mass market I don't think many users would care very much who owned it.'

Facebook's Chandlee points to another advantage enjoyed by social media that should certainly please the traditionalists. 'We are fiscally very conservative, we keep our employee base low. Plenty of people here went through the dot.com crash; they know what that felt like and they don't want it to happen again. Comscore says we're the third most popular website in the world, and we've done that on less than 1,000 employees—fewer even than Google.'

So will social networking ever pay? Almost certainly, yes. You may not share the desire to broadcast your entire personal life to the world on Facebook, or share your every waking thought with the Twitterati, but a lot of people do—these are some of the fastest-growing businesses on the planet. 'I'm optimistic that sites with mass scale, and well-differentiated niche sites, will do well,' says Hoberman. 'The middle market will struggle.'

After all, as Michael Wolff admits: 'You have to say that if it's not possible for someone to make money out of the intense engagement of all the millions of people who use social network sites, we might as well all give up.'

Good point. Someone should Tweet it.

ADS, DATA AND APPS—WHERE THE MONEY COMES FROM

For a medium that prides itself on novelty, the lion's share of revenue generated by social networks still comes from a traditional source—advertising. Despite the hunt for alternative sources of income, this won't change quickly. 'For the foreseeable future,' says Facebook's Blake Chandlee, 'advertising will remain the dominant revenue stream.'

The received wisdom is that if people in social networking mode are less receptive to ads than those merely browsing, but social networks know a great deal about the habits and proclivities of their users. That kind of data should allow them to identify precisely targeted audiences, something the internet has long promised but never quite delivered. Hence the ongoing battle over who can do what with all the personal data that users type into social network pages. 'So far, a lot of online advertising has not really added much to what can be achieved in a magazine,' says DFJ Esprit's Nic Brisbourne. 'That will change.'

So expect to see a raft of more sophisticated techniques, from product placement via interactive ads to the 'engagement' model, which tries to make ads more palatable by encouraging feedback from users. Some professional-interest sites have better data than mass-market rivals.

There should also be a good business in selling data on what people are saying about brands to corporate clients—'analytics'. 'It comes down to whether you can influence people's buying behaviour without upsetting them. I think the answer is yes,' says PROfounders' Brent Hoberman.

The other possibility is in the topsy-turvy world of apps—small pieces of software designed to run on top of a social network and to do something users find fun or useful: Tweetdeck on Twitter, for example, or Facebook Connect.

Developers don't get charged for using the underlying platform to sell their app. So although Twitter itself makes no money, several developers are doing very nicely off the back of it. Will Twitter use some of its war chest to snap up the most successful apps?

2

"Does Social Sell?"
Doing Business in the Digital World

Editor's Introduction

It used to be that a company was considered tech-savvy if it had a decent Web site. Nowadays, if the CEO doesn't have a Twitter account and a few hundred followers, the firm might as well be selling typewriters by candlelight.

While most major companies have taken steps to establish themselves on social networks, some question whether it's worth the investment. After all, it takes time and money to Tweet and court Facebook friends, and doing these things doesn't guarantee higher sales or other such quantifiable benefits. What's more, on-line marketing can be risky, as companies that are too pushy with their sales pitches may alienate consumers. Mastering social media requires a careful balancing act, and as the articles in this chapter attest, even well-established firms are struggling to find their footing.

In "Reaping Social Media Rewards," this chapter's lead entry, Lyndsie Bourgon explains how Starbucks is using Foursquare to promote customer loyalty. The coffee giant now offers discounts to "mayors," or people who check in most frequently from certain locations, and in doing so, they're giving Frappuccino fanatics a financial incentive to stop in for regular refills.

Up next, John Soat draws on survey results and expert opinions to answer the "7 Questions Key to Social Networking Success." Addressing the issue of ROI, or return on investment, Soat paraphrases the philosophy of Internet consultant Dan Shust, writing, "It's about conversations, not messaging; relationships, not salesmanship." In other words, companies need to look beyond conventional metrics when it comes to judging the effectiveness of their social-media campaigns.

With "Deleted, De-Friended: Social Media Great for B2B Until You Misuse It," the subsequent piece, Brian Shappell offers more tips for businesses looking to expand into social media. He warns against posting "buy my stuff" messages and urges companies to avoid writing about anything that may be deemed offensive. Shappell also says social networking is "not the entirety of anyone's business," adding that companies shouldn't devote too much time to updating their LinkedIn or Facebook pages, lest it appear their employees have nothing better to do.

Companies approach social networking in different ways, and while some dedicate entire departments to digital marketing, others leave the blogging to top executives. In "The Tweet Life of CMOs," the next article, Barbara Lippert looks at how some company heads are navigating the tricky world of Twitter, crafting 140-

character postings that are creative and informative without being blatantly promotional. "It's a very interesting juggling act," president of the firm Euro RSCG PR, tells Lippert.

In "Can You Measure the ROI of Your Social Media Marketing?" the next piece, Donna L. Hoffman and Marek Fodor explain why the "show me the return" philosophy common among executives is too narrow. Because on-line relationships with consumers are "interactive," the authors write, they often take time to develop. Hoffman and Fodor outline what they believe are the three crucial objectives of social media: brand awareness, brand engagement, and word of mouth.

The chapter concludes with "Does Social Sell?" Brian Morrissey's look at how three companies—Pepsi, Dell, and H&R Block—have successfully used social media. Morgan Stewart, director of strategy and research for the marketing company ExactTarget, again downplays the importance of ROI, telling Morrissey there are other reasons to invest in digital promotion. "Companies using reputation as a measure of success are more likely to be shifting budget there," Stewart says. "That tells you something about the mind-set."

Reaping Social Media Rewards[*]

By Lyndsie Bourgon
Canadian Business, July 20–August 16, 2010

Glen Sloan is the mayor of Starbucks, though he admits he didn't do all that much to earn the honour.

Every morning Sloan, a motorcycle mechanic, orders a hot chocolate at the Starbucks on the corner of College Street and Euclid Avenue in Toronto's downtown. As he's standing in line for his travel mug to be filled, he uses his iPhone to maintain his "mayorship" via the website Foursquare.

Foursquare is a social network that members use to "check in" at businesses and other locations they often frequent. The person who checks in the most is thereby crowned the "mayor" of that location.

Recently, Starbucks began using Foursquare to offer the mayors of each of their stores a $1 discount on their drink of choice.

"I think platforms like Foursquare offer a real opportunity for loyalty programmes," says Phil Barrett, the vice-president of digital and mobile at Toronto's marketing communications agency BStreet.

"In the past, businesses would send coupons to homes, and maybe you'd go or maybe you wouldn't," says Barrett. "With Foursquare, you're motivated to go back time and again to maintain mayorship and get points. It drives beneficial behaviour for the retailer."

According to a statement from Starbucks, Foursquare represents a natural evolution of its social-media strategy. "What's great about Foursquare is that it links the real-time, in-store experience to the online community," it said.

Sloan agrees. "It brings the Internet into the real world," he said. "You can go and have a tangible experience instead of vicariously living through people. It's more like a morale boost."

At last tally, Foursquare had about 1.8 million users—a relatively small number compared to Facebook and Twitter—but the website has become part of a geopositioning social-media phenomenon, and is growing by about 15,000 users a day. On July 2, the website hit a milestone—over one million people checked in that day. Then, the next day, it reached that number again.

The company recently announced that it had locked down a new round of $20 million in venture funding, led by Silicon Valley's Andreessen Horowitz. And while its business model remains a work-in-progress, marketing deals with location-based branded companies such as Starbucks are a clear priority for driving revenue.

Those who use Foursquare often refer to it as a game, because the process of checking in earns users online badges and honours, depending on frequency. According to Barrett, that's the true business opportunity.

"The real opportunity isn't for mayors—that's limiting and short-sighted," he says. "Knowing that the top 5% of customers generate the majority of the revenue, it's a whole new loyalty platform. And it's a lot cheaper than Aeroplan."

He adds that Foursquare discounts are not foolproof: "The disadvantage is you now have employees becoming mayors and preventing the best customers from enjoying rewards." In Canada, it's still early days in terms of businesses utilizing Foursquare. Especially compared to the U.S., where Barrett says he's seen businesses offering everything from free drinks to happy-hour discounts to those who check in.

"It really is something that could take off," he says. "What [these businesses] want is foot traffic, and [Foursquare] will drive it in."

7 Questions Key to Social Networking Success*

By John Soat
Information Week, January 18, 2010

Social networking true believers use words like engagement, responsibility, and transparency that smack of the Internet's hippie days in the late 1990s, yet social networking has proved to be much more than a passing fancy. The exploding numbers associated with the most popular sites like Facebook and Twitter inspire awe in even the most jaded statisticians. Time spent on social networks increased 277% in the United States last year, according to media research firm Nielsen, and Twitter itself grew more than 500%.

Now the social media category is primed to emerge as the most significant business enabler since the Internet itself. Organizations must ask themselves seven important questions about their plans for leveraging social networking over the next 12 months. Their answers may spell the difference between success and failure in the coming decade.

1. ARE MY COMPETITORS CONTINUING TO INVEST IN SOCIAL NETWORKING?

Measuring yourself against your competition isn't the best way to decide strategy, but it's a fair question given the flash-in-the-pan potential of social networking. And the answer is yes.

"I'm hiring," says Christopher Barger, director of social media at General Motors. That's the good news. The bad news is that, last July, Barger had five people in his social media group at GM; today, there's only him. Barger says part of that reduction is due to attrition but says some has to do with his "immerse and disperse" strategy for spreading social media awareness and expertise across the automaker. People with whom he worked over the last year are now placed in the company's communications, design, performance vehicle, and emerging technology groups.

While GM isn't typical in terms of attrition—the company went through some financial difficulty last year; you might have read about it—it's typical in its desire to maintain its investment in social networking. According to a Deloitte survey of more than 400 companies, conducted late last year with Beeline Labs and the Society for New Communications Research, 94% of respondents intend to maintain or increase their investment in enterprise social networking tools this year.

For its second annual "Tribalization Of Business" survey, Deloitte polled companies that maintain online communities of 100 members to more than 1 million, created on their own sites or on public social sites such as Facebook and MySpace. About 60% of those communities are less than a year old.

2. WHERE'S THE ROI?

This is the $64,000 question. And it's not easy to answer because it depends on what it is you're trying to accomplish with your social media strategy. "Right now it's owned by the marketing division and looked on as a low-cost or no-cost way of amplifying your marketing message," says Ed Moran, director of product innovation at Deloitte.

Except social networking isn't a marketing activity in the one-to-many, shotgun-blast approach that traditional marketing is built on. Or it shouldn't be.

"Sales isn't necessarily the end goal," says Dan Shust, director of emerging media for Resource Interactive, an Internet consulting firm. Shust is talking specifically about Facebook fan pages, a grassroots effort brought to light when a Coca-Cola page created by two Coke fans became a social media phenomenon. Corporate marketers quickly realized the potential; Resource Interactive helps companies develop and support Facebook fan pages built around brands or products.

Shust says social network marketing is about engagement: fostering a community of individuals who represent the human face of a company or organization. It's about conversations, not messaging; relationships, not salesmanship.

All that doesn't lend itself to hard ROI numbers. "That's a challenge in most marketing models," says Barbara McDonald, VP of marketing for the Public Relations Society of America. "When we incorporate social media into our campaigns, we get better lift, but it's hard to track."

ROI shouldn't be so difficult, insists Deloitte's Moran, and it isn't when it comes to other ways social media can be used by companies. Take customer service, which Moran says is an underused opportunity to leverage the relationship-building and community spirit of social networks. The cost of customer support is easy to calculate and should be familiar to most executives. When a customer has a problem resolved in an online community, either by a corporate representative or especially by another community member, and as a result the customer doesn't call the support line, the cost savings can be measured.

3. WHICH WAY WORKS BEST?

Social media is still an amorphous concept, represented by the microblogs, wikis, forums, chat rooms, and RSS feeds found on thousands of corporate and organizational Web sites, as well as by the familiar sites such as Friendster, Facebook, and Flickr.

There are legendary corporate success stories. Starbucks, for example, started an online community called My Starbucks Idea that lets registered members suggest ideas for products and services and comment and vote on the ideas of others. It also features feedback by Starbucks representatives on actions taken in connection with those ideas. At last count, the site had garnered more than 20,000 ideas for new coffee products alone, and another 60,000 ideas for everything from merchandise to new locations. Ideas implemented range from frequent-buyer cards to low-calorie snacks.

The public social networks are less familiar territory for most companies. Joel Comm, CEO of InfoMedia, a social media consulting firm, recommends that companies maintain a four-pronged public networking strategy: Facebook, LinkedIn, Twitter, and YouTube. While there are many, many other social network sites—and more every day—these four have emerged as the dominant players.

Comm, author of *Twitter Power: How To Dominate Your Market One Tweet At A Time* (Wiley, 2009), has his personal favorite—Twitter—where "a little goes a long way," he says. As an example, he points to Comcast's Frank Eliason, whom he credits (as have others) with turning around the company's dismal customer service reputation, exacerbated by an embarrassing video that hit YouTube a couple of years ago called "A Comcast technician sleeping on my couch," by using his corporate Twitter account, Comcastcares.com. Eliason has more than 36,000 followers on Twitter and has generated more than 39,000 tweets. "What they're paying this one gentleman is generating huge returns for them," Comm says.

What the public sites don't allow is "complete control over content," says Tom Erickson, CEO of Acquia, which distributes and supports Drupal, an open source software platform used in developing social media sites. Drupal lets companies incorporate blog, search, and wiki capabilities in their online communities, and directly integrate various forms of content such as video. With Facebook, Twitter, and other public sites, "you're limited in the type of content and placement and style," Erickson says.

Most observers agree that companies must develop a dual social media strategy that incorporates homegrown online communities and involvement with the public social networks.

4. HOW DEEP WITHIN MY ORGANIZATION SHOULD SOCIAL NETWORKING BE ALLOWED TO PENETRATE?

This is a sticky question, for several reasons. First, corporate culture is historically closed and conservative. Second, some high-profile incidents relating to employee abuse of social networks have put the fear of God into some executives regarding reputation management and legal exposure.

And there's still a whiff of the old complaints of workplace distraction that accompanied the introduction of e-commerce sites. Morse PLC, an IT services company, touted research late last year that it claims demonstrates that the use of social networks at work costs U.K. businesses 1.38 billion pounds (U.S. $2.23 billion) a year in lost productivity.

Nonetheless, many companies are driving social media deep into their organizations. General Motors offers a video course on its intranet that introduces neophytes to the basics of social networking and the company's policies concerning it; about 3,000 GM employees have viewed that course. A more advanced course offered by Barger's group trains employees to become social media proselytizers and teachers; about 500 have completed that training.

The objective, for GM and every other company that embraces a wide-open social networking strategy, is twofold: Let subject matter experts interact directly with customers, potential customers, and partners; and promote authentic voices as company representatives in the community.

5. IS IT NECESSARY TO HAVE A CORPORATE POLICY AROUND SOCIAL NETWORKING?

Yes, and it needs to be three things: short, simple, and clear. Many companies, including IBM and Intel, have made public their policies concerning the use of social networking tools. A Web search will uncover a list of them.

The Public Relations Society of America will make its policy, covering about 30,000 members, available next month, says VP of marketing McDonald. That policy, based on one introduced earlier this year by Australian telecom company Telstra, embraces the "three R's"—representation, responsibility, and respect. Representation means that you're forthcoming about your affiliation and agenda, so that "people have context," says McDonald. Responsibility means that what you share is factually accurate and relevant, and that you strive to "find the expert" to best answer a query or concern. Respect involves "being civil and understanding," she says.

While social media are an excellent vehicle for generating ideas, those ideas must get to the people in the organization who can make the best use of them. "We're not convinced that a lot of the ideas that come in actually get to the right people in the enterprise," Deloitte's Moran says.

That's because at most companies, the social media function is almost exclusively owned by a single department: marketing. Instead, Moran says, companies should create centers of excellence to disseminate the ideas culled from social networks and online communities—on products, markets, talent, trends—to the right people who can act on them.

6. WHAT CAN SOCIAL MEDIA TEACH ME ABOUT INTERNAL COLLABORATION?

Social networking woke up companies to the way people want to interact with each other, and the ways they don't. "The corporate intranet has become a place where corporate documents go to die," says Srinivas Balasubramanian, CEO of Photon Infotech, an IT consulting firm.

Photon Infotech last year helped Johnson & Johnson overhaul its intranet by adding social media functions. In fact, a growth area for the consulting firm is a product that Balasubramanian says "gives you everything that Facebook and Twitter and YouTube give you on top of SharePoint."

At least one veteran Web 2.0 developer thinks companies should let employees use Facebook, LinkedIn, or Twitter, whichever they choose to get their jobs done, rather than force them "onto captive social networks, or monolithic enterprise platforms." Chris Richter is founder and CEO of startup Socialware, which sells software that controls employees' interactions with public social sites. The company's risk manager module, for instance, monitors and stores content sent by employees to outside social networks and can block anything proprietary or objectionable.

Still, if companies think social networking is about technology, they're missing the point, says John Faber, chief operating officer of af83 Inc., a social media services company. Transparency and knowledge flow are key, yet companies are using social networking techniques to re-create closed, segmented, hierarchical structures and still expecting social media-type benefits. "It won't work," Faber says.

7. WHAT'S NEXT?

Two words that come up often as social media trends are measurement and analytics—as in, is there a way to measure interest and involvement, and to derive insights from raw social networking data? "All this user-generated content is being collected," says Ari Lightman, a marketing consultant. "The idea is to mine through this content to look for correlations."

Those correlations can serve corporate interests in several ways. For instance, they can shed new light on a company's constituency. Toward that end, about a third of respondents to Deloitte's "Tribalization" survey are attempting to capture data on "lurkers," nonactive members of online communities. The idea is to track what these low-profile people might do with the information they get in those forums, such as go off and make purchases or recommendations to friends or comment on other sites.

Online communities can be analyzed for market trends. Tech and entertainment companies are investing heavily in this area, says Marshall Toplansky, president of WiseWindow, which specializes in so-called sentiment analysis services.

One underexploited area of social media analytics has to do with product development—mining online communities for ideas and trends related to product areas. That's mainly because, once again, social media are considered a marketing function, notes Deloitte's Moran. Among the business objectives listed in Deloitte's social media survey, respondents ranked "bring outside ideas into organizations" fourth, behind generating word-of-mouth, increasing customer loyalty, and increasing product/brand awareness.

Mobility is another social media opportunity. GM's Barger says one of his priorities this year is to help company employees make use of Foursquare, which offers smartphone users location-based information-sharing in a Twitter-like format.

Look for more use of public social networks and a movement away from corporate online communities and destination sites. It's the opposite of the "build it and they will come" strategy.

An early harbinger of that trend is a tool developed by Resource Interactive called Off The Wall that lets potential customers on Facebook fan pages receive product inducements through the Facebook news feed and then buy that product directly from the Facebook wall. Resource Interactive's Shust says people have moved on from looking at the Web as a series of destination sites and are "now really starting to exist on the Internet." And while engagement is still the main purpose of social media, he explains, there can be a logical conclusion: "Engagement, and then eventually sales."

When it comes to using social media for business gain, the potential is there—perspective is what's needed. Instead of taking a narrow view, advises consultant Lightman, organizations must use social media to collaborate, innovate, and unlock "knowledge repositories that they didn't know existed."

Deleted, De-Friended[*]

Social Media Great for B2B Until You Misuse It

By Brian Shappell
Business Credit, April 2010

Social media has come a long way in a very short time. From humble beginnings last decade as a means primarily for high school or college-aged computer users to communicate with friends, social media options such as LinkedIn, Facebook and Twitter now are more a necessity than a forward-looking luxury in the business world. Even President Barack Obama, who used social media heavily during his 2008 presidential campaign, continues to engage his constituents through such online platforms.

"You have to go where people are," said Hazel Walker, president of the Referral Institute of Indiana. "If your customers or colleagues are on social networking sites, why would you not be there? It doesn't make sense not to."

However, with so much information out there, social media is a bit like the technological Wild West and carries virtually as much danger to your business if used in a haphazard manner. Despite the widespread growth of such sites, and accompanying stories of embarrassment upon misuse, too many users from credit professionals to vendors make the mistake of treating social media as casual media. When applied to B2B relations, it's anything but.

"Most businesses are not using social media strategically or masterfully," said Nadia Bilchik, of Atlanta-based Greater Impact Communication. "You have to remember you're constantly being branded whether you're conscious of it or not."

HAVE A PLAN

Before using social media well, the management of any business needs to familiarize themselves with the various platforms, which can vary greatly both in

---

[*] Reprinted with permission of *Business Credit Magazine*, the magazine of the National Association of Credit Management.

options and the perception. Think of three of the most used platforms with the following in mind, said Bilchik, who will speak about social media as well as improving executive presence during sessions at NACM's Credit Congress next month: LinkedIn is the Internet equivalent to a business meeting, Facebook is akin to a house party or barbecue and Twitter is a soapbox. David Nour, managing partner of Atlanta-based Nour Group Inc. and author of the book *Relationship Economics* agrees, and he likens the most of the remaining social media options as "bars you don't really want to go into."

Perhaps most importantly, a business needs to have a firm plan before dipping into these Internet waters. In that a company has to have established in advance its goals of using social media, who is going to manage its platforms, whether or not someone from outside the company will be hired to manage those efforts and how to ensure the messages are consistent with the planned image.

One of the more common tales of misusing social media is posting too infrequently. It's commonplace for a well-versed user to post a minimum of two to three times per week with content relevant to your followers/potential business associates. Walker, who presented an NACM teleconference on social networking in March, is all too familiar with allowing one's posting habits to fall by the wayside, along with readership.

"I had started up a great blog and didn't post on it for two months—readership fell dramatically and it took such a long time to rebuild that," said Walker. "People will abandon you. So, if you take the time to build it up, you'd better be paying attention and putting content up as much as possible. If your competitors are putting up a lot of content, you will lose customers to them."

She says businesses that move into social media without a plan face a similar fate. Additionally, it's inadvisable for unfamiliar users to begin Tweeting, for example, without talking to people who use the platform frequently and know all its ins and outs. It can be one of a business' more technology-savvy employees, a college-aged intern or even a family member in their teens. Learn from their expertise and apply it.

NOT A SALES CIRCULAR OR HERO SHEET

At their core, social media platforms are about cultivating relationships, not just about steadily downloading one's own ideas and information about products or services. A key part of building relationships in such an online environment is immediacy, not necessarily in how quickly a given relationship grows but, rather, in necessity to respond to comments or queries made on or through the social media site. Forgetting that is a significant faux pas.

"Not responding to a Twitter message quickly is like not responding to an email for a month. People get the sense that you're not responsive, not paying attention," said Nour. "It's probably better to not jump in at all than to jump in and leave or fall asleep at the switch."

Regardless of how often businesses post or respond to their followers/associates/ friends, Nour and Walker agree that the most blatant misuse of social media is pelting users with sales messages. Remember: no one is jumping onto Twitter or Facebook to read what Walker calls "buy my stuff" messages. It's much better to use the tool more to educate the consumer and encourage intelligent dialogue focused on topics on which you can offer knowledge, said Walker. These approaches build a positive brand image and customer/client loyalty far more than consistently pushing product or services at people.

"The worst thing to do is sell because it unequivocally turns people off," said Nour. "There's a fine line between educating and making something your personal billboard where you're the hero of every story. That gets old to people in a hurry."

STAY PROFESSIONAL

One might think it's a no-brainer to keep any information that can be viewed as controversial off a social media page. But it's shocking just how often people continue to get themselves in trouble—at work, with family and friends or with the law—through online writings or photographs. Examples range from the downright stupid to the seemingly innocent or innocuous. Consider two of Walker's favorite examples out of Indiana in recent months: In one case, a group of police officers were recently fired after posting pictures of themselves drinking beer and playing with guns simultaneously. In another, the head of a public relations firm spurred ill will with sore-loser talk after her favorite football team, the Indianapolis Colts, lost in The Super Bowl.

"She made a mean comment about New Orleans and the Saints . . . Yeah, that didn't really help her firm," said Walker. "And, as a PR professional, she actually created a major PR faux pas for her own business."

Even if something is meant to be funny or playfully sarcastic, written communications don't have the benefit of facial or body expressions. Thus, the point of the message can often be taken out of context as offensive, especially when something is impulsively posted on a site instead of being well thought out. A good rule of thumb is treating every social media message with the same care and attention to detail that goes into meeting a business contact in-person for the first time.

"If you don't want it to be found by someone, anyone, do not put it online," said Nour. "Even if you delete it after an hour, someone may have seen it or it's on someone's server. It's somewhere out there."

In the end, if using the platform as a means of positive B2B communication, the user on the other side generally doesn't want to hear about your religious, political and societal views—so, don't try to spoon-feed them to followers. Even non-business stories that appear inoffensive to just about anyone can put a user in the wringer.

"You shouldn't even discuss things like Tiger Woods through social media because you never know who you're talking to," said Robin Jay, president of the Las

Vegas Speakers Bureau and Nevada-based firm Two Birds Inc. "If I make a comment about Tiger, I don't know if this client is cheating on his wife. He could think I believe he's despicable, too."

In short, focus almost solely on business items, especially when forging new business relationships through social media, and stick with the facts.

DON'T OVERDO IT

While social media is an increasingly crucial part of doing business in the modern age, it's not the entirety of anyone's business. As such, think about whether it's a good idea to have potential business partners holding a view that someone at your business is reading or posting on Twitter, LinkedIn or Facebook all day.

"Your behavior with social media is apparent and transparent," said Bilchik. "In a B2B sense, you're a person I want to be trusted or relied upon. You never want to send the message that 'I'm too busy being frivolous and doing other things.'"

The Tweet Life of CMOs*

By Barbara Lippert
Mediaweek, September 13, 2010

Lord knows, it's a social media free-for-all out there. CMOs—and in some cases their marketing brethren, from "brand ambassadors" to "chief social marketing officers"—seem to be spending more time tweeting than the Situation does tanning.

"We've all had to learn to be copywriters," says Marian Salzman, president, North America, Euro RSCG PR. "And [tweeting] has to be 140 characters, minus a hashtag. And it can't be self-promotional [and has to have] just enough creativity that it doesn't look like a commercial sponsorship. It's a very interesting juggling act."

So why even do it? "I think it can make a difference in categories that are poorly understood or that have had challenges, like automotive and retail banking," says Dorothy Crenshaw, head of Crenshaw Communications. "Done right, it's very humanizing, a way to be authentic and a way for followers to engage and find common ground."

Obviously, there are many CMOs who get it, and they are too numerous to mention. But some lesser knowns—as well as a usual suspect—are being social in ways others might find helpful to learn about before (or after) jumping into the world of social networking. The most important quality that unites them: the ability to relate to their followers.

Steve Fuller, CMO for L.L. Bean, walks the line between professional and personal in pretty much a pitch-perfect way. He has a scant 980 followers, but, more interestingly, he says he follows (and presumably listens to) about the same number.

Sometimes, for things like customer complaints, Fuller gives specific responses. He also manages to blend the personal with the not too promotional while still pushing the L.L. Bean brand image, such as with this tweet: "The woman sitting next to us at the airport is making earrings. They look remarkably like Royal

Coachman fishing flies." And this one, which included a photo: "Thursday night climb of Mount Fuji with Japan staff."

Another nice approach comes from Lisa Gavales, CMO of Express, the lower-priced fashion brand. Gavales, who has 20,689 followers, even weighs in on fashion choices: "Totally agree, very difficult decision! Lovin' everything about that coat!" She also responds to very specific customer product questions: "Just heard back curcumfrance [sic] 375 mm (14.76 inches) for our mini wedge boot."

She often offers a "Pick of the Day" that no doubt helps sell the line, and occasionally posts codes for discounts and coupons.

The only cavil I have with Gavales and Fuller is with their choices of avatars: Fuller uses a copy of the catalog and Gavales the Express logo. To really connect with their followers, they should be less corporate and use photos of themselves—the human face of a brand.

When it comes to the art of the tweet few surpass Ted Rubin, chief social media officer of OpenSky, a site that helps to monetize the businesses of mommy bloggers. His life is an open book, and this includes his frank discussion on his blog of his very painful divorce.

Rubin's best known for building the cosmetics company e.l.f. (eyes, lips, face) with almost no media budget by using the Internet and his rabid, indefatigable social media skills. He built powerful relationships with mommy bloggers and YouTube posters, and "met" magazine writers in the Twittersphere, which translated to print profiles. In turn, he leveraged the power of his followers to get a brick-and-mortar foothold in Target. Now he's doing the same kind of networking for OpenSky.

When tweeting, Rubin, who has more than 30,000 followers, likes to fire off nuggets of wisdom that resonate with his audience. One example: "Women hold famly shoppng purse strings, so no mattr what ur product, u shud b talkng 2 women." (When keeping things to 140 characters, the English language sometimes suffers.) He also gives advice, such as: "Dont expect to build trust if ur only responsive to ur audience every now and then."

Barry Judge, CMO at Best Buy, was an early advocate of social media. This led, in part, to BB agency Crispin Porter + Bogusky developing the award-winning "Twelpforce" (a combination of "tweet" and "help") campaign, which draws on the power of some 2,500 employees to answer consumer tweets. (The service seems to work better on Facebook, but I guess "Felpforce" doesn't have the same geeky ring.)

Two years ago, in an in-house video, Judge said, "For our brand to be relevant . . . we've got to live digitally with our communication and the products we sell." But the reality is that living digitally can be difficult to keep up. Judge discovered the inevitable, recently noting in his blog, "Writing a blog gives you newfound respect for journalists who do this for a living. It's hard work!"

And that's not a bad thing—if it helps to weed out those with little to offer.

Or the ones looking for powers in numbers: Before you know it, a few innocent answers to "What are you doing?" can lead to wearing epaulettes and a messianic drive to have more followers than Ryan Seacrest. For the record, he has more than 3.4 million. (Are they called tweeps?) At a Yahoo presentation at Cannes this year, Ben Stiller joked that Seacrest tried to sell him his list. Actually, it's a list not a few marketers wouldn't mind having.

Can You Measure the ROI of Your Social Media Marketing?[*]

By Donna L. Hoffman and Marek Fodor
MIT Sloan Management Review, Fall 2010

As managers become more comfortable with including blogs and social networks as part of their integrated marketing communications, they have naturally turned their attention to questions regarding the return on investment of social media. Clearly, there is no shortage of interest in the topic. A quick Google search recently for "ROI social media" returned over 2.5 million hits, many seemingly relevant. Internet marketing and online retailing conferences now devote attention to ROI issues, and managers are asking themselves every day, "What's the ROI of [substitute social media application here]?" Blog posts, white papers and case studies prepared by social media gurus, consultants and industry analysts abound, yet the answer remains largely unsatisfying. That isn't good, especially when the CEO and CFO are demanding evidence of potential ROI before allocating dollars to marketing efforts.[1]

We understand the pressures and the desire to quantify the return generated by investing in social media, but we believe most marketers are approaching the issue the wrong way.

Effective social media measurement should start by turning the traditional ROI approach on its head. That is, instead of emphasizing their own marketing investments and calculating the returns in terms of customer response, managers should begin by considering consumer motivations to use social media and then measure the social media *investments* customers make as they engage with the marketers' brands.

Handling the measurements this way makes much more sense. It takes into account not only short-term goals such as increasing sales in the next month via a social media marketing campaign or reducing costs next quarter due to more responsive online support forums, but also the long-term returns of significant corporate investment in social media.

We will explain our reasoning in detail and suggest some guidelines for better integrating social media into your overall marketing strategy, but first a quick example of the kind of radical rethinking we believe is called for.

TURNING YOUR THINKING UPSIDE DOWN

In calculating social media ROI, most marketers start by measuring the cost of launching a blog, for example, and then seek to calculate the return on sales, say, from that social media investment. But a company could also start by thinking about what marketing objectives such a blog might satisfy (e.g., brand engagement), why its customers would visit the blog (e.g., to learn about new products) and what behaviors they might engage in once they got there (e.g., post a comment about a recent consumption experience) that could be linked to the company's marketing objectives.

These behaviors then can be considered (and measured) as customer investments in the marketer's social media efforts. *This suggests that returns from social media investments will not always be measured in dollars, but also in customer behaviors (consumer investments) tied to particular social media applications.* Consumer investments include obvious measures such as the number of visits and time spent with the application (the blog in this case) as well as more active investments, such as the valence of blog comments and the number of Facebook updates and Twitter pages about the brand. These investments can then be used to measure key marketing outcomes such as changes in awareness levels or word-of-mouth increases over time.

Although what we are proposing might seem radical, we believe you have no choice.

Traditional media measurement seems almost quaint in today's dynamic and increasingly complex media environment. Marketers are struggling with social media measurement partly because the frameworks are still largely driven by "reach and frequency" and are ill-suited to the interactive media environment.

On one side are the managers in the trenches whose experience and gut feelings tell them that social media are important, even as they struggle with how to quantify this. On the other side is top management, who may not be 100% convinced about the value of social media or fully understand them—and even if they "get it" in principle, they still want to see the numbers. This tension explains the constant questioning about ROI in emerging advertising media like Twitter.

While managers certainly need hard numbers to know whether their investments are paying off, they represent a narrow "show me the return" focus rooted in a traditional mainstream media. This narrow focus has two problems. First, it is oriented to the short term ("show me how my company's tweets will improve sales next quarter"). Developing meaningful relationships with customers takes time because online relationships involve interactive "conversations,"[2] and some managers still do not fully appreciate that they are entering a brave new world of "relationships" with customers.

This is a world in which customers are fully in *control* of their online experiences and where their motivations lead them to connect online with other consumers while they *create* and *consume* online content, much of it user- —rather than marketer- —generated. These four key motivations—connections, creation, consumption and control—drive consumer use of social media.[3] This "4c's" perspective is important because it leads to a consumer-oriented framework for evaluating social media. *Most managers still consider social media applications as "just another" traditional marketing communications vehicle. That is a mistake. The social media environment is largely consumer- —not marketer- —controlled.* And marketers who don't understand that do so at their peril. (See "The Worst That Can Happen Is Worse Than You Think")

Second, and more importantly, the narrow focus ignores more qualitative objectives—such as the value of a tweet about a brand—that flow from the unique capabilities of the Internet and have no obvious analogues with traditional media metrics. This is a powerful point that is often overlooked.

Both these things call for a different way of thinking about how to measure social media. Let's talk about how you might do it.

SOCIAL MEDIA OBJECTIVES DRIVE SOCIAL MEDIA METRICS

As a first step, marketers should focus on objectives that explicitly recognize the value of operating in the social media environment. Most managers feel pressure to emphasize traditional objectives such as direct sales, direct cost reductions or increases in market share from social media. Ultimately, of course, outcomes like these are the bottom line for any manager. And a marketer who wants to know the immediate effect on sales of a particular social media campaign can do so relatively easily by tracking the revenue generated from the dollars spent, even if tying social media actions directly to sales is difficult. It is becoming increasingly obvious that social media can lead to real cost savings, such as when customers serve as their own version of a company's toll-free help desk through FAQs on user forums. It is also clear that social media can improve the efficiency of market research efforts when, for example, marketers set up online prediction markets to crowdsource new ideas or mine online forums that allow customers to comment on product concepts and offer improvements for existing products.

Sales, cost efficiencies, product development and market research are obvious objectives, but in our development of appropriate social media metrics we want to emphasize objectives that take advantage of the distinctive characteristics of social media. In the social media environment, marketers have unique opportunities to develop social media programs that tackle awareness, engagement and word-of-mouth objectives. Social media applications can fulfill any of these objectives, where the appropriate set of metrics depends on the objective. (See "Relevant

Metrics for Social Media Applications Organized by Key Social Media Objectives," p. 73.)

To get an ROI estimate, managers would link the social media metrics to an additional set of proxy benchmarks (e.g., the likelihood of future purchase by a user engaged with the company's brand through a specific social media application, or the reach of a specific word-of-mouth element and subsequent conversion to future sales). For example, a popular personal care brand ran a large-scale integrated ad campaign on MySpace in the second quarter of 2008 and used matched consumer panels to link online social media behavior to survey measures of purchase intent as well as actual in-store sales. The results showed an ROI of 28% for the ad campaign.[4]

As this example shows, companies are starting to see some success measuring the ROI of their social media experiments, including some that offer the consumer a relatively complex social media experience. For example, in 2007, Kellogg created an integrated digital media experience for the "Special K Challenge" featuring a support website that offered consumers the opportunity to customize a diet using Special K cereal, participate in online forums with pointers from experts, join a Yahoo! e-mail support group and click through to Amazon.com to purchase the cereal. Kellogg, which was able to translate those website interactions and click-throughs to market response over 18 months, found that the online ROI for Special K cereal was twice as large as that from television.[5] Vocalpoint, Procter & Gamble's social networking site, has over 350,000 members who talk about P&G products; by linking these customer investments in brand conversation to sales, the site is credited with market response increases of up to 30%.[6]

To be sure, there is some complexity involved in calculating the ROI of a sophisticated social media campaign, not necessarily limited to determining the size of the test and control samples and the ability to match online customer profiles with offline purchases. However, even small-scale social media efforts can benefit from plugging in segment-level estimates and proxy measures to quantify how the customer investments from brand awareness, brand engagement and word of mouth affect the purchase decision funnel and, ultimately, the bottom line. We expect that over time the number and quality of the necessary inputs will increase, but marketers can find even rough proxy estimates useful in the meantime to generate the calculations necessary to link marketing investments to customer investments and market response.

Below we discuss three social media objectives and provide several examples of each.

Brand Awareness Traditionally, brand awareness is measured through tracking studies and surveys. Online, however, marketers have a number of ways to track brand awareness.

In the social media environment, every time a person uses an application designed by or about the company, the company gains increased exposure to its brand, often in highly relevant contexts. For example, several days before Election Day 2008, Starbucks ran a spot on the "Saturday Night Live" show as well as on

YouTube, promoting a free coffee giveaway. Twitter mentions of Starbucks sky-rocketed, averaging a mention every eight seconds, which translated into a sizeable increase in brand exposure.[7] Such usages enhance and strengthen associations of the brand in customers' minds through increased exposures. Thus, brand awareness is a key social media objective.

Another example is Naked Pizza, a New Orleans, Louisiana-based business catering to health-conscious pizza lovers, which tweeted about its pizzas in 2009 and successfully drew around 4,000 followers in just a few months. The company also kept track of sales that were spurred by a billboard outside its shop encouraging customers to follow it on Twitter. The microblogging campaign's success culminated in the company breaking its one-day sales record, with more than 68% of its sales coming from customers who were Twitter followers. Also on that day, 85% of the company's new customers claimed they had been motivated to buy from Naked Pizza because of Twitter.[8]

Finally, in what have rapidly become classics in the social media sphere, K-Tec's blender brand Blendtec posted a series of humorous demonstration videos in which the company's founder, Tom Dickson, posed the question "Will It Blend?" and then proceeded to blend iPhones, glow sticks, golf balls and many other products previously thought unblendable using his line of hardy blenders. The "Will It Blend?" campaign quickly went viral and as a result saw its sales grow fivefold. The BlendTec videos have now been viewed more than 100 million times on YouTube.

Brand Engagement Brand engagement can be enhanced through social media in various ways, and the results can be strikingly positive. In an effort to engage its customers, Southwest Airlines revamped its "Nuts About Southwest" blog with podcasts, videos and other social media tools. Visits to the new and improved blog rose by 25%, page views increased 40% and visitors stayed 26% longer on the company's website. The blog engaged customers on touchy subjects like assigned seating and used the results from 700 posts as a virtual focus group.[9]

Target leveraged the social networking aspect of Facebook by encouraging its customers to join and participate in an online environment devoid of any apparent self-serving sales pitches. Target tracked the success of its social media campaign by monitoring membership sign-ups. On their own, thousands of members generated significant buzz with regular posts, which in turn motivated numerous others to join and participate on the networking site. A Facebook application called "Circle of Moms"—which let mothers post messages, arrange carpools, set up back-to-school checklists and click through to promotions on the Target site—generated more than 20,000 visitors in six weeks.

For its 125th anniversary, Gretsch Guitars held a contest on its MySpace page to find the next best unsigned independent band. Nearly 900 bands entered the contest, and over 55,000 site visitors voted for their favorite bands. By soliciting participation from both musicians and their fans, Gretsch engaged its target customer and raised awareness of the brand more broadly.

These highly engaging social media campaigns involving user-generated content likely generate commitment on the part of the consumer, reinforcing loyalty to the brand and making the customer more likely to commit additional effort to support the brand in the future. The bottom-line rewards for this kind of engagement may be observed through delayed sales. Traditionally, marketers measure engagement through customer surveys. Online, marketers can use one-time versus repeated interactions or active participation compared to passive consumption of social media as proxy measures.

Word of Mouth Once consumers are aware and engaged, they are in a position to communicate their opinions to other consumers. Satisfied and loyal consumers communicate their positive attitudes toward the brand itself or toward the social application created by the company (be it a Facebook application or group, a Twitter presence, a blog or a YouTube video) to new, prospective customers both online and offline. Dissatisfied and disgruntled customers may also share their negative attitudes toward the brand or poor social applications, as when technology journalist Jeff Jarvis blogged in 2005 about the shoddy customer service he received from Dell—his own "Dell Hell" that spread like wildfire on the Internet and mainstream media—and Dell saw its customer satisfaction score drop five points in one year.[10] On the positive side, Japanese gaming company Square Enix started an online community to stir up interest in its North American release of Sony's Playstation 2 video game "Dragon Quest VIII: Journey of the Cursed King." The North American online community was a success, drawing more than 14,000 members to join its forum, with 30% recruited via word of mouth from existing members; 40% of the online community pre-ordered the game. By the end of 2009, the video game had sold 510,000 units in North America.

In 2009, Burger King asked members of its "Whopper Sacrifice" Facebook application to un-friend 10 of their Facebook friends in exchange for a free sandwich. Though later pulled, the reverse word-of-mouth campaign resulted in members unfriending a total of 234,000 Facebook friends. These abandoned friends monitored by the application received alerts informing them that they had been sacrificed for a Whopper. The offbeat campaign resulted in significant word of mouth for Burger King.

Traditionally, companies can estimate word of mouth through surveys that measure the likelihood of recommendation or can use customer satisfaction, loyalty and purchase likelihood as proxies for word of mouth, but online, word of mouth can be measured directly. More sophisticated methodologies are often required to measure word of mouth because a significant amount can occur either offline or online via private communication, where direct measurement is impossible. User-generated content can also embed consumers' favorite brands (such as in a video on YouTube or a photo posted on Flickr) and contribute to word of mouth—and companies can organize such experiences on behalf of their consumers. For example, Atrapalo.com, one of Spain's leading online travel agencies, included on its site a way for consumers to share travel videos and customer photos.

WHY YOU WANT TO DO IT THIS WAY

The advantage of starting with consumer motivations, as opposed to trying to figure out what social media application to use, is that it makes clear how seemingly disparate applications are actually quite similar if they share the same underlying motivations for use. This makes the job of creating integrated marketing campaigns not only less overwhelming for the manager but also much more closely tied to online consumer behavior.

In other words, the question is not whether to blog or tweet, but what objectives need to be achieved and which set of tools with their corresponding metrics can best achieve them.

PATHS TO EFFECTIVE SOCIAL MEDIA STRATEGY

Once managers have a set of objectives in place for their social media efforts and understand that consumers are motivated to make investments in companies' social media efforts through their interactions with the brand, the next step is to consider the strategic options for social media measurement.

Our simple 2 × 2 framework, which assumes the manager has a social media effort ongoing, neatly summarizes the choices managers face as they strive to develop social media strategy and suggests better (and worse) paths toward social media success. (See "Strategic Options for Social Media Measurement[, p. 74].")

Let's start with the "dead end." In this scenario, the marketer has only a limited ability to measure his social media efforts (fuzzy) and believes that his efforts are not working (failing). Managers find themselves in this quadrant as a result of the "throw it on the wall and see what sticks" strategy and perform arbitrary changes with no way to measure their impact. Because measurement is fuzzy and the effort's effectiveness appears to be failing, the manager has little insight or idea on what to do. The outcome is fairly predictable: The manager will give up on social media efforts or continue efforts that involve random adjustments without data support. This quadrant is a dead end. You don't want to get stuck here!

Next is "measure and adjust." In this scenario, the marketer has a reasonable ability to quantify his social media efforts, and these measurements lead him to believe that his efforts are not working (failing). This is distinctly different than the "dead end" scenario, because even though the manager does not believe he is succeeding, at least he is making some attempt to measure social media effectiveness. Since the components are being measured, there are probably some good clues about what is going wrong. This means the manager can evaluate and adjust the social media strategy accordingly. If the manager can do this well, he can move toward the "iterate for success" quadrant.

In that space, the marketer has both a reasonable ability to measure his social media efforts (quantifiable) and the belief that his efforts are working (succeeding).

Since the components are being measured, the manager can purposefully iterate to improve even more. This is hard to do but obviously worth the effort.

The other path is "naïve optimist." Here, the marketer has only a limited ability to measure his social media efforts (fuzzy), yet believes that his efforts are working (succeeding). We believe most marketers actually start here. They believe social media are worth the effort, but are not quite sure how best to measure their efforts. This quadrant is tricky because although it is a reasonable place to start, you want to move out of it as fast as possible so you don't get stuck here.

Managers have two good options for moving from "naïve optimism" to "iterate for success" and one poor choice. Let us examine the poor choice first.

If the manager does not change anything, he will likely migrate to the "dead end." This is because the lack of measurement will eventually lead to deterioration in the effort's effectiveness over time, particularly as competitors are able to do it better.

There are two better options. First, the manager simply starts to measure social media efforts, discovers things are not working as well as they could be ("measure and adjust") and then directs his efforts toward "iterate for success." In the shorter path, the manager starts measuring and discovers the efforts are succeeding, moving directly to "iterate for success" from "naïve optimism." In either case, the goal is to move away from fuzzy measurement and toward quantifiable metrics where the manager can get a real handle on what is working and what is not and then follow the best path that will get him where he needs to go.

DONE RIGHT, SOCIAL MEDIA STRATEGIES PUT THE
BRAND TO WORK FOR CUSTOMERS

Reducing social media strategy to a mere measurement problem would be a mistake. Although measuring the ROI of social media efforts is important and necessary, it is far more important that managers make sure their social media efforts are effective, even if the state of ROI measurement may be less than satisfactory. In order to maximize the effectiveness of their social media efforts, managers must recognize two important facts of social media life when implementing social media campaigns.

First, while it is certainly true that consumers have much greater control over their online experiences, managers also have—and must exercise—a fair amount of control over the rules and framework for brand participation in social media. For example, a manager can control who posts to a blog devoted to the company's brand. More generally, managers certainly have at least some control over the rules and the participatory framework of how consumers will engage with their brands in the social media space.

Second, managers must appreciate that the social media environment is highly dynamic and rapidly evolving. While this may seem obvious, it is mostly overlooked when campaigns are conceived and launched. Many managers still approach social media as if the practices—and consumer behaviors—are largely fixed. Social media-savvy managers know this is not the case, but traditional beliefs about how to reach consumers and potential consumers die hard.

Our premise is that social media efforts that are developed in the context of the 4c's—connections, creation, consumption and control—that underlie consumer motivations to participate will lead to higher ROI because the company's marketing investments can better leverage the active "investments" its customers will make as they engage with the company's brands. These investments can take the form of blog comments, registration and active participation to become a part of a brand-related community, private endorsements of a brand or product (a tweet or retweet, Facebook comment, review, blog post or offline recommendations to friends) and the like. While the content of consumers' interactions is largely out of managers' control, setting up the framework to facilitate that interaction is squarely in their control.

How managers design, launch and actively manage their social media campaigns plays a large part in determining whether and how consumers will participate and interact. Savvy managers understand that there is a feedback loop. They don't sit back once the social media campaign begins. Instead, they listen carefully because they know that consumers not only "consume" the campaign, but can comment on it ("create"), share it with their friends and anyone else ("connect") and provide their uncensored thoughts about it ("control") for any and all to view. And this listening must then lead to action. For example, if a consumer posts a question to the manager's blog, someone with a face in the company must reply. If a video is uploaded, someone must monitor the Twitter stream for comments and be prepared to react if problems appear.

Traditional marketing metrics with narrowly defined ROI tend to lead to social media campaigns that maximize short-term benefits for the brand (or the manager!), without worrying too much about customer motivations and the long term. The result tends to be campaigns that expect the customer to work for the brand. In contrast, effective social media strategies put the brand to work for the customers by satisfying their needs to create, consume, connect and control in the social Web.

In a well-designed social media campaign, consumers are likely to spread viral videos, create additional brand-related content, tweet about the brand and post about their experiences on Facebook. The social metrics that reflect these kinds of social media behaviors are important not only because they let marketers measure the bottom-line impact of their social media efforts, but also because they focus marketers' attention on social media strategies that take into account the objectives of both the brand and the online customer.

There is reason to be highly optimistic about improving the effectiveness of social media. The social Web is a highly measurable environment, and it is a relatively simple matter for a manager to measure the number of product reviews, blog posts and comments, retweets and appearances in the social network timelines of the company's brands. At the same time, managers are often able to measure click-throughs to transactional websites, as well as capture the number of leads generated or conversion rates for online sales. While there will still be those situations in which behavior cannot be completely and accurately traced (e.g., offline purchases or offline word of mouth), we think that carefully planned social media campaigns afford phenomenal opportunities for relatively easy and cost-efficient measurement of customers' online investments in a company's brands.

DONNA L. HOFFMAN *is the Chancellor's Chair and Professor of Marketing at the A. Gary Anderson Graduate School of Management, University of California, Riverside.* **MAREK FODOR** *is the cofounder of Atrapalo, one of Spain's leading travel agencies, and was formerly its chief technology officer. Comment on this article at http://sloanreview. mit.edU/x/52105, or contact the authors at smrfeedback@mit.edu.*

ACKNOWLEDGMENTS

This research was supported by a grant from the UCR Sloan Center for Internet Retailing. The authors thank Mark Manalang for his research assistance.

REFERENCES

1. Lenskold Group, "2009 Lenskold Group/MarketSphere Marketing ROI and Measurements Study" (Manasquan, New Jersey: Lenskold Group, 2009).

2. D.L. Hoffman and T.P. Novak, "Social Media Strategy," in "Handbook on Marketing Strategy," ed. V. Shankar and G.S. Carpenter (Northampton, Massachusetts: Edward Elgar Publishing, in press).

3. T.P. Novak and D.L. Hoffman, "Roles and Goals: Consumer Motivations to Use the Social Web" (paper presented at the INFORMS Marketing Science Conference, Cologne, Germany, June 19, 2010).

4. L. Liftman, J. Nagy and N. Wortman, "Advertising on Social Networks Drives In-Store Sales," 2008, www.thearf.org.

5. E.B. York, "Kellogg Says ROI on Digital Trounces TV by 'Factor of 2'," Advertising Age, Sept. 6, 2008.

6. B. Cummings, "J&J Takes Baby Steps Toward Social Media," Brandweek, Apr. 13, 2008.

7. C.C. Miller, "New Starbucks Ads Seek to Recruit Online Fans," New York Times, May 18, 2009.

8. C. Baldwin, "Twitter Helps Dell Rake in Sales," June 12, 2009, www.reuters.com.

9. P. Berg, "Southwest Airlines: Nuts About Online Communication" (presentation at the Inbound Marketing Summit, Boston, May 27–28, 2009).

10. K.T. Williams, "Case Study: Dell Hell," Feb. 7, 2009, www.docstoc.com.

THE WORST THAT CAN HAPPEN IS WORSE THAN YOU THINK

Marketers often think the worst thing that can happen during a marketing campaign or support forum is no activity or response. They are wrong. The "rules of engagement" and the dynamics of interaction in the social media world are often quite different from traditional marketing.

Several companies that are considered marketing experts have learned the hard way that even well-intentioned social media efforts can go embarrassingly wrong. And while social media blunders may not necessarily negatively impact sales, managers need to be mindful as the results of social media experiments gone awry live on, just a Google search away, for years to come.

Case Study: *Raging Cow.* In 2003, Dr. Pepper/7UP elicited consumer anger with its Raging Cow campaign. The company enlisted a group of six teenagers and 20-somethings to post favorable reviews and spread positive word of mouth about its new flavored milk drink, without disclosing that the enlisted bloggers received incentives like product samples, T-shirts and gift certificates. On the surface, the blogs looked impartial and did not appear to be affiliated with the company or the drink, except for a few obligatory links to the Raging Cow site. But closer examination by a group of suspicious bloggers revealed that the company was behind the blogging effort. The marketing campaign was subsequently attacked in the blogosphere. Bloggers started a boycott, and the product disappeared.

Case Study: *Motrin.* Johnson & Johnson's Motrin brand launched a video campaign in 2008 targeted to "baby-wearing" mothers. This was a 45-second commercial in which the voice-over of a supposed mom talked conversationally about the burdens of wearing your baby in a body sling. A number of mothers were so offended by the video, which was viewed as both condescending ("Wearing your baby seems to be in fashion" was the opening line of the spot) and exploitive in promoting Motrin as a cure for the back-breaking pain of baby wearing, that they took to Twitter and the blogosphere to criticize the brand in real time. Riding off the momentum of enraged tweets from baby-wearing defenders, the "Motrin Moms" debacle immediately became a top trending topic on Twitter Search. But instead of quick damage control, Motrin did nothing. Only after mainstream media coverage, during which countless social media experts weighed in and branded the effort with a unanimous thumbs down, did Kathy Widmer, McNeil Consumer Healthcare's vice president of marketing, finally offer a limp apology. What's particularly relevant here is that the bulk of these events unfolded over the course of 24 hours on a weekend.

RELEVANT METRICS FOR SOCIAL MEDIA APPLICATIONS ORGANIZED BY KEY SOCIAL MEDIA OBJECTIVES

This table organizes the various social metrics for social media by classifying them according to social media applications and social media performance objectives. While it is not exhaustive, it should give marketers a useful starting point for measuring the effectiveness of social media efforts because all of the metrics listed are easily measured.

SOCIAL MEDIA APPLICATION	BRAND AWARENESS	BRAND ENGAGEMENT	WORD OF MOUTH
Blogs	•number of unique visits •number of return visits •number of times bookmarked •search ranking	•number of members •number of RSS feed subscribers •number of comments •amount of user-generated content •average length of time on site •number of responses to polls, contests, surveys	•number of references to blog in other media (online/offline) •number of reblogs •number of times badge displayed on other sites •number of "likes"
Microblogging (e.g., Twitter)	•number of tweets about the brand •valence of tweets +/– •number of followers	•number of followers •number of @replies	•number of retweets
Cocreation (e.g., NIKEiD)	•number of visits	•number of creation attempts	•number of references to project in other media (online/offline)
Social Bookmarking (e.g., StumbleUpon)	•number of tags	•number of followers	•number of additional taggers
Forums and Discussion Boards (e.g., Google Groups)	•number of page views •number of visits •valence of posted content +/-	•number of relevant topics/threads •number of individual replies •number of sign-ups	•incoming links •citations in other sites •tagging in social bookmarking •offline references to the forum or its members •in private communities: number of pieces of content (photos, discussions, videos); chatter pointing to the community outside of its gates •number of "likes"
Product Reviews (e.g., Amazon)	•number of reviews posted •valence of reviews •number and valence of other users' responses to reviews (+/–) •number of wish list adds •number of times product included in users' lists (i.e., Listmania! on Amazon.com)	•length of reviews •relevance of reviews •valence of other users' ratings of reviews (i.e., how many found particular review helpful) •number of wish list adds •overall number of reviewer rating scores entered •average reviewer rating score	•number of reviews posted •valence of reviews •number and valence of other users' responses to reviews (+/–) •number of references to reviews in other sites •number of visits to review site page •number of times product included in users' lists (i.e., Listmania! on Amazon.com)
Social Networks (e.g., Bebo, Facebook, LinkedIn)	•number of members/fans •number of installs of applications •number of impressions •number of bookmarks •number of reviews/ratings and valence +/–	•number of comments •number of active users •number of "likes" on friends' feeds •number of user-generated items (photos, threads, replies) •usage metrics of applications/widgets •impressions-to-interactions ratio •rate of activity (how often members personalize profiles, bios, links, etc.)	•frequency of appearances in timeline of friends •number of posts on wall •number of reposts/shares •number of responses to friend referral invites
Video and Photosharing (e.g., Flickr, YouTube)	•number of views of video/photo •valence of video/photo ratings +/–	•number of replies •number of page views •number of comments •number of subscribers	•number of embeddings •number of incoming links •number of references in mock-ups or derived work •number of times republished in other social media and offline •number of "likes"

STRATEGIC OPTIONS FOR SOCIAL MEDIA MEASUREMENT

Every manager's goal should be to move away from fuzzy measurement and toward quantifiable metrics. That way, a manager can understand what's working and what's not—and revise the approach accordingly.

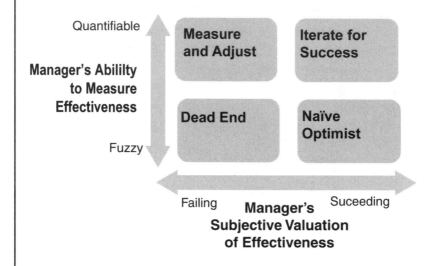

Does Social Sell?*

By Brian Morrissey
Adweek, February 15, 2010

For all the excitement about social media, there's a specter hanging over its use by companies. Is all this Tweeting, blogging and Facebooking paying off? For some proponents, the question is irrelevant. They agree with the view encapsulated in the social media bible The Cluetrain Manifesto—markets are conversations. Companies have to participate in the conversations where they're happening, ROI be damned. Their dismissal of metrics is summed up in an oft-repeated question, "What's the ROI of putting on your pants [. . .] in the morning?"

Those kind of pithy ripostes are music to the ears of the social-media faithful at conferences and on blogs, but they're unlikely to impress budget-strapped CMOs who, while eager to find new ways to reach consumers, are under more pressure to prove their efforts are pushing the business forward. Measurement remains the single greatest challenge to social-media adoption by companies. While digital channels and online interactions offer a plethora of data points, they don't come with a set playbook for assigning value. Marketers have grown comfortable with formulas like gross ratings points and frequency, time-tested formulas for building brands in traditional media. Yet with social media, what's a Facebook friend worth?

"The value of social media is it's the richest data set that's ever existed," says Dan Neely, CEO of Networked Insights, a Wisconsin-based analytics company that uses social media to help clients make marketing decisions. "You can use this data for many things."

The two sides of the social-media measurement debate are at the forefront as many marketers plan to ramp up their social-media budgets in 2010. According to an ExactTarget survey of 1,000 marketers, 70 percent said they plan to increase spending in social media, but less than 20 percent said they could effectively measure ROI. The seeming schizophrenia is because marketers using social media tend

---

to blend "art and science" in their measurements, according to Morgan Stewart, ExactTarget's director of strategy and research.

"ROI isn't the thing dial's pushing people to social media," says Stewart. "Companies using reputation as a measure of success are more likely to be shifting budget there. That tells you something about the mind-set."

Here's what three marketers well versed in social media are doing to measure their participation and justify new investments.

PEPSI: THE SPEED OF DIGITAL CULTURE

At a time when many brands are stuck in experimentation mode in social media, Pepsi is placing a staggeringly large bet on it. Pepsi was absent from the Super Bowl for the first time in 23 years, redirecting money to an ambitious social marketing-centered program called Refresh Everything that will direct $20 million to charities. According to Pepsi execs, the program is appealing because it rested on four big trends: crowdsourcing, doing good, sharing and transparency.

Refresh Everything is the culmination of years of social-media work done by Pepsi, the perpetual No. 2 behind Coca-Cola in the soft drink market Pepsi's still a big spender in traditional media—it spent $89 million in U.S. advertising on the brand in 2009—but Coke out-guns it by a 33 percent margin. Social media, offering a more level playing field, is where Pepsi is making its stand with one of the largest commitments to the space yet seen.

Yet Pepsi execs are at pains to point out that Refresh Everything is not a social-media campaign per se. Rather, it uses social media as glue to hold together a wider push that includes traditional elements like TV spots, says Bonin Bough, PepsiCo's director of social media. It even includes a dash of Pepsi's usual celebrity tie-ins with the inclusion of Hollywood stars Demi Moore and Kevin Bacon, and New Orleans Saints quarterback and Super Bowl hero Drew Brees.

When it comes to measurement, Bough's team has developed a scorecard with different elements that tie back to brand health and relevance. It will gauge, via standard research methods, whether people's perception of Pepsi changed. Pepsi is using social monitoring tools to track share of voice and mentions in social media and traditional media, as well as harder engagement metrics like visits to the Refresh site, time spent, submissions and votes. It will try to gauge whether the program makes an impact in communities. The overall aim is to follow in the footsteps of decades of Pepsi marketing. "Our goal is to skate to the center of culture," says Bough. "Right now, digital is culture."

Pepsi has the advantage of experience to draw upon. It has launched several social-focused efforts for brands. Tropicana created the Trop 50 community site with Blogher last year to reach women bloggers. Mountain Dew launched Dewmocracy, which designated to consumers its marketing plans. "We've already gone through the experimental phase," notes Bough.

While Refresh Everything is a risk, Pepsi has drawn the notice of Coke. Soon after Pepsi announced Refresh Everything, Coke began a Facebook campaign and now donates $1 to the Boys and Girls Clubs of America for each visitor and every time a virtual gift is sent.

DELL: FROM SILENT TO IDEASTORM

In five years, Dell went from being the poster boy of ignoring the emerging social Web to becoming a model for how to orient a company around social media. Its journey began in 2005, when Facebook was barely beyond a dorm room project. Problems with Dell customer service percolated on blogs under the moniker "Dell Hell." The company, founded by Michael Dell with a focus on customers, reoriented itself to be more responsive.

It's gone on to become a social media star, ranked by Vitrue as one of the 10 social-media brands of 2009. It has built a strong social-media team that focuses on entwining those technologies within all aspects of its business, from customer service to marketing to research. Its activities include racking up $6.5 million in sales through Twitter, connecting with 3.5 million consumers on social sites and its own, and soliciting consumer input through sites like Dell IdeaStorm and Dell Tech Center.

"When we first jumped headfirst into this, we started with engaging and listening to consumers," says Manish Mehta, vp of social media and community at Dell. "Hopefully that moved the needle. The business will at some point question how this is helping the P&L. That's why taking a step back and finding the value drivers is so important."

The company's push into social channels left it with a conundrum: How could it evaluate efforts that were taking place all over the company to see if they were worth the investment? This fall, Dell's social-media team mapped out a defined framework to guide those decisions. It identified a set of value drivers for the customer and for the business, looking for programs that overlapped the two sets. For consumers, Dell identified drivers like connections, recognition and advice. For its business, its drivers are things such as revenue, brand health, share of voice and customer sentiment.

"They are light years beyond what others are doing," says Aaron Strom, CMO at social-media firm Powered in Austin, Texas. "They spend a lot of time thinking through how to translate that into real dollars. Quite frankly a lot of companies haven't done a good job at that."

Take the Dell Tech Center, one of the company's less sexy social initiatives. The Tech Center is an online community for IT managers to go and connect directly with Dell engineers. Dell tracks its success based on fundamental metrics, like members, questions posed and answered, and traffic to the site. It also charts how many large-enterprise customers have interacted with the site through a post-purchase survey. Yet one of the key metrics is harder to define: evidence that it's helping deals close quicker and stripping out costs.

"We've found our salespeople are referring prospects in there," says Richard Binhammer, a senior manager on Dell's social-media team. "It's shortening the sales cycles."

Binhammer and Mehta agree the key to pushing forward with social media at the company is a commitment at senior levels. As a tech company that sells most of its products online, this is easier at Dell, although there's still work to do, Mehta admits.

"We want to make this be completely embedded into the fabric of the company," he says.

H&R BLOCK; TAXING PROBLEMS

When H&R Block launched an ambitious social-media outreach campaign in 2008, it followed some textbook advice: fish where the fish are. So it went on Twitter looking for frustrated taxpayers, offering them help. Instead, the company found reticence among potential customers who didn't want to air their problems on Twitter.

This year, H&R Block changed course, abandoning one-on-one Twitter contact in favor of building a Q&A community site, Get It Right, which replaced a more standard blog the company did last year. The Get It Right site required H&R Block's social-media team to recruit and train 1,000 tax pros to answer questions. It looked to local managers to nominate tax preparers to participate. Early results are promising: Get It Right has signed up 65,000 members and answered 50,000 questions, with the big tax push still to come.

"We're outpacing where we thought we'd be," says Zena Weist, director of social media at the company.

The challenge will be tracking these queries back to sales. H&R Block, after all, makes most of its money by getting people into its offices. Weist only recently joined the company. With few internal resources, the company has needed to pare back its social programs, emphasizing Twitter and Facebook less, for instance. The decision was hard but necessary, Weist says, since H&R Block can't promise to answer tax questions posed on Facebook. Instead, it is using Twitter and Facebook mostly as broadcast vehicles, hoping customers who have come to Get It Right then tell their networks they were helped.

H&R Block is trying to steal a march on competitor TurboTax, from Intuit, which has a team of experts dubbed Team TurboTax answering questions on Twitter. "A community wants a one-to-one relationship where they can continue to come back," Weist says. "That's not what Twitter is. You don't have continuous dialogue."

To figure out if the strategy's working, Weist is tracking visits, time spent, registrations and questions asked. The company will conduct Dynamic Logic surveys to gauge brand favorability changes in visitors. It's also trolling social sites for the number of brand combinations in social media and their sentiment. There's also value in knowing many of the people contacting the company online wouldn't call in, thereby saving H&R Block money. The metrics can, at times, be "squishy," Weist says, but the opportunity in social is worth the tradeoff.

"If your word of mouth isn't positive, forget about brand awareness and consideration," she says. "If word of mouth is bad, there is no consideration."

3

Tweeting for a Cause:
Social Media Meets Politics and Activism

Editor's Introduction

Given that political discourse in the United States often centers on sound bites, it's not surprising that social networking—characterized by 140-character Tweets, quickie Facebook status updates, and other such bursts of information—has become a major part of modern campaigning.

In the aftermath of the 2008 presidential election, much was made about how Facebook, Twitter, and Meetup had helped propel Barack Obama into the White House. Indeed, Obama's team relied heavily on these sites, using them to post news updates, mobilize volunteers, and perhaps most importantly, raise hundreds of millions of dollars. "They made online the central nervous system for their organization," Pete Snyder, co-founder and CEO of New Media Strategies, tells writer Michael Learmonth in "Social Media Paves Obama's Way to White House," the piece that begins this chapter's look at social media's role in politics and activism.

When Obama seeks reelection in 2012, he may find himself up against a member of the Tea Party, a conservative group whose female constituents, dubbed "mama grizzlies," have adopted social media as their primary means of organizing. In "Can the Mama Grizzlies Pull Off a Twitter Revolution?" the next article, Noreen Malone explores whether social-networking sites spur meaningful political action, as the Tea Partiers suggest, or simply lessen "the level of motivation that participation requires," leading to empty gestures, as journalist Malcolm Gladwell asserts.

Gladwell's views also figure prominently in the next entry, Frank Rich's "Facebook Politicians Are Not Your Friends." Rich starts by restating the "idealized narrative of digital democracy," recounting how YouTube sank the career of a Virginia senator and helped Obama defeat Hillary Clinton—a better-known candidate with deeper pockets and stronger party connections—in the 2008 Democratic presidential primary. As the piece progresses, however, Rich focuses on the "less salutary counternarrative," arguing that social-networking sites spread misinformation and stand little chance of taking down candidates with "big lies and big money."

If it remains to be seen whether social media can actually influence the outcome of elections, candidates aren't taking any chances. In "In Social Media Election, the GOP Capitalizes," the next selection in this chapter, Jake Coyle reports on the 2010 midterm elections, highlighting the ways in which politicians—Republicans in particular—used on-line resources to get out the vote. According to Lee Rainie, director of the Pew Internet and American Life Project, social networking is now "inextricably a part of the political communication landscape." The numbers bear this out, and 74 percent of congressional candidates with more Facebook friends than their opponents won on election night.

In "What You Need to Know About Social Networking," this chapter's next entry, Pam Greenberg and Meagan Dorsch present eight helpful tips for politicians looking to capitalize on social media. The first step, the authors write, is to "know the tools," or gain an understanding of how, say, Facebook differs from Twitter, and what types of users frequent each site. "At no other time in history have we been able to use technology to connect with so many people at one time," Greenberg and Dorsch write, concluding that social networking, though not without its risks, is worth the effort.

In "Road Kill Social Media: What's Hot One Day Can Cool Off in a Hurry," the subsequent article, Mark Hrywna turns to the world of nonprofits, exploring the ways in which PETA, Oxfam, and other such organizations are promoting their causes on-line. According to one survey, 86 percent of nonprofits are on Facebook, while 60 percent have Twitter accounts. Mirroring the trend among individual users, many agencies are moving away from MySpace, which has experienced a tremendous dip in popularity.

Social Media Paves Obama's Way to White House[*]

Presidential Run Raised the Bar for Campaigns, Offered Plenty of Lessons for Consumer Brands

By Michael Learmonth
Advertising Age, March 30, 2009

"The point isn't for people to come to your site and do cool stuff, it's to help you accomplish your core goals," said Joe Rospars, who served as new-media director for Barack Obama's presidential campaign.

In a world of me-too web campaigns and get-me-one-of-those gimmicks, marketers could do well to follow the advice of Joe Rospars, who helped Barack Obama tap Facebook, Twitter and Meetup in his bid to win the presidency. While there may be no greater sales story for social media than that of Mr. Obama, the campaign never used the tools just to show it could; it used them for the real, often unsexy, heavy lifting they provided.

To recap: $500 million raised online from 3 million donors, most in increments of less than $100; 35,000 groups organized through the website My Barack Obama; 1,800 videos posted to YouTube, garnering 50 million views; and Facebook's most popular page, with gagillions of friends.

Mr. Obama's team had respect for the technology and knew how to use it. Rather than cloister the web staff in a room stocked with Mountain Dew and Twizzlers, Mr. Obama's various web "gurus" had real power in the organization, and the internet was used in every aspect of the campaign: PR, advertising, advance work, fundraising and setting up organizations in all 50 states. Indeed, the web allowed Obama to mount the first true 50-state campaign in years, rather than just rally the base and focus on a few battleground states, or even counties.

"They made online the central nervous system for their organization; smart brands are going to start doing this," said Pete Snyder, co-founder and CEO of New Media Strategies. "The ripple effect of this will be felt for years to come."

Digital tools allowed the campaign to communicate directly with voters on an unprecedented scale, bypassing the forms and filters of traditional media. And because digital had been an integral part of the plan from the start, the Obama team made it look easy—and that became quickly apparent when his challengers rushed out me-too efforts that looked amateurish by comparison.

The campaign was uniquely adept at using the right tool for the right purpose. For example: Much was made of the Obama campaign's use of Facebook, Meetup, YouTube and Twitter, but the most powerful tool in Obama's digital arsenal was probably his 13.5 million-strong e-mail list.

Blue State Digital had My Barack Obama up and running the day Obama declared his candidacy. About 1,000 groups organized in the next few hours; among them were the groups that became the biggest and most powerful as the bruising primary battle with Hillary Clinton wore on. "Our guiding philosophy was to build online tools to help people self-organize and then get out of their way," said Facebook co-founder Chris Hughes, who joined the campaign to help it use the tool to organize younger voters. "The technology was more a means of empowering people to do what they were interested in doing in the first place."

Tens of thousands of young people downloaded voter-registration forms on Facebook; when a supporter used Obama's phone-bank tool to call undecided voters, it appeared in her friend feed.

Sure, it didn't hurt that Mr. Obama also had a consistent message, an intuitive read on the country's outlook and an ability to see beyond his base. And he and his target audience were in sync with social media. His supporters, like social-media proselytizers, seemed given to an optimism not typically seen in the political world, talking up the candidate's strong points and overlooking the weaknesses. "Transparency," for example, was a buzzword for both crowds. It remains to be seen how much real transparency will help marketers, but Mr. Obama took no chances. Despite a fondness for the word, his core campaign messaging was as tightly controlled as previous efforts by George W. Bush.

When the campaign ended, Mr. Rospars returned to Blue State Digital, where he and co-founder Thomas Gesemer are looking to apply the lessons of the campaign for nonprofit organizations and for brands—but perhaps not all causes or brands.

"We are progressive in nature and interested in staying on the non-evil side of the business," Mr. Rospars said.

The digital organization built for the campaign has been turned over to the Democratic National Committee in the form of a new group, Organizing for America, and tasked with continuing to cultivate the grass-roots movement that swept Mr. Obama into office. Naturally, the group will be powered by tools developed by Blue State Digital.

Mr. Hughes, the Facebook co-founder, took a job with Mr. Obama's ad agency, GMMB, as a strategic adviser.

When it comes to applying the lessons of the campaign to brand marketing, there are plenty of opportunities, but as brands such as Skittles and Motrin have shown, not every tool is appropriate for every marketer, and a two-way conversation with the public can get, well, complicated.

"A lot of what we learned is applicable, but not all," said GMMB partner Greg Pinelo. "Barack Obama is not a shoe. He is the first great political leader of the 21st century. I do think the lessons of social engagement and two-way conversation apply to a broad range of entities."

Can the Mama Grizzlies Pull Off a Twitter Revolution?[*]

By Noreen Malone
Slate Magazine, October 14, 2010

"But how do the hash tags work, exactly?" "How can I link my blog to my Face-book page?" The questions were directed at me and came from a retired female cop from upstate New York. Our dining companions, seventysomethings from North Carolina, asked for my professional media expertise. They hadn't yet joined Twitter but planned to after all they'd heard about it at the Smart Girl Summit, a recent conference of conservative—mostly Tea Party—women. They listened eagerly to my answers, then even more eagerly as featured speaker Michele Bachmann told the group that 61 percent of independent voters distrust the "lamestream" media, that the media are even angrier than the Tea Party. The ex-cop blogger clapped loudly and politely passed the rolls my way.

The Smart Girl Summit, attended by about 250 (largely women, with a smatter-ing of husbands and male speakers), grew out of a blog started by a stay-at-home mother. One of the featured speakers, Dana Loesch, a rising conservative pundit and home-schooling mother, initially grabbed attention for her blog, Mamalogues, which she still maintains in addition to her TV and radio work. Another, Rachel Campos-Duffy, a *Real World* alum, has maintained her media presence through a combination of mommy-blogging and TV punditry. One attendee, a hairdresser turned full-time mother, grabbed national attention during the 2008 election for her blog, Moms4SarahPalin.

The new wave of Mama Grizzlies believes—and they have some evidence to prove it—that social media is the key to their success. In nearly every session I sat in on, the speaker drove home the point that the easiest way to work for the Tea Party was to be active on Twitter and Facebook—this was the sort of political or-ganizing that a busy mom could do, without even leaving the house. And by many measures, women already dominate social media: They outnumber men nearly 60 percent to 40 percent on Facebook and Twitter, and married women between 35 and 50 are the fastest-growing group of social-networkers. Their usage also tends to be more relationship- and communication-driven, less "transactional." "Nontraditional media will give you the courage to tell your story," one speaker said, echoing a blogger who told me she thinks women are more bold behind the safety of our computer screens.

None of them mentions a recent *New Yorker* article on Twitter activism by Malcolm Gladwell, which would dampen their cause. Gladwell is thoroughly skeptical of its effectiveness, comparing Twitter activism in Iran and Moldova unfavorably with the activism of the 1960s American civil rights movement. The key distinction, according to Gladwell, is that "Social networks are effective at increasing *participation*—by lessening the level of motivation that participation requires" rather than effecting actual change. And true, that's exactly what the online Grizzlies emphasize, how easy it is to be part of the movement online.

Gladwell concedes that "[t]he drawbacks of networks scarcely matter if the network isn't interested in systemic change—if it just wants to frighten or humiliate or make a splash." But is that true of the Tea Party moms? Yes, their poll numbers are relatively unpromising for the November general election. But they seem to still want to turn their online power into noise on the streets. The group that sponsored the conference also sponsored the first Tea Party rally last year, and the point of the summit was to take "weak-tie" online bonds and turn them into real-life connections (which, Gladwell says, drive effective activism). To get people to move from just being part of an inchoate network and to think about becoming leaders within a movement. To have women meet the people they'd been retweeting on Twitter, so that maybe they'd volunteer for the other's candidate of choice, or even her campaign. To spawn more organizations, more networks within a network. According to Loesch, "Activism is just as much building relationships as getting out there."

The conference itself, by the way, got most of its publicity through its social media presence—that's where almost everyone I talked to said they'd heard about it and where I was tipped off to it, too. And the organizers told me they were able to attract such high-profile speakers—Bachmann, Liz Cheney, Anita MonCrief—because of a larger-than-life, influential Twitter presence. And when they all get together in person, as Hanna Rosin wrote in *Slate* earlier this year, "the movement feels like a real tea party." It's social, it's fun for these women; it flies in the face of the bowling-alone trend.

Of course, before the Tea Party, there was Obama's '08 campaign, famous for its online grass-roots activism, which candidates on both sides have imitated to mixed results. It's still unclear what works, though the Tea Party has especially embraced the home phone-bank along with social media, instead of flashy but less effective—and far more expensive—iPhone apps and the like. This particular conference included seminars on how to obtain old voting data for your precinct, how to crunch the numbers and decide when a precinct was winnable, what to say when talking to undecideds, what sort of voter fraud to be on the lookout for, even how to lay the groundwork for your own campaign. (Another Twitter-activism critique from Gladwell: "It shifts our energies from organizations that promote strategic and disciplined activity and toward those which promote resilience and adaptability. It makes it easier for activists to express themselves, and harder for that expression to have any impact.") There have been plenty of conservative women's organizations before, of course—think the Eagle Forum—but over and over, panelists emphasized that those groups hadn't adapted and that these new tactics were reaching a new audience, a new generation, the "new media." Look no further than Sarah Palin's tweeting for evidence of how large and loud that bullhorn can be: She is followed by fewer than 300,000 users, a relatively modest number given her celebrity, yet her remarks often propel a whole news cycle.

This brand of social activism also happens to perfectly dovetail with the brand of conservative feminism that was being promoted at the conference: You can maintain your duties as a wife and mother but also become involved in the movement through making phone calls, handing out flyers, running for school board if national office seems too disruptive to your family. ("Start small, build big" was another theme—school board leads to county leads to state, etc.) You can organize an entire conference and run a highly trafficked Web site but, since those activities are not professionalized, still call yourself a stay-at-home mom. And those "maternal" skills—organization, communication—are just as good, if not better than, a high-powered professional résumé in a movement that's asking for foot soldiers. (But high-powered résumés are OK, too—cf Liz Cheney.)

Women who stayed at home with their kids might not be able to then land a gig at, say, the *National Review* if they'd wanted one, but in this movement, the blogs they might start and the tweeting they can do are valued more than "lamestream" coverage. Or at least that's the message. Whether the message—tweeted, facebooked, direct-mailed, blogged—can actually turn into reality remains to be seen. "Victory," said a Smart Girl organizer, setting up for the long view, "is in planting the seed."

Facebook Politicians Are Not Your Friends[*]

By Frank Rich
The New York Times, October 9, 2010

"The Social Network," you're understandably sick of hearing, is a brilliant movie about the Harvard upstart Mark Zuckerberg and the messy birth of his fabulous start-up, Facebook, circa 2004. From the noisy debate over its harsh portrait of Zuckerberg, you'd think it's a documentary. It's not. Its genre is historical fiction— with a sardonic undertow. The director David Fincher and the screenwriter Aaron Sorkin are after bigger ironies than the riddle of Zuckerberg, a disconnected geek destined to spawn a virtual community of 500 million "friends." You leave the movie with the sinking feeling that the democratic utopia breathlessly promised by Facebook and its Web brethren is already gone with the wind.

Nowhere, perhaps, is the gap between the romance and the reality of the Internet more evident than in our politics. In the idealized narrative of digital democracy, greater connectivity has bequeathed more governmental transparency, more grass-roots participation and even a more efficient rendering of political justice. Thanks to YouTube, which arrived just a year after Facebook, a senatorial candidate (George Allen of Virginia) caught on camera delivering a racial slur was brought down swiftly in 2006. Not long after, it was the miracle of social networking that helped enable Barack Obama's small donors to overwhelm Hillary Clinton's fat cats, and his online activists to out-organize her fearsome establishment pros.

But you can also construct a less salutary counternarrative. For all the Obama team's digital bells and whistles, among them a lightning-fast site to debunk rumors during the campaign, Internet-fed myths still rage. In a Pew poll in August, 18 percent of Americans labeled the president a Muslim—up 7 points since March 2009. The explosion of accessible media and information on the Web, with its potential to give civic discourse a factual baseline and hold politicians accountable, has also given partisans license to find only the "facts" that fit their prejudices. Meanwhile, wealthy candidates like Carly Fiorina, the former Hewlett-Packard chief executive running for Senate in California, have become adept at buying up prime Google-YouTube advertising real estate to compete with digital stink bombs tossed by the rabble.

The more recent miracle of Twitter theoretically encourages real-time inter-connection between elected officials and the citizenry. But it too has been eas-ily corrupted by politicians whose 140-character effusions are often ghost-written by hired 20-somethings, just like those produced for pop stars like 50 Cent and Britney Spears. When the South Carolina governor Mark Sanford was pretending to hike on the Appalachian Trail during his hook-up with his mistress in Argentina last June, his staff gave him cover by feeding his Twitter account with musings about such uncarnal passions as "Washington D.C. financial recklessness."

At least Obama and Ron Paul have admitted they don't write the Twitter feeds in their names. It took journalists poring through financial disclosure forms to discover that Sarah Palin had paid a Los Angeles blogger $22,000 to script her "Internet messaging." We must take it on faith that her former running mate, John McCain, an admitted computer illiterate who didn't use e-mail just two years ago, is now such a Twitter maven that he dashes off aperçus about MTV's Snooki to his followers.

Just as "The Social Network" hit the multiplexes, Malcolm Gladwell took to *The New Yorker* with a stinging takedown of social networks as vehicles for meaning-ful political and social action. He calculated that the nearly 1.3 million members of the Facebook page for the Save Darfur Coalition have donated an average of 9 cents each to their cause. He mocked American journalists' glorification of Twit-ter's supposedly pivotal role during last year's short-lived uprising in Iran, suggest-ing that the rebels' celebrated Twitter feeds—written in English, not Farsi—did more to titillate blogging technophiles in the West than to aid Iranians in their struggle against totalitarian rulers.

"With Facebook and Twitter and the like," Gladwell wrote, "the traditional re-lationship between political authority and popular will" was supposed to be up-ended, so it would be "easier for the powerless to collaborate, coordinate, and give voice to their concerns." Instead, he concluded, we ended up with the reverse: social media increase the efficiency of the existing order rather than empowering dissidents. In his view, social networking is far less likely to recreate the civil rights movement of the 1960s than to track down missing cellphones for Wall Streeters.

Gladwell's provocative Internet critique is complemented by a much-buzzed-about independent movie—in this case, an actual documentary—that was released shortly before "The Social Network." No one will confuse this ham-fisted film, titled "Catfish," with a Fincher-Sorkin production, but it's highly unsettling none-theless. It tells of a 25-year-old Manhattan photographer who strikes up a devoted Facebook friendship with a small-town Michigan family whose 8-year-old daugh-ter is a painting prodigy. When the photographer seeks out his virtual friends in the real Michigan, it's inevitable that he and the audience will learn the hard way, as the *Times* film critic A.O. Scott put it, that cyberspace is a "wild social ether where nobody knows who anybody is."

Even if Gladwell and "Catfish" are overstating the case, they certainly have one if you look at the political environment in our election year of 2010. The Internet in general and social networking in particular have done little, if anything, to hobble those pursuing power with such traditional means as big lies and big money. Perhaps what's most remarkable this year is the number of candidates who have tried to create fictitious avatars like the Facebook impostors in "Catfish." These candidates and others often fashion their campaigns to avoid real reporters (and sometimes real voters). Some benefit from YouTube commercials paid for by impossible-to-trace anonymous donors. In this wild political ether where nobody knows who anybody is, the Internet provides cover, not transparency.

Go online, and you'll discover that many of those now notorious false fronts for oil billionaires and other corporate political contributors have Facebook pages. We don't know who has written checks to Crossroads GPS, the more shadowy wing of American Crossroads, the operation concocted in part by Karl Rove to raise $50 million to attack Democrats. (There's already $32 million in the bank, $10 million more than was spent by Swift Boat Veterans for Truth in 2004.) But the American Crossroads page on Facebook sure looks like a bottom-up populist movement, festooned with photos of thousands of ordinary folk voting their "like" of the site. The Save Darfur Coalition page may have infinitely more friends, but it's American Crossroads that has real clout in the real world even if nobody knows who is behind the screen.

What you might call our "Catfish" Congressional candidates are a perfect match for the phantom donors. The power of the Google search hardly deters those politicians intent on fictionalizing their identities. Richard Blumenthal, the Democratic senatorial candidate in Connecticut, repeatedly implied in public speeches that he had fought in the Vietnam War, though he'd served only stateside. Mark Kirk, the Republican senatorial candidate in Illinois, inflated his own military history, bragged of a nonexistent teaching career, and exaggerated his derring-do in a teenage boating accident. Ben Quayle, an Arizona G.O.P. Congressional candidate with no children but a history of writing under a nom-de-porn on a racy Web site, burnished his wholesome image with a campaign photo in which nieces stood in for his nonexistent daughters. In each of these cases it was old-fashioned analog reporters, most of them working for newspapers, who finally penetrated the falsehoods.

When Christine O'Donnell ran an ad last week with the improbable opening line "I'm not a witch," we once again had to marvel at the Delaware primary triumph of a mystery candidate with a falsified résumé, no job, and apparently no campaign operation beyond out-of-state donors and out-of-state fans like Palin "writing" Twitter endorsements. O'Donnell's Facebook page is by far the most palpable presence of an aspiring senator who shuns public events and the press in Delaware. In a brave new political world where candidates need only exist in virtual reality, it's no wonder that Donald Trump believes he's qualified for public office because of his relative gravitas as a heavy on a television "reality" show.

and parties not in power look for innovation when trying to communicate with voters in new ways."

The reverberations the Internet can have on an election cycle have been well-known at least since Howard Dean let out an unusual battle-cry during the 2004 presidential election. But 2010's election was the first where social media was virtually ubiquitous.

In 2008, Facebook had one-fifth the active members it now has. Twitter was nascent, its news value not yet realized. Location-sharing services such as Foursquare and Gowalla didn't exist or had just been created.

This year, most major candidates had a Facebook page. Election night results went directly to smart phones. And everything—the campaigns, the ads, the voting—was filtered through social media.

More than 12 million clicked Facebook's "I Voted" button on Tuesday, more than twice the 5.4 million from two years ago.

Asked if Facebook is contributing to a heightened awareness of elections, Adam Conner, associate manager for privacy and global public policy at Facebook, said that he'd "like to think that we are."

"It's important when the message comes from places like Facebook but I think it's really exciting when people's friends are telling them, 'Hey, it's an election. Make sure you vote. Make sure you participate, it's important to me,'" says Conner.

Networks and news organizations sought to weave social media into their coverage. Reporters and TV anchors tweeted through the night. ABC partnered with Facebook, NBC posted video on Twitter and CBS worked with Google. *The Washington Post* was the first news organization to sponsor a "promoted trend" on Twitter with the hash tag "Election."

The flow of Twitter updates from selected sources was enough to usurp TV coverage for some users.

"By 'tuning into' Twitter on election night, I was able to get timely updates on the races that mattered to me from people I've already decided that I trust," said Mark Rosch of New Mexico. "Social media, particularly Twitter, gave me the ability keep up with the far-flung contests I was most-interested in, as well [as] getting more information more quickly on local races."

Foursquare encouraged users to vote by awarding a special "merit badge" to those who went to polling places. More than 50,000 of its 4 million users received it.

Facebook, Twitter, Foursquare and others used their power to get out the vote, supplying easy links for locating one's nearest polling place. That could have helped voter turnout, which was projected at 42 percent of registered voters, about 1.2 percentage points higher than the 2006 midterms.

Mindy Finn, co-founder of the online political media firm Engage, said politicians are spending less than 5 percent of their budgets on social media. She cautioned overestimating its effect.

"Do we assign impact to people talking to their friends and neighbors in the same way we assign impact to people knocking on doors and making phone calls for a particular candidate or political party or cause?" said Finn. "On a basic level, it's the same and things haven't changed. Friends are still contacting friends and neighbors are still talking to neighbors."

One of the most buzzed-about candidates of the election didn't win. Christine O'Donnell, the Tea Party candidate who ran for the Senate in Delaware, had the most-viewed politician channel on YouTube. (YouTube counted 450 candidates with official channels.)

Her campaign ad in which she began by saying, "I'm not a witch," was watched by millions. It was parodied on "Saturday Night Live," set to song in a popular "Auto-Tune the News" video and creatively co-opted by countless YouTubers with their own political messages to distribute.

Those clips, combined with the many older videos of O'Donnell that circulated widely, made her one of the most viral candidates—yet she still lost badly to Democrat Chris Coons.

Facebook claimed correlation between social media buzz and election success. It said that 74 percent of House and Senate candidates with more Facebook fans than their competitors won on Tuesday.

The social networking platform also co-hosted a town hall meeting with ABC News. The sight was telling: a room full of people on laptops gazing at a giant Facebook "buzz wall."

They were far from alone in their Internet-tethered election experience. Akamai Technologies Inc., which delivers about 20 percent of the world's Internet traffic, showed traffic peaking around 6 p.m EDT at over 5.6 million global page views a minute. That's one of Akamai's highest traffic rates in five years of measurement—even more than during President Obama's election night win in 2008.

Come two years and the next presidential election, social media is likely to be vital territory sought by Democrats and Republicans.

"In 2012, this will be a very contested battlefield," says the Pew Internet's Rainie. "It's not a sidelight to politics right now. This is a central venue."

What You Need to Know About Social Networking*

By Pam Greenberg and Meagan Dorsch
State Legislatures, July 2009–August 2009

Blogging. Tweeting. Facebooking. If you think these are terms only teenagers are familiar with, think again.

The use of social media sites, or tools of Web 2.0, spans generations. The first social networking site, SixDegrees.com, was created in 1997, followed by sites such as BlackPlanet, Friendster and MySpace. But today, the most popular site is Facebook, with more than 200 million members worldwide.

In the United States, the number of adults with a profile on a social networking site has more than quadrupled in the past four years—from 8 percent in 2005 to 35 percent in December 2008—according to Pew Internet and American Life Project surveys. Time spent on social networking and blogging sites is growing at more than three times the rate of overall global Internet growth. And the fastest growing segment of users is women over age 55.

Candidates for school boards, city councils, state legislatures and even the president of the United States have used social networking tools.

More than 35 state legislative caucuses across the country are using social networking sites such as Facebook, MySpace and Twitter. These new interactive communities allow politicians to have direct, unfiltered communication with voters and constituents. Legislators are also using social media as a campaign tool that can influence debate, help build name recognition, gain supporters and motivate volunteers around elections.

Are social media for you? Below are eight things you should know before setting up your own site. These tips can help you sucessfully manage your site daily.

---

1. KNOW THE TOOLS

The number and types of tools in the social media arsenal are expanding each day. Remember when the term blogger was new? Knowing that the largest age demographic on Facebook currently is 18 to 24, and 35 to 49 on Twitter, may help you decide which tools to use.

Also keep in mind which tools are considered public and which ones can be picked up by search engines. On Twitter, postings are usually visible to anyone who wants to view them, although "followers" can post replies and are more likely to view updates. Texas Senator Dan Patrick's Twitter account includes frequent updates about what's happening on the floor, opinions on bills, notes about rallies or events, and references directing readers to his Facebook page for more details. Patrick's followers post thank yous, opinions on bills and a few jabs, as well. In contrast, Facebook and other social networking sites are for members only, and interactions are between only friends.

2. FOCUS ON YOUR PURPOSE

Knowing your purpose will help determine which tools you select and how you use them. Maryland House of Delegates Minority Leader Chris Shank looks at social media as new ways to communicate with constituents and to reach out to new groups and a younger demographic, as well as to keep people connected to what is going on at the statehouse. "Facebook is a powerful medium to help my constituents," says Shank.

Representative Marko Liias of Washington announces events and invites his supporters to campaign parties, victory celebrations and community events using Facebook's events feature, which allows his supporters to register an online RSVP. He posts his opinions on his Facebook page where his supporters can give a "thumbs up" or "thumbs down."

3. DIFFERENTIATE BETWEEN PERSONAL AND PROFESSIONAL

Do you want people to get to know you as a public official or as a private person? If you set up your sites as "Representative Smith," rather than "Joe Smith," consider the 80/20 rule. That's the advice from Brad Blake, social media director for Massachusetts Governor Deval Patrick. It means 80 percent of the content should be work-related, and only 20 percent personal.

On Facebook, a "Politicians" page allows people to connect with you as "supporters" rather than "friends." It also has a "Government Official" designation for those who want to keep their official duties separate from their political activities.

4. DEVELOP A COMMUNICATIONS PLAN

Can you integrate social media into your communications plan? Many communications offices have explored this avenue as a way to keep the public informed about activity in the legislature. Media coverage of statehouses has dwindled over the past several years, as blogs and other new media have exploded. Using social media tools can help close that gap in coverage.

Arkansas Representative Steve Harrelson believes there are three compelling arguments for using these tools: They are immediate, unfiltered and transparent. Social media, he says, give you a way to get messages out quickly, and as events occur, to say what you want without worrying how it will be filtered or interpreted.

If you decide to set up a Twitter or Facebook account, remember to let people know. You can include "widgets" or little icons for many of these social media sites on your own webpage. You also can add tag lines in emails or send out a press release.

5. IDENTIFY YOUR AUDIENCE

If a large percentage of your constituents are online or are younger people, the likelihood is high that they have a social media account.

Research indicates that those plugged into this new media are more likely to volunteer, donate, promote candidates and join causes through online and word-of-mouth advocacy. And they send and receive more political text messages than the general population.

One of the biggest mistakes politicians make, according to some experts, is not paying attention to who is coming to their sites. They recommend keeping track of who signs up for updates and who is coming to events listed on your sites. They also suggest connecting with the leading online political voices—the new media gurus—in your community.

6. SET YOUR LIMITS

As of today, social networking sites are free and generally easy to sign up for and use, but keeping up with and integrating the sites into a comprehensive communications plan can be more difficult. The social networking culture is all about real time contact and regular, if not frequent, updates. According to the Internet marketing blog Hubspot, the average number of "tweets," or messages, per day is around four. If you are unable or unlikely to keep your Twitter, Facebook or MySpace accounts updated regularly, you may be better off without them. But there are tools that can make keeping up easier. For example, TweetDeck, Seesmic and other applications allow you to post to Twitter and Facebook simultaneously.

7. KNOW THE SECURITY RISKS

Social networking sites create a perfect opportunity for hackers and online fraud-sters, according to security experts. Some schemes trick users into believing they are receiving messages from friends, and lead them to click on links to fraudulent sites that can collect passwords or personal information or download malware and viruses to users' computers. Up-to-date antivirus software and caution when open-ing attachments and following links in emails are essential. Social networking sites also often have security pages with updates about current threats or pages where users can report scams or possible viruses.

8. BE FAMILIAR WITH YOUR UWS AND POLICIES

Privacy policies and terms of service agreements of social networking sites can vary considerably. In addition to understanding the policies before using the sites yourself, consider including a disclaimer on your own website if you provide links to social networking sites.

Elected officials also need to be careful about how they deal with comments that others post on their sites. Wes Sullenger, writing about legislators' blogs in the Richmond Journal of Law and Technology, cautions that legislators using govern-ment-owned equipment or networks are government agents and, as such, cannot censor citizen comments.

Freedom of information laws also can come into play on social networking sites. Legislators who discuss public business could find they are subject to public meet-ings and records laws.

The rewards involved in using social media could balance out the potential risks, At no other time in history have we been able to use technology to connect with so many people at one time. If you are thinking of diving into social media, now is a great time! Everyone is learning how to swim at the same time, and the social networking world is forgiving. Test the waters and find out if social networking is for you.

A VIRTUAL TOOLBOX

Social networks are interactive online membership communities on the Web where individuals can create an online profile, connect to other users, and share interests and activities through online messaging, email, photos, video, blogs or discussion groups.

- Facebook, MySpace, Ning, BlackPlanet: These are a few of the hundreds of social networks where individuals create a website profile, add photos and graphics, send emails, post messages, and link their profile with friends".
- Twitter: This is the most popular "micro-blogging" service that allows people to stay connected through the exchange of short (140 characters or less) updates.
- LinkedIn, Plaxo: These are business-oriented sites where users create a professional online identity, exchange ideas and opportunities, and stay informed through contacts and news.
- YouTube, Flickr, Picasa: These are examples of video-sharing websites where users can upload, view and share photos and video clips.
- Delicious, Digg: These are social bookmarking and aggregation sites where users find, store and share content, and vote and comment on others' links.

Road Kill Social Media[*]

What's Hot One Day Can Cool Off in a Hurry

By Mark Hrywna
The Non-Profit Times, August 1, 2010

In just less than a month, the "Skinned Alive" campaign by the People for the Ethical Treatment of Animals (PETA) had garnered 98,000 fans, driven almost entirely through social media, primarily Facebook and Twitter. MySpace? Not so much.

Only a few years ago, MySpace was essentially neck and neck with Facebook in a battle for social networking supremacy. These days it seems to be falling into the niche category while Facebook boasts more than 400 million users worldwide and Twitter has seen fast-paced growth during the past year. Nonprofits, it seems, are following the same lead.

In the second annual survey of nonprofits' use of social networks, MySpace saw a 45 percent dip in year-over-year usage. Only 14 percent of organizations surveyed, compared to 26 percent last year, reported a presence on MySpace, according to the Nonprofit Social Network Benchmark Report, which was compiled by Portland, Ore.-based NTEN, ThePort Network of Atlanta, Ga., and Common Knowledge in San Francisco, Calif.

Meanwhile, other social networks continued to see increased participation, such as 86 percent of nonprofits responding they were on Facebook, compared with 60 percent on Twitter, 48 percent on YouTube and 33 percent on LinkedIn.

In another survey of nearly 500 nonprofits by Portland, Maine-based Idealware, Facebook (73 percent), Twitter (56 percent) and video-sharing sites (49 percent) were the most widely used social media channels. MySpace was ranked lowest for outreach and enhancing existing relationships.

---

* Reprinted with the permission of *The Non-Profit Times*. Nonprofit executives can receive a free subscription by going to www. nptimes.com.

DIFFERENT PLATFORM, SAME TECHNIQUES

The basic fundamentals of fundraising remain regardless of the medium. "Just because email comes along doesn't mean direct mail is going out the window," said Paul Phillips, online fundraising manager for the PETA Foundation. "Everyone reinforces everything else," he added.

"Our engagement in Twitter became much deeper and a much larger part of our overall social marketing scheme," Phillips said of the "Skinned Alive" campaign. "We probably will look for folks who use Twitter to reinforce what we're doing across other social channels more," he said.

PETA's strategy isn't so much about shunning MySpace as it is about simply going to where constituents are, Phillips said. The nonprofit can still be found on MySpace, although the number of fans on the network is about 10 percent of the total on Facebook. "Chalk it up to constituents moving to a social media channel they're most comfortable with," he said. "If we have one-tenth the voice on MySpace that we do on Facebook, that's entirely the driving factor of why Facebook is the central piece in this campaign. It's much more a matter of where the audience is more active. We're going to take PETA's message to whatever channel constituents want us to," he said.

"A lot of the tools we provide should work across social media platforms. Part of the nature of social media is letting the crowd take the message to their friends and family," said Phillips. Even if something comes along that turns out to be "the next Facebook," there usually are enough compatible elements and tools that will migrate to another network.

"Social networking is in large part about going to where our constituency is. At Oxfam America, we're not focusing on MySpace as much because our constituents left it for Facebook and Twitter," according to Megan Weintraub, new media manager at Oxfam America. The growth of Oxfam's community in MySpace has slowed significantly during the past 12 to 18 months while its presence on Facebook and Twitter has exploded.

It's almost inevitable that something will come along eventually to knock even Facebook off its perch. Five years ago, it was Facebook versus MySpace in a duel of rival social networks. Before that, there was Friendster and MeetUp, and other social networks that were the shiny, new toy at some point.

Jeff Patrick is often asked which social networks nonprofits should join. "When a new wave of things happen, it usually happens in a certain way, and understanding that helps people get a handle on that," said Patrick, the president and CEO of San Francisco, Calif.-based Common Knowledge. "Certain things tend to happen when new technology comes in; a bunch of players hit and some evolve as mainstream players," he said.

When social networks started to take off about five years ago, there was MySpace and Facebook but also thousands of other networks. "As each one of those develops their solutions, their base of consumers, each tends to develop the company, the product and the customer base," Patrick said. As each gets bigger, they get dominant players in each area. Years ago, the social networking space was still shaking out but today, there are strong indications of who will be dominant.

Precursors to MySpace and Facebook were Friendster and MeetUp, which were social networking focused in 2000. "They got outdated and usurped when Facebook and MySpace were incrementally more social. They were just better, more shiny," Patrick said. "They failed to see the real potential in the social networking software," he said, and the two still exist but are not considered state of the art.

LinkedIn might not be as popular as Facebook but it is solidifying its lead as the social networking platform for professionals, according to Patrick. And while it might still be too early to tell, FourSquare, a spin-off of Twitter, is making its case in the mobile social networking space.

WHEN THE BUZZ WEARS OFF

A common misconception is that people assume since media coverage has slowed that something is no longer viable or even exists, according to Susan Tenby, online community director at San Francisco-based nonprofit TechSoup. A case in point is Second Life, a virtual world where you can control your avatar and buy virtual land.

"At the beginning, everybody thought they had to be there because it was the sexy, new technology; there was nothing else like it," Tenby said. Those organizations that figured out a use for it are staying in Second Life. "They're the ones who tested it . . . and are staying," she said.

Since 2008, 1,900 avatars have spent 15,000 hours at Second Life's Nonprofit Commons, run by TechSoup. A campaign to raise money for Haiti generated $7,000 in virtual donations, and the American Cancer Society's Relay For Life raised $300,000 last year in Second Life. "It's successful because it's so well known. There's huge muscle behind their following in real life," Tenby said.

Some smaller nonprofits have stepped away from Second Life and other social networks, either because they're taking a break from social media, loss of staff or moving to their own simulation. "It's about meeting people where they're at. Find out where your community is," Tenby said. It's not really about finding a new tool, it's about going where people are, she said.

Patrick said nonprofits must determine how they want to use the social network, whether for fundraising or community building. "When you make the choice and invest in it, it has to be there tomorrow," he said, so nonprofits have to prognosticate to some extent. "After four or five years, winners are beginning to evolve and will continue to advance in this space," Patrick said.

Weintraub expects location-based social networking will play a greater role in organizing volunteers and events for the organization's outreach work, but "the jury is still out on which product will take the lead and be used most widely by the constituents we are cultivating," she said.

It took email several years to get to a point where Patrick was confident that it could raise money for nonprofits. "We're getting to that place on Facebook; we're not quite there . . . that likely will be solidified in the next few years," he said.

Before dumping one technology or social network altogether, Patrick suggests checking that it's really not valuable for your nonprofit. For instance, he said MySpace appears to have some people they can't reach other ways. MySpace tends to still attract youth and minorities.

"Don't just follow what the market trend is because it might not look as you originally imagined, you might have to adapt," Patrick said. "If after doing that it's clear that it's going to be decreasingly less value for you here, falling away, cut your losses and do your best to migrate those folks to something else," he said. "There's no point in sticking around with something that's not going to work."

Rather than adopting one network, figure out what demographic you want to reach with this message and decide what network you're going to use to do it. "When you do that, you're customizing to a network and an audience," Patrick said. Each social network will reach an intended market versus arbitrarily picking something that you think will be the network for the rest of your life, Patrick said. "It's not going to be. Twitter and Facebook are going to go away, we just don't know when and what'll replace it," he said.

"No one wants to do business on 10 different platforms. You'd rather have a few places that work really well; that are more cost effective. Industry focuses on several, then accentuates those. That's what's being called widely adopted," Patrick said.

Tenby suggested nonprofits use content across a broad range of platforms. "Show them that it's not one tool or the other," she said, "a way to connect these tools so you have a constellation of social networks and . . . consistent branding," she said.

4

Tweeting is Fundamental:
Social Media in the Schools

Editor's Introduction

According to the Kaiser Family Foundation, nearly three quarters of students in grades 7 through 12 have at least one social-media profile. In the coming years, that figure is likely to climb even higher, as a study by NielsenNetView indicates that, from 2004 to 2009, children aged 2 through 11 increased the time they spent on-line by 63 percent.

As young people flock to social networks, educators find themselves facing a number of difficult questions. For starters, do Facebook, Twitter, and other such sites have educational merit? If so, do the potential benefits outweigh the risks? How should a teacher respond if a student sends a friend request? Do districts have the right to tell their employees how to conduct themselves on-line, during non-school hours? The articles in this chapter consider these and other questions, examining how schools across the country have responded to the rise of social media.

In "Social Networking Goes to School," the first entry in the chapter, Michelle R. Davis looks at how schools have benefited from both existing social-media services, such as Ning, and custom platforms that are more easily monitored. While Davis highlights several schools that have found innovative uses for social networking, she also interviews experts staunchly opposed to its use. "Facebook is too much of an intrusion into students' personal and social lives for educators to be using it as an educational method," Montana Miller, an assistant professor of popular culture at Bowling Green State University, tells Davis.

The chapter continues with "Social Media in the Classroom—For Kindergartners(!) Through High Schoolers," Renee Ramig's tutorial on the age-appropriate use of social-networking tools. Now that social media has gone mainstream, Ramig writes, "schools should reflect this reality" and teach students about technology they're sure to encounter later in life.

Ramig would get no argument from the Cincinnati-area educators Denise Smith Amos profiles in "Schools Get on Web 2.0 Bandwagon," the final selection in the chapter. Amos visits several teachers who have made effective use of social media, including an English teacher who shows his class YouTube videos and a German teacher who encourages her students to leave voicemail messages on Google Voice.

cluding the fact that many schools still block access to such sites within their walls. School officials must also confront the uncertainties and questions surrounding privacy issues, proper management, and cyber security when they open their doors to social-networking sites.

But it's a world that some educators are realizing students feel at home in and is unlikely to disappear. A study by the Washington-based Pew Research Center's Internet & American Life Project released early this year found that 73 percent of Americans ages 12 to 17 now use social-networking websites, up from 55 percent in 2006.

"Social networking is not going to go away," says Steve Hargadon, the creator of the 42,000-member Classroom 2.0 network on Ning, a popular site among educators. He's also a social learning consultant for the ed-tech company Elluminate, based in Pleasanton, Calif.

"These are so powerful in terms of learning," Hargadon says of such tools.

In some schools, social networking has changed the way educators teach and students learn, says Silvia Rosenthal Tolisano, the 21st-century-learning specialist at the private, K–8 Martin J. Gottlieb Day School in Jacksonville, Fla. In January 2009, Tolisano launched her "Around the World With 80 Schools" project. The goal was to introduce her school's students to peers in countries around the globe. She built a social-networking site using Ning for teachers from all countries who wanted to participate, eventually attracting 300 members.

Tolisano says she sets up a meeting between classes using Skype. Students prepare a list of questions (What's the weather like there? How big is your town or city? What continent are you on?) and chat with students in Canada, Finland, New Zealand, and Spain, among a long list of others.

The Florida students also have different jobs to do during the call. One might be a photographer, documenting the meet-and-greet. Others place the location of the class they're talking with on a Google map. Still other students might serve as Twitter "back channelers," who send out tweets—the short messages Twitter is designed to convey—as the live event is happening. Classes even added "fact checkers," who go back to make sure the information provided is accurate. One group of Gottlieb students had just read a book about Orca whales, Tolisano says, and wanted to know more, so they contacted a class in British Columbia, where whale watching is a common pastime. Within a week, the British Columbia students hopped on a boat and shot video of a pod of Orcas, which they sent to the students in Florida, Tolisano says.

"It creates a global awareness that there is a wider world out there and that we are not alone," Tolisano says. "They find it's just as easy to collaborate with a class in England as with the class next door."

In addition, Skype is so simple to use that just about any teacher can typically handle it with a few minutes of training and minimal equipment. It's nearly as simple as dialing the phone, but on the computer.

Social networking can mean using ready-made platforms like Ning or Facebook, but it can also be about networks that schools create specifically for their students.

Project K-Nect, a grant-funded program that uses smartphones as teaching tools in a handful of North Carolina school districts, allows students to instant-message their peers and teachers with questions on math homework at any time of the day or night. Students can also post questions and answers to school math blogs, where a student struggling with algebra could find several classmates willing to walk him or her through a problem or even post video of the best way to solve it.

"The idea that kids would post blog items on solving linear equations was treated as a laughable concept" by the adults before the project launched, says Shawn Gross, the managing director for Digital Millennial Consulting, an educational technology firm based in Arlington, Va., that oversees Project K-Nect. "The first week we had 75 students post videos on solving linear equations." Social networking among students has become one of Project K-Nect's most popular features, he says.

At New Milford High School, it was the idea of keeping in touch with parents that first prompted Principal Sheninger to look into Twitter during the last school year. That first foray changed his professional life. After tweeting to parents for a few month he began to reach out to other educators and collaborate. "At that point, the way I used social media" metamorphosed, he says. "I used it to look for new ideas and new resources, to forge new relationships, and as a means of public relations."

But Sheninger found his students weren't as entranced by Twitter as he was. In fact, the Pew study bears that out: It found that only 8 percent of teenagers online say they ever use Twitter. The Pew study found that 37 percent of 18- to 24-year-olds were using Twitter, the largest percentage of any age group. Members of New Milford's student government suggested Sheninger create a Facebook page for the high school instead. In April, the school site was born.

While students haven't become enamored with Twitter yet, it has become a hot spot for educators to find professional development and resources. One of the most popular types of educator events on Twitter are "Ed Chats"—one-hour conversations that take place every Tuesday around a particular topic. The chats are the brainchild of several educators, including Thomas Whitby, a co-creator of a 3,700-member Ning site called The Educator's PLN, for "professional learning network."

Social networking is allowing teachers, who often feel isolated in their classrooms, to revolutionize the way they connect with others, says Whitby, a former English teacher who is now an adjunct professor of education for secondary English at St. Joseph's College in New York City.

Teachers are "finding out about a whole wide range of options beyond what is done in their own building," he says. "People are trying more things based on recommendations from teachers around the world."

They can get those recommendations every Tuesday at 7 P.M. Eastern time during Ed Chat. Moderators choose a topic, and for an hour educators everywhere can ask questions and chime in. All chat contributors "hash tag" or label their comments with "#edchat," to make sure they appear on a Twitter stream. The event was so popular that creators had to set up an Ed Chat for earlier in the day (starting at noon Eastern time) to accommodate international teachers in differing time zones.

A recent Ed Chat tackled alternatives to traditional grading. Some of the comments, limited to Twitter's 140 characters per tweet, included a suggestion for rating creativity and innovation. One tweet mentioned a pilot program evaluating students on individual learning goals. Someone else asked, if a student is "working at 100% of his ability and is failing, do we grade on achievement or ability?"

Whitby says that after the chats, which sometimes receive more than 2,000 tweets in an hour, many educators discuss the topics in greater depth on their blogs.

Steven W. Anderson, an instructional technologist at Clemmons Middle School in the 52,000-student Winston-Salem/Forsyth County school system in North Carolina, says social networking is revolutionizing the way teachers improve their skills.

"In the past, professional development has been so formal and rigid. You go to these events scheduled by the district because this is what they think you need," says Anderson, an Ed Chat moderator. "With social networking allowing teachers to connect one-to-one and one-to-many, they have the professional development that they really desire."

In fact, Ning, a social-networking platform, is full of sites dedicated to different specialties—everything from geography to teaching English as a second language or first-year teachers.

On Twitter, Anderson says, he's constantly being pointed to different Web sites and applications that can aid teachers. And if a teacher has a question or needs a recommendation for a site, Twitter can help with instant suggestions.

"Twitter is like a giant conference that's on all the time," Anderson says. "I always know I can find something I can use. That's huge." Teacher Shelly Terrell, who writes the blog Teacher Reboot Camp, says she's found value in different types of social-networking sites when it comes to professional development. Terrell, who is currently teaching in Germany at the German-American Institute, also holds weekly field trips into the virtual world of Second Life for teachers new to the site.

"I take the teachers to a safe ground," she says. "If you're on your own in Second Life, you might end up where you don't want to be as an educator."

In Second Life, a virtual world where users interact as avatars, or electronic representations of themselves, the North Carolina Community College System has developed an island for teachers to show them how to work with audio and video. Though Terrell can't visit that world with her students, since users are required to be at least 18 years old, she says the virtual field trips can be beneficial for teachers, particularly in "experiencing" other countries.

If she takes teachers to Second Life's virtual Venice, for example, they can ride a gondola, meet people speaking Italian, and observe the way people dress and the culture.

But many educators who see the value in social networking face significant obstacles to incorporating it into their school days.

Both Twitter and Facebook are blocked by many school computer networks. Even Sheninger, who has had great success with his school's official Facebook page, says the site still isn't accessible from inside the school's walls.

"One thing I ran into a lot in the U.S. was filtering or blocking," says Terrell. To use some social-networking sites or tools, "I had to get the technology director and let him know specifically what I was using it for, and it was a long process getting sites unblocked."

In addition, some district officials remain skeptical that such social-networking tools really benefit education, worried that they just open the door to Internet-security problems and the possibility of cyber bullying.

In April, the principal of Ridgewood, N.J.'s Benjamin Franklin Middle School, Anthony Orsini, sent out an e-mail to his students' parents asking them to bar their children from using social-networking sites to prevent online bullying. "There is absolutely no reason for any middle school student to be a part of a social-networking site," Orsini wrote in the e-mail.

Also in April, Utah's 68,300-student Granite school district barred teachers and students from "friending" each other on Facebook. And Louisiana state law requires all school districts to document every electronic interaction between teachers and students through a "non school-issued device, such as a cellphone or e-mail account."

But it remains unclear what all of that means for social-networking tools and sites being used for purely educational purposes.

Montana Miller, an assistant professor of popular culture at Bowling Green State University, in Ohio, and a Facebook expert, says not only have educators put their careers at risk with inappropriate exchanges with students on sites like Facebook, but she also believes it's not the sort of place for any educational exchange.

"Facebook is too much of an intrusion into students' personal and social lives for educators to be using it as an educational method," she says. "I'm not against collaborative, online education with students, but I am against merging their personal home, private family world with something that is required for a class activity. Millions of things can go wrong."

Schools also need to pay close attention to federal laws like the Children's Online Privacy Protection Act of 1998, or COPPA, which seeks to protect children's privacy and bars most children under 13 from participating in many websites. Education officials should also consider other federal laws like the Children's Internet Protection Act, or CIPA, which requires schools to provide Internet filtering to prevent access by students to offensive content over the Internet, and the Family Educational Rights and Privacy Act, or FERPA, which protects the privacy of student information.

In fact, most social-networking sites like Facebook and Ning require users to be at least 13 to participate. That's why private wikis or blogs or other social networking tools designed for school use can often be more beneficial in such situations, says Terrell, the teacher and blogger. For example, she often uses a tool called Voice Thread with even her youngest students. That free service allows users to leave voice comments about pictures, video, or drawings, and it enables users to doodle or draw on the screen as they comment.

In Terrell's case, she had her kindergartners create a book in Voice Thread with a kindergarten class in Turkey. The youngsters drew "pages" and then spoke into a microphone to record parts of the story.

"Parents are very big on privacy, and this can be private," Terrell says of Voice Thread. "It gives the teacher control in terms of filtering."

But Terrell says fears about how to proceed with social-networking sites and tools should not prevent educators from using them.

"If you don't take that golden opportunity to teach students about the responsibility of using these things, you lose a teachable moment," she says. "If schools block them, they're preventing students from learning the skills they need to know."

Social Media in the Classroom—For Kindergartners(!) Through High Schoolers*

By Renee Ramig
MultiMedia & Internet @ Schools, November/December 2009

Twitter, Blogger, Facebook, MySpace, Ning: How do we help our students learn the social skills needed to understand what it really means to live and participate in a global community? How do we incorporate this into our schools and classrooms? How do we keep ourselves and our students safe?

Social networking sites are mainstream media for many tweens, teens, and adults. There are even social networking sites that attract kids as young as 5 years old. This is the reality of the world we live in, and schools should reflect this reality. We need to help students become effective communicators, offline as well as online.

AT THE YOUNGER END, SAFETY IN NUMBERS

For students in grades K–3, find ways to use online social networking tools with the entire class. Pair up with another school. Together as a class, post online messages that students in the other school respond to. For very young students, try a network such as Voice Thread, which uses recorded messages rather than typed ones. By second grade, you can move to blog or wiki sites that are text-based. Encourage parents to read what has been posted too. Have class discussions about social networking. Students even as young as kindergarten have heard of Facebook and Twitter, so seize this opportunity to talk about what these sites are and how they are similar to what you are doing in class. Discuss what is good to post online and what should only be shared with people the students know in person.

By upper elementary, students are ready to have individual accounts. A great way to start is to post "thinking questions" students can respond to in a social networking format. Remember to give students guidelines on ways they can respond.

For example, they should not just say that they agree with what a certain student said. They should be specific and say what they agree with and why. Use specific examples in class of good posts and not-so-good posts.

As students become more confident using a social network to interact with each other, branch out and create a social network for kids from several classes, even moving outside of the school into networks where kids from several schools can communicate. Here are some things to remember, especially as you branch outside of your classroom:

- Keep the network private, allowing only the students you chooose to have access.

- Decide if you want parents to have access, and, if you do, give them their own accounts.

- Monitor the network regularly.

- Share both appropriate and inappropriate posts, discussing why something should not have been posted (and remember to remove inappropriate posts).

- Be specific on what the network is to be used for and what it is not to be used for.

- As with grades K–3, discuss popular sites such as Facebook and MySpace that are used by older kids; discuss how they are similar to what happens in class.

FOR THOSE 'EXPERIENCED' MIDDLE SCHOOLERS

Middle school students can be a tricky group when it comes to social networking tools. By sixth grade, about 40% of the students will already have experience using social networking tools at home or at a friend's house. If students have not been using social networks in school during grades K–5, they will often need to have a lot of guidance on how to use them appropriately. Start with a network that only the students in your class have access to. Be very specific on what your expectations are when using the online social networking tool. Monitor it often, and share appropriate and inappropriate responses with the class.

DISCUSSION EXTENDERS

Using social networks to begin or extend class discussions is a great way to start using them in middle school. For example, if you wanted to discuss how the design of the pyramids affected the way the ancient Egyptians lived, post a question about it on the network, along with links to online resources—websites and videos—for students to check out. Students can then do a little research and post their responses. The next day in class, bring up the responses and use them to start a class discussion.

You can also have students use the network to continue a discussion started in class. Remind students to stay on topic. In the beginning, it is best to continue posting questions students are responding to rather than just allowing them to get on the network and chat. (It is amazing how quickly middle school kids get off topic. Even though they know a teacher is monitoring their online communication, without guidance and lots of reminders they will post just about anything.)

As you and your students gain experience, you can expand the networks to more students—other students at the school in the same grades, multigrade levels, or even to students in other schools. Remember to restrict the network so that only students you want to have access can get on, and monitor it regularly.

HIGH SCHOOL MEGA-USERS

By high school, about 90% of kids will have used social networks. Since the kids are all 13 or older, you have many more options. Of course, having lots of options can become overwhelming. So as with elementary and middle school kids, make sure you are very clear about the purpose for using a specific tool.

In high schools, increasing numbers of teachers are using social networks and Web 2.0 tools, so students end up having to visit a lot of different sites each evening; each site will require its own username and password. If possible, talk to the other teachers in your school and try to agree on one or two social networking tools you will all use. Create a single network for multiple classes and, within that network, create groups that you can invite students to join. In that way, students can go to a single site and get access to the networks and groups they need for all of their classes.

A great use of social networks in high school is as a place for students to post questions related to their homework. Teachers as well as other students can then respond. Teachers can see which students are asking questions and which are offering responses.

In secondary school, as in middle school, social networks continue to be a great tool for starting or continuing classroom discussions and responding to "thinking questions." It remains essential, however, for teachers to regularly monitor the networks, removing inappropriate posts and keeping a dialog open with students about appropriate use of the school social network.

FOCUS ON SAFETY

As we use more and more of these online tools, we want to continue focusing on student safety. Here are some common-sense concepts you can incorporate into your teaching that will help.

- Talk to your students about what should be kept private. As adults, most of us instinctively know not to share our phone number and address with people we have never met. But there is often a disconnect between "in real life" and "online" for kids, tweens, and teens. They usually feel they know the people they are talking with, and so they share personal information. Many sites have privacy settings. Learn what these are and help kids (and parents) use them appropriately.

- Become familiar with the online networks your students are using. You are the teacher, and you don't need to be using all the tools the students are using to set limits on how they are being used. However, it is difficult to have a conversation about Facebook or Twitter if you aren't using these tools yourself.

- Use social networking tools as part of the education process. Kids love using these tools, so embrace them for use at school. Demonstrate proper ways to use the technology. Use these tools to teach digital citizenship and media literacy.

- Understand the privacy laws and what they are designed to do and not do. Most of what you will hear is related to the Children's Online Privacy Protection Act (COPPA). In summary, this document, which is aimed at website providers rather than at parents or teachers, says sites must get parental consent before they can collect personal information from anyone younger than 13. It also allows parents to view online profiles for their kids younger than 13. To avoid issues relating to COPPA, many social networking sites have decided to limit participation to those 13 and older. There is currently no online-specific legislation directed to kids 13 and older. Some sites will comply with requests from parents of kids ages 13–17 to remove their information; other sites say it is up to the child to do this.

- Don't freak out and shut down access if you find kids doing activities that are disturbing. Use this as a time to talk with and listen to your students. Encourage dialogue. Remind your students why certain activities are not allowed. Help them to use the social networking tools appropriately.

Kids, tweens, and teens are using social networks regularly. All predictions indicate use will continue to increase, so it's also increasingly important that we find ways to incorporate them into schools. Only in this fashion will we be able to teach kids how to use them well.

Schools Get on Web 2.0 Bandwagon[*]

By Denise Smith Amos
The Cincinnati Enquirer, August 29, 2010

Nearly three-quarters of online teens use social-networking sites at least once a week, national polls show.

Now a growing number of teachers in Greater Cincinnati and Northern Kentucky and nationwide are joining, rather than fighting, the tide.

It's a new day for social networking in schools, experts say. Schools until recently were cracking down on most uses of online social networks during the school day.

This fall, more schools in the Cincinnati region are channeling YouTube, Facebook and other social sites to market themselves to potential students, parents and taxpayers. And more teachers are Tweeting, Skyping, blogging and "wiki-ing" with students for educational purposes that can span the world.

At St. Xavier High, for instance, a sophomore history class last May "Skyped" with a minister who lives in what was East Berlin. Talking face-to-face, he described his boyhood under Hitler, his adult life under communism and now, in post-Cold-War Germany. The sophomores, though born after the Berlin Wall fell, asked lots of questions, including his impressions the first time he saw bluejeans.

Principal David Mueller saw the class and wrote to parents recently: "I felt like I did when watching the live telecast of the first moon landing. I realized that we had crossed into a radically changed world."

Classrooms are changing, but it's taking time and patience for educators to harness the many social networking—or "Web 2.0"—technologies that experts say can open students to educational opportunities around the world.

For now, those classrooms are still in the minority. A national survey last year showed 70 percent of districts still ban or block Facebook, YouTube and other social network sites.

"We block instead of teach," says Will Richardson, an education technology expert, teacher and author from Flemington, N.J.

"Right now, very few kids have adults in their lives who are teaching them how to learn in these (social network) spaces. They don't need us to teach them how to use Facebook (aside from the safety aspects), but they do need models and opportunities to connect with other people from around the world with whom they can learn."

But reports about Internet pedophiles, cyber bullying, and sexting still scare educators and parents. And there are too many social networking tools for teachers and schools to master and employ on a large scale—not without some help to make them safe for youngsters, said Mary McCaffrey, CEO of a TH(i)NQ Ed, a Carbondale, Ill., company that markets such services and programs to schools.

"There's a huge interest in using these technologies in school, but the reluctance is from the work that it takes, how easy they are to use, and whether or not you might be opening up a security issue or a PR issue for your district," she said.

For instance, YouTube's video category "School fights" is still popular, with students posting hundreds of videos of school fights.

New Richmond schools last year briefly unblocked Facebook for a few days, "until the high school discovered students going to the library just to check and update their Facebook pages," said Enos Pennington, district spokesman.

Now it's blocked, though the district still uses its Facebook pages for school board updates and alumni, sports and PTO groups. It also posts school videos on Teachertube.com.

Students can get around school firewalls and blocks, warned Russell Fox, a Simon Kenton High English teacher, so teachers might as well guide students through the Internet morass.

Fox shows his classes YouTube videos of famous people—or historic re-enactors—delivering famous speeches. His Broadcast students produce YouTube videos of mostly school news, short skits and training videos.

"YouTube has a lot of garbage on it," he said, "but it also has a lot [of] really good stuff on it."

As more teachers gain confidence using Facebook, Linked In, and Twitter for personal use, more are trying them for educational uses.

"You see a lot more teachers blogging or using Facebook as a tool," Wiegele said. "If we want to be able to relate to our kids, I think we kind of have to. We're not all as curmudgeon-y as people like to think."

Susan Reinhardt, a German teacher at Moeller High in Kenwood, can get some social network benefits in a more protected environment. She plans to use Google Docs this year to let students collaborate and create versions of German fairy tales. Students can edit their shared documents without emailing back and forth, Reinhardt said, and she can see who is doing the work.

She also plans to use Google Voice to get students to leave her voicemail messages in German that she can grade and replay in class.

More schools should direct social networking and Web 2.0 tools toward education, Richardson says.

"In one sense, the Internet is a library," he said, "but . . . we're not just checking out books; we're writing them, in many cases together with people half a world away."

WEB 2.0 GLOSSARY

Web 2.0 describes technologies and Web applications that allow people to access and create Web content, and communicate and collaborate together.

Examples teachers use:
- Skype: Internet-based software that enables people to communicate through voice and video for free.
- WebQuest: An inquiry-oriented lesson or format that is Internet-based. Teachers share lesson plans and designs on websites. Students learn critical thinking, problem solving, research skills and technology skills via web-based assignments.
- Animoto: A video creation tool, free for educators, that allows teachers and students to create video book reports, capture field trips and help each other study.
- Google Docs: A free Web-based word processor, spreadsheet, presentation, form and data storage service that allows users to create and edit documents online while collaborating in real-time with other users.
- Moodle: Free, open-source e-learning software that helps educators create online courses and collaborative lessons.
- Wikis: Software programs that let people create, remove and edit content on a Web page, or collections of information that can be edited by multiple people within a group. (Wikipedia is an example.)

NETWORKING SITES

- Weblogs: Online journals created by a person or organization and often cover specific topics. By discussing and linking to each other's posts, bloggers can form networks. Technorati is a popular search engine for blogs.
- Ning: A website that lets you create your own social networks and place blogs, videos, photos, surveys and other applications.
- Twitter: A microblog social network environment.

SOCIAL NETWORKING AT LOCAL SCHOOLS

- At Seven Hills' campuses, first-graders will Skype to explore life in India while second-graders will study China and Japan by communicating with pen pals via blogs and emails. Fourth- and fifth-graders will partner with students in Spanish-speaking countries, and some science students will partner with others in Alaska on projects ranging from the earth's magnetic field to solar energy to bird migrations.
- Cincinnati Country Day's videoconferencing has linked kindergartners to the Cleveland Museum of Art, older students studying Shakespeare to Globe Theater actors, and other high schoolers to Nick Clooney. The school is on YouTube, Twitter, and Facebook, and its student newspaper is a constantly updated blog, www.scrollonline.net.
- Oak Hills High will for the second year "broadcast" its football games on the Internet but this year will let people tweet on the site, which last year attracted more [than] 4,000 hits.
- In Forest Hills, sixth-graders have Skyped with a soldier in Iraq, while a Spanish class talked with kids in Spain.
- St. Ursula Academy's 125 "student ambassadors" will blog for prospective students.
- St. Mary School in Hyde Park lets its Stock Market Club and students who traveled to Costa Rica for a science program maintain blogs.

5

Bullied, Spied On, Fired, Never Hired:
The Dangers of Social Media

Editor's Introduction

Mark Zuckerberg, the founder of Facebook and arguably the most controversial figure in the history of social media, likes to talk about "openness." He lists it among his interests on his own Facebook page, and he claims to have created his massively popular digital network as a means of fostering communication. To hear him tell it, Facebook's hundreds of millions of users want a service that allows them to share with friends, family members, and anyone else they've welcomed into their circles the most intimate details of their lives.

That's the utopian view. Zuckerberg's critics—some of whom went as far as to organize Quit Facebook Day on May 31, 2010—take a more cynical stance. They argue that for all his rhetoric about openness, the 26-year-old billionaire is really interested in exploiting users to make a profit. Facebook earns its money through advertising, and thanks to its half-billion members, each with a unique profile, the site is brimming with valuable consumer data. If, for example, the makers of a new horror movie want to ensure a strong opening weekend, they can pay Facebook to direct their advertisements at users with a known interest in such films. Even if Facebook doesn't share its data with advertisers, consumer watchdogs say this type of targeted advertising constitutes a violation of users' privacy.

That word—privacy—is one that comes up again and again in this chapter, which focuses on the dangers of social media. In the leadoff article, "Why We'll Never Escape Facebook," James Cowan examines some of the major complaints that have been lodged against Zuckerberg's creation. When Facebook adds new features, Cowan explains, it often makes privacy an "opt-in" function, meaning that if users don't want to share photos, profiles, status updates, shopping habits, and other pieces of personal information with the general public, they have to manually change default settings. Doing so can be complicated, and while Facebook has apologized several times for failing to properly explain new features, the company hasn't changed its ways. "Zuckerberg finds it easier to ask for forgiveness, rather than permission," Cowan asserts.

Advertisers aren't the only ones with an interest in Facebook profiles. According to the 2009 CareerBuilder survey Eileen Morgan Johnson cites in "Social Media: Its Use by Employers in Pre-Employment, Employment and Post-Employment Situations," the next piece in this chapter, 45 percent of hiring managers use social-media sites to evaluate potential employees. That's bad news for anyone who has ever posted a photo of a crazy college beer bash or written a derogatory blog entry—even in jest—about a former employer. As Johnson explains, employers are prohibited from basing hiring decisions on race, sexual orientation, and other such factors, but if they see a Facebook photo of an applicant drinking or using drugs, they may be within their rights to disqualify that individual. Johnson also touches on how companies monitor employee use of social-media sites and work to prevent information leaks.

In "Addicted to Facebook," the next entry in this chapter, Scott Kerbs profiles a woman who nearly let her obsession with Facebook games destroy her family. As Kerbs reports, social-media addiction is a growing problem, and many people spend hours a day engaging in what they mistake for genuine human interaction. "It's easier than a real relationship," addiction specialist Aaron Shaw tells Kerbs. "It's human nature to go after the easier thing."

While MySpace and Facebook offer some users a sense of community, they're not always hospitable places. In "Cyberbullies Ramp Up the Taunting—Anonymously," the final selection, Roger Neumann looks at how teenagers are using social media to spread gossip and pick on one another. "We know that people will do things as part of a group or when they're anonymous, rather than face-to-face," Binghamton University psychology professor Brandon Gibb tells Neumann. "They're more likely to be mean."

Why We'll Never Escape Facebook[*]

By James Cowan
Canadian Business, June 15, 2010

After a spring of skirmishes between Facebook, its users, international privacy watchdogs and Internet activists, two things have become clear:

1. You should quit Facebook.
2. You probably won't.

The case for quitting is strong. Critics allege Facebook changes privacy policies at whim, makes it difficult to control personal information and hoards users' data. They also claim that Mark Zuckerberg, the company's 26-year-old founder is a false prophet who claims his generation values openness, and casts anyone who cares about privacy as an old-fashioned fuddy-duddy.

These arguments are made convincingly and often. Yet users don't seem to care. The site added 30 million new users in May alone, according to Inside Network, a research firm. More than 912,000 Canadians joined the site in May, a 6% hike in membership, along with close to 7.9 million Americans. Facebook this spring overtook Google as the most visited site in the world. Roughly 55% of the people who visited a social networking site last month used Facebook, compared with 16% who used YouTube, the second-most-popular site in the category. Roughly 41% of all Americans now use Facebook; in Canada, the number now sits at 47.9%. Facebook will soon have 500 million users, more people than live in the United States, Canada, the United Kingdom, France and Spain combined.

Whether we like it or not, the battle over privacy has already been fought. Facebook won. "The days of being anonymous on the Internet are gone, unless you take steps to be anonymous," says David Fewer, director of the Canadian Internet Policy and Public Interest Clinic. "You used to have to give your permission to be tracked. Now, these businesses have models where you opt out of being tracked. The onus has switched."

Facebook is different from almost any other product or service in the enormous degree of emotional and time investment it demands from its users. The average American Internet user in January spent 14 minutes on Facebook each day, up from 11.5 minutes just four months earlier. It's become a cornerstone of people's lives, a component of their identity and not something they'll toss away over abstract concerns over who might see their baby photos. Protest movements may claim a few defectors, regulators may impose minor restrictions that will prove useless in the face of the Internet's rapid change, and competitors may promise better networks, but Facebook is currently a Goliath without a David.

Zuckerberg has long cast the transition to "opt-in" privacy as a social good rather than a part of Facebook's business model, which it clearly is. Famous for his unvarying wardrobe of T-shirts and hooded sweatshirts, Zuckerberg looks and talks like a spokesman for the Internet generation. Born in 1984 and raised in the suburbs of New York, Zuckerberg was a geek from the get-go. (He had a *Star Wars*-themed bar mitzvah.) He was MVP of his private high school's fencing team, can read and write in five languages and arrived at Harvard in 2003 with a heap of academic awards.

Neither his sartorial sense nor sense of humour has evolved much since university; he reportedly wears rubber sandals to board meeting, and his business card once read: "I'm CEO . . . bitch." David Kirkpatrick, author of *The Facebook Effect*, an authorized history of the company, writes, "It's not that he sets out to break the rules; he just doesn't pay much attention to them." (You'd be forgiven for thinking that Zuckerberg doesn't sound like the ideal candidate to serve as gatekeeper of one of the world's fastest-growing databases of personal information.) He has never been a compelling public speaker—he lacks the zeal of Steve Jobs or the earnest thoughtfulness of Bill Gates—Zuckerberg still occasionally ventures forth to preach the virtues of a more open world. "People have really gotten comfortable not only sharing more information and different kinds, but more openly and with more people. That social norm is just something that has evolved over time," he told a technology conference in January. Zuckerberg's own Facebook bio reads: "I'm trying to make the world a more open place" and lists "Openness" among his interests.

Unfortunately, only 381 out of Facebook's half-billion users share that particular interest, a bit of trivia which begins to hint at the flaw in Zuckerberg's rhetoric of openness. Facebook has not simply benefited from the zeitgeist—it has shaped the zeitgeist to suit its own needs. Since its founding in 2004, it has prodded and cajoled people into making their information more public, forcing online culture to conform with its own corporate interests. The company thrives on advertising revenue, on pooling users' information and using that data to target ads at very specific demographics. Knowing your age and gender helps somewhat. Knowing that you enjoyed the last Black Eyed Peas record, shop at the Gap, went to the University of Toronto and love to garden helps more. Facebook knows who its members are dating, when they break up, when they change jobs and when they move.

"Facebook's patrons are not its customers. We're its product," says Fewer. Facebook displayed 176.3 billion ads in the first three months of 2010, more than industry leader Yahoo, according to comScore, a market-research firm. Forecasters predict Facebook will exceed US$1 billion in revenue this year, up from roughly US$650 million in 2009. With its market valuation more than doubling in less than a year, from US$10 billion in July 2009 to US$22 billion last month, Facebook needs users to keeping on sharing.

And people, so far, seem happy to share. There are now 25 billion bits of information, from web links to photo albums, shared on the site each month. When Zuckerberg announced in April changes designed to strengthen connections between Facebook and the wider web, the company further increased the size of its online real estate. By introducing the company's familiar "Like" buttons on outside sites, even more people would engage with Facebook, increasing its appeal for advertisers. The "Like" buttons on IMDB, a movie information site, were used more than 350,000 times in their first two weeks, while 100,000 sites used new software to link themselves with Facebook. The NHL's site, for example, saw traffic from Facebook increase 80% as users viewed pictures, articles and videos. Meanwhile, the new "instant personalization" feature, which uses Facebook data to personalize users' experiences on outside websites, means Facebook could soon find itself at the hub of everything from online dating to travel sites to polling. "These are ultimately the places where Facebook is going to make money on their services: connecting with other people, connecting users with advertisers and sharing information," says Michael Gartenberg, a partner with the Altimeter Group, a California-based technology advising firm.

Critics don't hate these new services so much as the way they were implemented. Controversy came when Facebook decided it would subscribe all its users to the new service, forcing them to opt out if they didn't want their likes and dislikes shared with the wider web.

While many of the concerns expressed in the media and online are valid, some are also sheer paranoia, likely driven by a misunderstanding of how Facebook handles the information it collects. Advertisers are never handed a list of users in their chosen demographic. Instead, Facebook promises to show the ad to the appropriate users and then reports on the results. Because of this, it doesn't really matter whether a person's hometown or love of Italian cooking is made public or private. Facebook still knows—and targets its ads accordingly. "The targeting is not affected by whether your information is available to everyone or just friends, or friends of friends," says Debbie Frost, director of communications and public affairs for Facebook. "The advertisers never learn anything about our users. If I'm a manufacturer of tents, and I want to target people ages 20 to 30 who like camping, then I can do that. The report I get from Facebook says my ad was shown 80,000 times to people who fit that demographic."

While Facebook doesn't sell users' information to advertisers, it remains unclear what happens to the personal data harvested by the dozens of games, quizzes, personality tests and other time wasters that clutter Facebook. Produced by third-party developers, these games do not necessarily adhere to Facebook's privacy rules, meaning that cute virtual pumpkin patch you've been tending could be a front for a data-mining operation. And even if users didn't partake in these third-party applications, their information could still be collected if friends were playing. In a recent FTC filing, U.S. privacy groups complained about Facebook's relationship with third-party developers, deriding its decision to allow them to now retain users' information for more than 24 hours. This is one of the largest complaints about Facebook, that ever-shifting privacy commitments mean users sign up expecting one level of protection, only to have the rules change in six months. It is not unlike Ford selling you a car, then showing up six months later and announcing you can no longer have air bags. The company has made commitments to no longer tinker with users' privacy settings—as it has done in the past—and to try to maintain a more consistent privacy policy in the future. "We've made a commitment that once you've made those choices, new products and services will align with what you choose," Frost says.

But Facebook still benefits from cultivating users willing to share more and more information. Each time someone lists an interest or clicks a "Like" button, that information gets added to the database, slowly creating increasingly sophisticated profiles of Facebook users and making it possible to focus advertising with pinpoint precision. If you don't like being treated as nothing more than a set of ad-consuming eyeballs, the solution is not to tighten your privacy settings. It's quitting Facebook altogether.

Zuckerberg's business strategy from the outset seems to involve transgressing first, than asking for forgiveness. People become addicted to the service and see that dependency exploited in subtle ways. So far, it's a strategy that has worked. Zuckerberg's first privacy snafu pre-dates Facebook. While at Harvard, he created an application called "Facemash," using information stolen from online campus directories. The Facebook prototype had a sophomoric twist; users were shown photos of two classmates and then asked to vote on which was more attractive. School administrators closed the site within days and hauled Zuckerberg before Harvard's administrative board on accusations of breaching security, violating copyright and breaching individuals' privacy. He was placed on probation.

When Facebook (or Thefacebook, as it was then known) launched three months later, Zuckerberg appeared to have a new found respect for privacy. Only students with a Harvard e-mail address could join, and they could limit access, barring everyone except other people in their residence if they wished. One of the company's earliest privacy policies stipulates: "No personal information that you submit to Thefacebook will be available to any user of the Web Site who does not belong to at least one of the groups specified by you in your privacy settings." Published in 2005, the policy is plainly written and less than 1,000 words. The company's current privacy policy is 414 times that size, making it—as myriad news stories have noted—longer than the U.S. Constitution.

The problem is not only that Facebook's rule book is increasingly complex, but also that the rules often change without warning. In 2006, Facebook introduced its "news feed" feature. Instead of having to visit friends' pages for news, information about breakups, job changes and other life events were aggregated directly on users' home pages. Having personal information suddenly broadcast bothered some users, and there was a rebellion. One million of the site's users joined anti-news-feed protest groups and plans fomented for a "Don't Log Onto Facebook Day." The uproar makes Facebook's current controversy look puny. One in 10 protested the news feed four years ago, which remains a central feature of day-to-day life on Facebook. In protest over recent privacy changes, over 28,000 Facebook users committed to deleting their accounts on May 31. That's only one in every 22,000 users.

If the news-feed fight makes current Facebook protests look impotent in comparison, it also made clear Zuckerberg's standard response to controversy. In the case of the news-feed backlash, Zuckerberg posted a message on the company's blog headlined "We really messed this one up." The news feed was designed to "provide you with a stream of information about your social world," Zuckerberg said. "Instead, we did a bad job of explaining what the new features were and an even worse job of giving you control of them." His words echoed an old politician's trick, apologizing for how his actions were interpreted rather than the sin itself.

Then, in 2007, the company introduced its Beacon program as part of its first big advertising drives. The service reported information about users' activities on partner sites. If you rented a movie from Blockbuster or purchased something at eBay, that information would appear on your Facebook page. Beacon spurred two class-action lawsuits—one against Facebook and its partners, another targeting Blockbuster—charging the service violated privacy laws because it required users to manually opt out of participation. Nearly two years later, Facebook paid $9.5 million to settle the suit and shuttered the Beacon program for good. However, it has already launched Facebook Connect, a similar program with better privacy controls. In 2007, Zuckerberg posted a now-familiar refrain on the company's blog: "We simply did a bad job with this release, and I apologize for it." Zuckerberg finds it easier to ask for forgiveness, rather than permission.

All Facebook's previous privacy battles were a mere prelude to what happened on April 21, when Zuckerberg strolled on to the stage at a developers' conference in San Francisco and let loose. He unveiled "instant personalization," which shared personal information with music site Pandora and Yelp, a review site, and then tailored the content displayed on those sites to the user's interests.

External websites are also now able to place "Like" buttons beside their content, allowing Facebook users to flag articles and information for their friends. Furthermore, software developers who make programs that run on Facebook, like the popular game Farmville or personality quizzes, would be allowed to store the information for more than 24 hours, a reversal of a previous company policy. Days before the developers' conference, the company began its push toward "Connected Profiles," which required information like a user's hometown, education and interests either be made publicly available or removed from the profile. The final change became a focal point for public anger, with allegations the company was forcing users to over-share about their lives. Users seem to forget that participating in Facebook is an option, not mandatory. It can't over-share information it's not told.

The controversy brought renewed scrutiny to Facebook's privacy policies as a whole. Rapid growth, a pile-up of new features and ad hoc responses to previous privacy concerns meant the site's privacy controls had become maddeningly complex, with users required to navigate 50 different settings and 170 different options. Soon, the media was reporting a "Facebook backlash," as publicity for Quit Facebook Day spread and high-profile geeks like pundit Leo Laporte, entrepreneur Jason Calacanis and Peter Rojas, the co-founder of Engadget, closed their accounts. A question-and-answer published in the *New York Times* with Elliot Schrage, vice-president of public policy, was meant to placate concerns but came across as dismissive. "We know that changing Facebook—something people have demonstrated is important to them—can be unsettling," Schrage wrote. Many disliked Schrage's tone, but the message was no different than Zuckerberg's in the past: we screwed up on the implementation, not the idea.

One could question whether Facebook goofed at all. The public embraced the changes announced in April. Yet, faced with a mounting pile of negative press, Zuckerberg announced changes designed to simplify the site's privacy settings. Nonetheless, the site's default settings still encourage people to share their status updates, photos and videos. Having been derided in the press, villainized online and even sued, Zuckerberg still contends the world still needs to become a more open place. "Maybe I'm in denial," a sweaty and shell-shocked Zuckerberg told a tech conference in early June. "I think our goals haven't really changed that much at all." Zuckerberg still casts Facebook as a public good, improving the world by encouraging us to open the blinds and let the sun shine in on our private lives.

Facebook's position, while self-serving, is not without merit. Only one-third of Internet users worry about how much information is available about them online, compared with 40% in 2006, according to recently released research by the Pew Internet and American Life Project. Just 4% of Internet users reported having something embarrassing posted online. Furthermore, 22% of all Internet users say that five or more pieces of personal information about them, such as birth date, home address or cellphone number are available online, with the number increasing to 32% for people between the ages of 18 and 32, or Zuckerberg's generation.

One of the most enduring myths about Facebook is that it exploits young people too stupid and inexperienced to know better. True, a recent study did find 42% of respondents between the ages of 18 and 29 could not answer a single question about privacy law correctly. But the same study found young people were just as likely to read sites' privacy policies as older respondents. Furthermore, the Pew study found people between the ages of 18 and 29 were most likely to limit the information about them on social networking sites, with 71% taking precautions compared with 62% of people between the ages of 30 and 49. "Young adults are more active in managing their online identities and reputations," says Mary Madden, a Pew senior research specialist. "While it may appear to older adults or the public at large that they're making choices that are very liberal, they are paying a lot of attention to their self-presentation."

This may all bolster Zuckerberg's case for openness while quashing the concerns of nervous privacy advocates fretting for our troubled youth. But if young people were the most savvy about social networking, they were also the most distrustful. When asked how much of the time you can trust social networking sites, 28% said "never," while only 2% said "just about always." (The largest cohort, 51%, said "some of the time.") In comparison, only 19% of users between 30 and 49 said they'd never trust Facebook or similar sites.

Privacy activists remain understandably skeptical about Facebook's true motives. Led by the Electronic Privacy Information Centre, a research group based in Washington, 15 similar groups filed a complaint with the Federal Trade Commission in early May, alleging Facebook's instant personalization program violated privacy rights by automatically subscribing users. On the day after Zuckerberg announced the company's latest concessions to privacy concerns, the groups, with names like the Privacy Rights Now Coalition and the Centre for Digital Democracy, held a conference call to explain everything that Facebook was still doing wrong. The list was lengthy, from forcing users to opt out of instant personalization to inadequate monitoring of outside applications. "We shouldn't lose sight of the fact that, despite the procedural improvements, the substance does remain largely unchanged," said Chip Pitts, president of the Bill of Rights Defense Committee and a Stanford law professor. "The default settings remain vastly more open to the world than the prior incarnations of Facebook that allowed it to get the 400 million, 500 million users that it now has." Four U.S. Senators in April sent a letter to Facebook demanding further privacy changes. In a press release, they declared social networking sites "a Wild West of the Internet," adding "users need ability to control private information and fully understand how it's being used." American activists look to Canada as proof that regulators can provide order to the lawless web. Canadian Privacy Commissioner Jennifer Stoddart last year wrung concessions from Facebook, including the introduction of a method to permanently delete an account. But the Internet moves quickly, and government regulators are lumbering. Even Fewer, whose Canadian Internet Policy and Public Interest Clinic filed the complaint that led to Stoddart's actions, says regulation is only a partial solution to the public's concerns. Further class-action lawsuits, like the ones that torpedoed Beacon, could have an effect. Ultimately, it will take the emergence of a viable competitor to force Facebook to change. "Competition in the marketplace provides the greatest incentives for businesses to provide secure, competitive products," Fewer says. "You've got a crappy product, you've got one that doesn't respect your privacy, you've got a product with weekly security issues—people will leave you when a new product comes along. Not even a better product, just a new one. The warts I don't know about might be better than the ones I do know."

Sadly, there is no social network yet ready to steal all of Facebook's friends. Media hype in recent weeks has focused on upstarts like Diaspora and Appleseed, but neither will be operational until this summer (at least). Existing competitors like

MySpace have already been deemed passé by the Internet elite. And even if a rival service emerges, the structure of Facebook will make it difficult for users to kick their habit. Zuckerberg has convinced Facebook users that openness means the freedom to share the trivialities of daily life. But on the wider Internet, openness has long meant the ability to move information freely from one spot to another with minimal hassle. And by that definition of openness, Facebook is remarkably closed. Anyone who has ever tried to export a photograph or a contact list knows that once information is fed into Facebook, it is remarkably difficult to dislodge. Having committed all this time to building a home on Facebook, it is unlikely that users will want to start anew elsewhere, even if Diaspora or MySpace or any of the other sites now billing themselves as privacy-friendly versions of Facebook prove viable. There are plenty of valid reasons to leave Facebook, but it's got some high walls around it. For its growing population, it may just prove easier to stay.

Social Media[*]

Its Use by Employers in Pre-Employment, Employment and Post-Employment Situations

By Eileen Morgan Johnson
New York Public Personnel Law, October 8, 2010

PART I: THE USE OF SOCIAL MEDIA IN PRE-EMPLOYMENT SITUATIONS

PRE-EMPLOYMENT SCREENING

Employers are taking advantage of the free information on social media websites and communication tools to screen applicants or to perform pre-offer due diligence on successful applicants. It's not just people in their 20's and 30's who have online profiles and the use of social media by human resource professionals is not a passing fad.

There are a variety of resources that can be consulted such as LinkedIn®, MySpace™ and Facebook. Users of these three sites create an individual profile that can include information about their work history, extracurricular activities, and contacts. Other sites such as Twitter™ and YouTube can also yield information on applicants that might be valuable in making a decision to extend or withhold an offer of employment. For those employers who are unsure about using social media sites, a simple search using Google™ or some other search engine can also yield potentially interesting information.

What are employers looking for? Social media profiles can provide a lot of valuable information. While an employer should not rely solely on these sites to verify information on employment applications, they can be used to discredit applicants or to provide another view of the person behind the resume or online application. Online profiles can provide information on the person's:

• Professional credentials

- Career objectives

- Maturity and judgment

- Abuse of drugs or alcohol

- Current employment status

- Red flags

A June 2009 CareerBuilder survey of 2,600 hiring managers found that 45% of them use social media in the hiring process. That was double the number of hiring managers that reported such use in 2008. What's more, 11% planned to start using social media for prescreening. Eighteen percent or almost one in five hiring managers surveyed reported finding information online that encouraged them to hire candidates:

- Profile - good feel for personality and "fit"- 50%

- Profile supported professional qualifications - 39%

- Candidate was creative - 38%

- Solid communication skills - 35%

- Candidate well rounded - 33%

- Good references posted by others - 19%

- Candidate received awards - 15%

However, twice as many (35%) hiring managers reported finding information that led them to not hire a candidate, including:

- Inappropriate photos or postings - 53%

- Postings on drinking or drug use - 44%

- Bad-mouthing previous employer, co-workers or clients - 35%

- Poor communication skills - 29%

- Discriminatory comments - 26%

- Lied about qualifications - 24%

- Shared confidential information from previous employer - 20%

POTENTIAL PITFALLS OF SCREENING

Screening with social media has some drawbacks. It can provide too much information about job applicants, including some information that cannot be considered in the employment decision. Some online content can be questionable in terms of its origin or truthfulness. Moreover, some employers are concerned about invading applicants' privacy.

TOO MUCH INFORMATION

Certain information that can be found in an applicant's online profile cannot be used as the basis for an employment decision. These include information on the applicant's race, religion, national origin, age, pregnancy status, marital status, disability, sexual orientation (some state and local jurisdictions), gender expression or identity (some state and local jurisdictions) and genetic information. While it is best to avoid obtaining or even seeing this information, it is often prominently displayed on social networking profiles.

A potential solution is to assign one person to review the social media sites who is not part of the decision making process. That person should filter out any information regarding membership in a protected class and only pass on information that may be considered in the hiring process. The most fundamental way to protect against discrimination claims in using information gleaned from social media sites in the employment decision process is consistency. Employers should keep records of information reviewed and used in any employment decision.

QUALITY OF INFORMATION

Online information is not always reliable. The first rule is to make sure that the person whose profile you are viewing is actually your job applicant. It is not unusual for people to have similar names or even the same name. If you have confirmed the identity of the applicant, keep in mind that there is a possibility that not all of the information in the profile is correct. Profile information might have been deliberately falsified by the applicant or a friend or significant other with access to the profile login information.

Employers should also recognize that any site provides a limited picture of the individual. Remember the intended audience. On sites like LinkedIn, the intended audience is other professionals. However, on Facebook and MySpace, profiles are often developed for close friends and family. And some people enjoy creating a new persona for their online life, one that has no relationship to who they are in real life.

INVASION OF PRIVACY

Employers have little risk that viewing applicants' profiles, blogs or other online postings will give rise to invasion of privacy claims. Users of social networking sites usually have the option to set privacy settings on their personal pages. Their personal pages can be available to any user of the network, or can be restricted to only individuals authorized by the user. A critical question to ask in evaluating an invasion of privacy claim is whether there was a reasonable expectation of privacy. To avoid the potential for liability, employers should avoid attempts at circumventing the privacy settings put in place by users. Only view information that is readily accessible and intended for public viewing.

GOOGLE™ AND OTHER SEARCH ENGINES

In a recent Monster.com report, 77% of employers surveyed reported performing a "Google" search on job applicants. Google is popular for the amount of information that can be discovered and the ease of use. In addition to the concern noted above that a Google search might return too much information, there are additional concerns about the quality of the information retrieved. The breadth of information that a Google search can produce has its own drawbacks including difficulty in identifying sources of search results.

As of now, employers are unlikely to incur liability based on Google searches of job applicants. To further protect against liability, employers should be consistent in their search practices, recognize the limits of online searches, and be sure the information they find actually relates to their applicants.

CURRENT LAW ON REVIEWING SOCIAL MEDIA SITES

There are no court decisions yet imposing liability for an employer's review of a social networking site in the pre-employment context. This is not a guarantee that such liability will not be imposed in the future. For now, the potential for liability is minimal in the absence of misconduct or discrimination by the employer. The potential for liability can be further reduced by:

- Being consistent in prescreening all applicants for certain positions or only those already selected for interviews

- Having someone other than the decision maker filter out protected class information if possible

- Keeping records of the basis for each employment decision

- Not circumventing privacy settings established on applicants' networking sites

If employers have any questions about whether information found through pre-employment screening should be used in the decision making process, they should consult employment counsel before using that information.

PART II: SOCIAL MEDIA IN THE WORKPLACE

THE USE OF SOCIAL MEDIA IN EMPLOYMENT
AND POST-EMPLOYMENT SITUATIONS

Social media is changing communications between employers and employees and among co-workers.

EMPLOYEE COMMUNICATIONS

The employee newsletter is out and the company Facebook group is in. Employees of the 21st century want a different relationship with their employer and co-workers than that of prior generations. They are used to receiving information that is current and relevant to them, and they expect the same ability to preselect and customize the information they receive in the workplace. Employees want to be able to ask questions and provide feedback to management. With more employees teleworking or working from multiple locations, they want the ability to communicate with their co-workers. Today's workers like to create their own news in their personal lives and share it with others electronically, and they expect to be able to do the same with their work lives.

The International Association of Business Communicators Research Foundation & Bucks Consultants surveyed 1,500 employers in June 2009. An astonishing 97% of the employers said that they frequently use social media to communicate with their employees. Of these, 19% reported occasional use, with only 1% reporting that they used social media rarely or never. Whether by company emails, an intranet website, Facebook group or other tools, clearly social media have become critical to employer/employee communications.

SOCIAL MEDIA USAGE POLICIES

Just as employers adopted Internet and computer use policies in the 1990's, now they are developing social media usage policies. These policies can be part of the company's electronic communications usage policy or a stand-alone policy. The key to an effective social media usage policy is frequent adaptation to new technologies and programs, new legal requirements related to both technology and the workplace, and communication with employees.

DISTRACTIONS AND PRODUCTIVITY

Employers worry about lost employee productivity due to the distractions of social media in the workplace. The temptations to communicate with their friends and family members are everywhere. Text messaging, cell phones and instant messaging provide near instantaneous dialogue which can be more interesting than the daily work assignments.

Twitter feeds and other alerts are used to notify blog followers when a new posting has been added. Younger workers are used to multitasking. They made their way through high school and college with laptops, iPods, and cell phones, and can write a paper, text a friend, and download music simultaneously while watching television and talking with friends. They want their work lives to function the same way their personal lives do with constant stimulation and communication.

Do employers have the right to force their employees to focus on the task at hand and not use social media while at work? The courts are still working that issue out, but at least one federal court has suggested that employers might have the right to prevent employees from accessing blogs while at work. Nickolas v. Fletcher, 2007 U.S. Dist. Lexis 23843 (E.D. Ky. 2007).

MONITORING

An employer might want to monitor its employees' online conduct while at work. The argument goes something like this: "The employee is on my time, in my facility, and using my computer equipment. Why shouldn't I be able to monitor what's going on?"

Any monitoring should be done with care. In Pietrylo v. Hillstone Restaurant Group, 2008 WL 6085437 (D.N.J. 2008), a Newark jury found that the employer violated the federal Stored Communications Act by secretly monitoring employees' postings on a private password-protected Internet chat room. This followed an earlier case, Konop v. Hawaiian Airlines, Inc., 302 F.3d 868 (9th Cir. 2002), where the court also held that secret monitoring by an employer of a password protected website visited by an employee while at work violated the federal Stored Communications Act.

However, earlier this year, the U.S. Supreme Court unanimously held that a public employer's review of an employee's text messages on an employer-issued device was a reasonable search under the Fourth Amendment. City of Ontario v. Quon, No. 08-1332, 560 U.S. ___ (2010). This case involved the use of a pager issued to the employee by the employer. The employer authorized a set number of text messages per month and allowed employees to pay for any overage. Employees were not prohibited from using the pager to send and receive personal text messages. The employer noticed that one employee had an excessive number of text messages and asked its service provider for copies of the text messages from that employee's phone. It found messages to the employee's wife and girlfriend. The employee claimed that his privacy had been violated. The lower court had held that the service provider violated the Stored Communications Act when it provided the employee's text messages to the employer. The Supreme Court reversed, holding that the employer had a right to see text messages sent and received on the employer's pager. While this case involved a public employer (and courts have typically allowed greater employer control of public employees), the court clearly stated that employees do not have an expectation of privacy when using equipment provided by the employer.

OTHER WORRIES

Employers have more serious potential issues than lost productivity to worry about. Social media tools present an easy method of accessing and communicating information. This can include the unauthorized disclosure of confidential information. While the concerns about unauthorized disclosure using social media tools are similar to unauthorized disclosure in more traditional ways, now the disclosure is at the click of a mouse to multiple recipients. Unauthorized disclosure can include the business plans and information of clients as well as those of the employer.

Unfortunately, social media tools can also be used to harass co-workers. What might be a harmless exchange of jokes or photos between friends can take on a new life when they are spread around the office. The seemingly innocent friend request on Facebook from a co-worker can take on new meaning. How does a female employee respond to a "friend" request from her male supervisor?

The technology behind social media presents another new challenge to employers, the inability to effectively respond to misinformation. A fleeting complaint lingers forever and can be accessed or rebroadcast by other employees or those outside of the company. Information remains in cyberspace indefinitely. The employer's response to misinformation or even a later retraction by the defaming party is unlikely to reach all who received the initial communication. Any communication issued by an employee is seemingly valid, even when the employee is a self-appointed company "spokesperson."

Employers might consider charging employees who misuse social media at the workplace with using company equipment inappropriately and follow appropriate disciplinary measures. The social media usage policy should provide for discipline for abuse of the policy and explicitly state that social media may not be used to violate other employer policies, including harassment and non-discrimination policies.

INTERNAL INVESTIGATIONS

In a June 2009 survey, Proofpoint asked US employers to report on internal investigations at their companies in the past 12 months. The results of the survey show that employers do have a reason to be concerned about leaks of confidential or proprietary information. Employers reported conducting investigations of leaks by:

- Email - 43%

- Blog or message board - 18%

- Video - 18%

- Facebook and LinkedIn - 17%

- Twitter or SMS texts - 13%

The same employers also reported on the results of their investigations, with a substantial number finding violations of company policies. The rates of employees disciplined or terminated for policy violations were:

- Email - 31% terminated

- Blog or message board - 17% disciplined, 9% terminated

- Video - 15% disciplined, 8% terminated

- Social networks - 8% terminated

- Twitter/SMS texts - no reported actions

EMPLOYER RESPONSES

Employers can take a number of measures to reduce the problems that can arise from the use or misuse of social media. As a first step, employers should remind their employees that they have no expectation of privacy when using the employer's electronic equipment or network. This includes employer supplied smart phones, voice mail, and email. Next, employers should review and update as necessary their Internet usage policies to include the use of social media and clearly state what employee actions will result in discipline or even termination.

To address the potential misuse of social media, a social media usage policy should prohibit the use of the employer's name by employees outside of official company communications. The policy also should discipline employees for posting any negative statements about the employer or any derogatory comments about the employee's co-workers or supervisors.

Whether it is two pizza parlor employees abusing food for their YouTube video or anonymous misstatements on a blog about a company's products or services, an employer's reputation can be easily and speedily damaged through the misuse of social media tools. Postings favoring the employer's competitors or slamming its customers, or, in the case of associations, its members, can also be detrimental and the intentional disclosure of confidential employer information can be devastating.

Employer social media policies should prohibit:

- Disclosure of confidential employer information

- Discrimination against or harassment of co-workers

- Using the employer's trademarks

- Infringing the intellectual property rights of others

- Making statements adverse to the employer's business interests or reputation
- Criticism of customers or business partners
- Statements supporting competitors
- Obscenity

LEGAL LIMITATIONS

Multijurisdictional employers may face inconsistent laws when trying to establish uniform policies for their employees. Some states prohibit an employer from acting with respect to employee activity that is not related to the employer or is not on working time. In addition, there are laws that protect concerted activity by employees—the protected right of employees to discuss common issues related to the workplace (these are the laws protecting labor unions). There are also laws that protect complaints related to the violation of workplace laws such as state and federal whistleblower laws. However, employees do not have a right to engage in activity injurious to the employer that does not fall within these limited exceptions. Employers should consult with counsel before establishing policies or taking steps to address the misuse of social media by their employees.

OFF-DUTY CONDUCT

Employers can tread over the line when they attempt to discipline employees for their off-duty conduct. Many states have off-duty conduct laws that prohibit employers from basing employment decisions on legal activities of employees outside of work time. Employers need to be aware of the state laws applicable to each of the jurisdictions where their employees are located to avoid violating these laws.

Postings complaining about the employee's work, the employer, supervisors, or co-workers or postings critical of the employer's product or service can be grounds for disciplinary action up to and including termination. For example, a teacher who was fired for an inappropriate MySpace page sued the employer and lost in Spanierman v. Hughes, 576 F. Supp. 2d 292 (D. Conn. 2008). Even when the conduct does not rise to the level of disciplinary action, it can cause the employer to question the employee's maturity or judgment.

POST-EMPLOYMENT

Former employees who left on their own or maintain a positive relationship with their former employer, supervisor and co-workers rarely raise concerns about the potential for harm to the employer through their online activities. However, the disgruntled former employee is a different story. Just as they are not concerned about the bridges they burn, these employees are not worried about the potential consequences of the statements they publish online or their tweets about their former employer, supervisor and even co-workers. The potential for a defamation claim against the former employee can be great. Alas, the opportunity to collect damages is not great.

Some employers have a real concern that confidential information will be released by disgruntled former employees. Requiring employees with access to confidential information, as a condition of employment, to sign a confidentiality and nondisclosure agreement which remains in effect following the termination of the employment relationship is one way to address this potential problem.

SOCIAL MEDIA NON-COMPETE

Employers who sanction employee blogs, Facebook groups, Twitter accounts, and other means of communicating through social media often do not think through the consequences of setting up these accounts with one employee as the face of the company.

What happens when the employee who has been regularly posting blogs on behalf of the company decides to leave? Who owns the profile? Who owns the content? More importantly, who owns the followers? Even if the now former employee does not object to the employer taking over his blog, what if the employer does not have the login name and password?

To address these issues, savvy employers are having their employees sign social media non-competition agreements. Under these social media non-competes, the profile, content and followers of a blog or other communication tool belong to the employer. These agreements are more akin to a non-solicitation agreement than a traditional non-compete.

They are difficult (if not impossible) to enforce but they clearly define the intent of the parties if the employer sees litigation (or alternative dispute resolution) as a necessary step to protect its brand or marketing position.

CONCLUSION

The now widespread use of social media in and outside of the workplace is not the end of the world as we know it. True, the situations employers can face are different, and small problems can very quickly magnify and multiply. But the sensible employer will respond appropriately, working with its employees to identify appropriate social media usage policies and exploiting the communication benefits that social media can bring to the workplace of the 21st century.

Addicted to Facebook[*]

Experts Worry Social Networking Sites Promote Habit-Forming Behaviors

By Scott Kerbs
The Spectrum (St. George, Utah), September 26, 2010

April Anderson has struggled against a powerful form of addiction, often sacrificing hours of her life to satisfy her cravings, but the St. George woman has not turned to alcohol or prescription pain pills.

Her "drug" of choice is the engrossing social experience of Facebook.

While online social networking platforms serve as useful tools for millions of users to stay connected with friends and loved ones, some experts believe a growing number of people are becoming addicted to the unique offerings of Facebook and Twitter.

With Facebook garnering more than 500 million users worldwide, addiction specialists and social media experts said the expanding prevalence of online social portals has led many to develop habit-forming behavior.

Anderson, 35, said she has struggled with addiction for about a year, often forgoing communication with her family while she spent four to six hours per day logged onto Facebook.

"I had no idea what my kids were doing because I was distracted with something else," Anderson said, describing how much of her life was consumed with electronic communication.

Although Anderson said she has taken steps to significantly reduce the social networking utility's firm grasp on her life, she still considers herself an addict.

The St. George mother is far from alone in her struggle with social media addiction, said Jennifer Jacobson, author of the book "42 Rules of Social Media for Small Business" and director of public relations for Retrevo, an online consumer electronics retailer that recently released a study focusing on the behavior of social media users.

Jacobson said the notion of social media addiction is a relatively new idea, but as technological advancements afford improved access to websites like Facebook and Twitter through computers and mobile phones, people are becoming addicted to the world's new social gathering venues.

"The technology is making it readily available," Jacobson said of social networking platforms. "It's essentially the new water cooler."

Illustrating the reality of social media's expanding role in people's lives, a March survey released by Retrevo found that 56 percent of social media users check Facebook at least once a day while 12 percent said they log on every few hours.

Jacobson said the survey also found that nearly half of social media users log on during the night or as soon as they wake up in the morning.

The immersive social experience of Facebook, which allows users to post status updates, comment on their friends' photos and communicate in a variety of other ways, sometimes promotes habit-forming behavior as some users begin to crave the instant gratification and sense of belonging offered in abundance through social media platforms, said Aaron Shaw, an addiction therapist in Loa who regularly works with teenagers who have developed addictions to social media and video games.

"People can get addicted to just about anything," Shaw said. "When it comes to something like social media you have those immediate dashes of pleasure. You feel like you belong."

Shaw said there are a variety of possible reasons behind social media addiction, with users often turning to Facebook and forming superficial relationships in an effort to relieve stress or escape from the difficulties of everyday life.

"Stress is a catalyst for most of our negative behaviors," he said, with many people using substances to relieve stress. "That substance can be alcohol or it can be Facebook."

Anderson said she was initially drawn to Facebook years ago in an effort to connect with friends and family, and while the website often provides healthy social interaction, it eventually began to consume her life when she discovered Facebook's innovative collection of social video games.

As she began playing Farm Town, a social game that tasks players with creating and maintaining virtual farms, Anderson said her addiction became firmly rooted and began to affect her personal relationships.

Spending virtually all of her free time harvesting virtual crops and interacting with other Facebook gamers in Farm Town and other games, Anderson said she neglected her husband and three children.

"She would get home from work and stay on the computer until bedtime," her husband, Holden Anderson, said. "It was a little irritating."

Many of the games available through Facebook are particularly addictive, Shaw said, often providing players with a rewarding sense of progression as they work to improve their virtual worlds or gain experience for their characters.

"That is one of the big factors that keeps people coming back for more," he said. "When you've got a farm mansion with cattle and goats, all of [a] sudden you're cool."

Shaw said many Facebook games also emphasize cooperative play, encouraging players to team up with others in an effort to reach a common goal. While interacting with other players often serves to build social skills, the form of online communication is often void of substance.

"It's easier than a real relationship," Shaw said of conversing with people through Facebook and social games. "It's human nature to go after the easier thing."

With little time for family outings as a result of her newfound obsession, Anderson's relationships with her children were also affected by her intense addiction to Facebook.

"I wasn't paying attention to what was going on around me," she said. "I was paying more attention to the games than whether or not they got their homework done."

She said her addiction often caused friction when her children sought to use the family's computer during her marathon gaming sessions.

"The kids would get so mad," she said. "It caused a lot of confrontation."

Shaw said it is often difficult for family members to cope with the behavior of a social media addict.

"It tells everybody where your priority is," he said, as social media addicts often ignore their friends and family to converse with hundreds of Facebook friends. "It makes people kind of feel less significant."

As her virtual farm continued to thrive at the expense of her family, Anderson said she recognized the severe impact of her addiction when her children's grades began to suffer, forcing the St. George woman to make a critical decision.

"You have to decide what's most important in life, Facebook or what's sitting right in front of you," she said while sitting alongside her husband and their daughter Eliza in their St. George home.

Anderson chose her family and successfully eliminated social gaming from her daily life.

Since quitting, Anderson said she has developed healthier relationships with her children.

"I'm a bigger part of their lives," she said.

While her virtual crops have wilted, Anderson said she continues to use Facebook to stay connected with friends and family.

"I'm still on there every morning," she said, sometimes spending as many as three or four hours per day on Facebook.

Anderson said she initially slashed her Facebook time to less than two hours per day, but after losing her job as an office manager several weeks ago, she now has more free time to spend online.

"I'm still addicted to Facebook, but not the games," she said.

Social media addiction is easily recognizable, Shaw said, as it is occurs whenever the behavior disrupts any facet of a person's life, including work.

SCHOOL AND INTERPERSONAL RELATIONSHIPS.

Routinely using social media platforms for three hours or more every day is also a key indicator of addiction, he added.

Shaw said he advises social media addicts to seek professional assistance and work with a therapist to develop healthier coping skills to prevent the behavior from damaging their real-life relationships.

While addiction is possible, Shaw said he encourages people to take advantage of the unique experiences offered by social networking utilities and online video games.

"It's something you can really enjoy," he said. "You can let it connect you to family and loved ones in a healthy way, but don't let it be all-consuming."

FACEBOOK FACTS

- Founded in 2004.
- More than 500 million users today.
- At current pace: 1 billion user mark would be reached in 2011.
- 1 billion users would mean 1 out of ever 7 people in the world.

FACEBOOK GAMES:

- More than 200 million people play games on Facebook each month.
- Americans spend 10.2 percent time online playing games.

TOP FACEBOOK GAMES:

- Farmville.
- Mafia Wars.

Source: The Nielsen Company.

Cyberbullies Ramp Up the Taunting—Anonymously[*]

By Roger Neumann

Star-Gazette (Elmira, N.Y.), June 13, 2010

Bullying, like so many things today, has gone high-tech.

Want to tell that boy you think he's gay? Send him a text.

Want to call that girl a slut? Do it by IM.

Want to challenge that kid to a fight and invite everyone at school? Post it on Facebook.

And don't forget to have your friends take photos with their cell phone cameras to document the event and share with others.

Pushing and punching in the halls, at lunch or on the bus? Well, yes, that still happens. But experts say that young bullies today are just as likely, if not more so, to use the latest in technology, often anonymously, to deliver their taunts and insults and challenges.

"Cyberbullying happens in all sorts of guises," said Celia Clement, school social worker at the Lehman Alternative Community School and Northeast Elementary School in Ithaca. She mentioned, specifically, instant messaging, texting, photo taking and shipping by cell phone, and online social networks.

"Physical bullying is being replaced by more relational bullying, where people spread rumors about each other," she said. "The most common form is to exclude them or to decrease their status, turning people against a person."

On the milder side, online postings, for example, can include comments about who's hot and who's not. But they can quickly become more personal.

"With girls, the rumors tend to be more sexual—calling someone a slut, perhaps," Clement said. "With boys, the rumors center around their sexual identity—calling someone a homosexual, for example."

An extreme example of relational bullying, Clement said, involved Phoebe Prince, the 15-year-old Massachusetts girl who authorities say was driven to suicide by bullies at school. The girl hanged herself Jan. 14, a tragedy that drew national attention.

ONLINE BULLYING

The latest in online bullying is a social networking site called Formspring.me. A May 6 article in *The New York Times* said the relatively new site has become "a magnet for comments, many of them nasty and sexual, among the Facebook generation."

The article said thousands of teenagers nationwide have set up free Formspring accounts over the past two months and linked them to their Tumblr, Twitter or Facebook accounts. Their online friends can ask questions or post comments without having to identify themselves.

Brandon Gibb, associate professor of psychology at Binghamton University, said anonymity gives online bullies a cover.

"We know that people will do things as part of a group or when they're anonymous, rather than face-to-face," he said. "They're more likely to be mean. And so, with technology like Facebook, or even some of the other social networking sites, or text messages or camera phones, you can instantly spread rumors or derogatory comments about people."

And he said the fact that something has been posted online can give it a kind of credibility.

"If you see something up on a website . . . your perception is that everyone knows, and now everybody hates you," he said. "And there's no way of contradicting that. I think that makes it a lot harder."

The Formspring phenomenon is so new that some school guidance counselors admitted they had not heard of it. Sara Vondracek, school psychologist at Horseheads Middle School, for example, said she knew of Formspring but thought of it only as a social networking site. She said she has not encountered any cases of bullying through that site affecting students at her school.

PARENTS' ROLE

Clement said it's tough for counselors and parents to keep up with advances in technology.

"What I try to do is keep on top of the newest types of problems that exist," she said. "But the problem with all this stuff is that we really don't know what's going on because the kids aren't willing to share."

For example, she said, "Texting happens 24-7. I hear that kids text all through the night. There's a lot of text addiction going on, and parents are not necessarily aware of it, and neither are teachers.

"Parents need to be aware of the fact that they can limit their child's cell phone use during the day. They can call the cell phone companies and ask them to restrict cell use during the day.

"Parents should have computers kept in an area that's more communal, so they can be watching for what's going on. There needs to be more discussion between parents and kids, and parents need to make their expectations known. All of that needs to be openly addressed between parents and kids and between schools and students."

TAKE CELL PHONES AWAY

Dr. Mary Muscari, an associate professor at Binghamton University's Decker School of Nursing, who has written parenting books, said she discourages the placement of computers in bedrooms or places where children can't be supervised, and she recommends having kids turn in their cell phones at night.

As for schools, they should have "an acceptable use policy so that kids are aware of what the expectations of their use of computers and cell phones are," Clement said.

"Cell phones have opened up a whole new range of problems for me as a police officer in schools," said Trooper Chris Cody, school resource officer for the Chenango Forks and Whitney Point districts. He said students often text during class, then fight later.

Schools have different policies regarding cell phone and computer use.

Students at East High in Corning are not allowed to have cell phones in school, Caulfield said. Binghamton High School prohibits the use of electronic devices during the school day, said Principal Albert Penna. At Horseheads Middle School, students must have their phones turned off and put away, Vondracek said.

Vondracek said her students have school e-mail accounts that are monitored "pretty intensely," with all social networking sites blocked. But she said schools have no control over what happens at home or elsewhere.

That's why Clement says it's important for parents to be involved.

"Adults need to be asking kids more questions," she said. "There needs to be a really clear process for kids and families who are experiencing any kind of bullying or victimization."

WHAT'S OUT THERE?

Facebook: A social networking website on which users can connect with friends and develop new ones and can send messages or update their personal profiles to notify others about what's going on in their lives.

Formspring.me: This relatively new service allows users to ask questions of others or make comments, without having to identify themselves. They can also post the questions and answers to their Facebook or Twitter account.

Tumblr: A blogging service that allows users to post text, photos, music, videos, quotes and links from a browser, phone, desktop or e-mail. Users can follow others and see their posts.

Twitter: This is a social networking and microblogging site that calls itself "a real-time information network powered by people all around the world that lets you share and discover what's happening now." Messages are called tweets.

6

The Social-Networking Phenomenon:
What It Says About Us, How It Affects Our Lives

Editor's Introduction

The term "social media" is something of a misnomer. There's nothing particularly social about sitting in front of a computer and posting status updates about your toddler's latest temper tantrum or what you ate for breakfast. In fact, some would argue that Facebook and other such sites promote antisocial behavior, particularly among computer-addicted shut-ins whose only interactions with the outside world occur via the Internet.

On the other hand, people who choose to sit at their keyboards and tell the world about the delicious scrambled eggs they just cooked must do so for some reason. It could be boredom or narcissism, but it could also be a genuine desire to connect with others and feel part of a community, however artificial. If this is the case, Facebook and Twitter might not be signs of humanity's unraveling, as some critics allege, but simply new forms of communication—ones every bit as valid as the letter, phone call, or email.

Either way, social media is a complex phenomenon, and as the articles in this chapter suggest, it both reflects and influences modern society. In "With Friends Like These," the chapter's first selection, Jeremy McCarter views Facebook as a response to the "American loneliness" writer Thornton Wilder spoke of in the 1950s. McCarter is especially interested in Mark Zuckerberg—not so much the real person, but the character in *The Social Network*. As McCarter sees it, Zuckerberg's Web site represents a misguided attempt to escape modern loneliness, rather than cultivate the kind of "fruitful solitude" Wilder advocated.

In "A Cyber-House Divided," the next entry, an *Economist* writer discusses whether "Peace on Facebook," a section of Zuckerberg's site that aims to "decrease world conflict" by promoting international and cross-cultural friendships, stands any chance of succeeding. The author presents arguments on both sides but ultimately says the Internet "is not magic," adding, "Anyone who wants to use it to bring nations closer together has to show initiative, and be ready to travel physically as well as virtually."

Turning from global affairs to matters far more mundane, Vanessa Grigoriadis continues the chapter with "Do You Own Facebook? Or Does Facebook Own You?" Grigoriadis describes using the site to reconnect with old friends and acquaintances, and while she initially enjoyed the process, she eventually grew tired of reading people's needy, mean-spirited, and often pointless postings. Still, Grigoriadis understands why such trifling exchanges are so valuable, particularly to Facebook's data-hungry advertising department. Having spent time on the site, she contemplates her contribution to the "social graph," or "map of every human relationship in the universe," she half-jokingly says Zuckerberg and company endeavor to create.

In "Curb Your Urge to Overshare," the next piece, Fernanda Moore catalogs what she considers the most annoying types of Facebook updates, taking to task those who brag excessively, provide graphic descriptions of physical ailments, apologize publicly for private missteps, and commit other such faux pas. According to social-media researcher Danah Boyd, people who overshare on-line do so for the same reason they do in real life: "People want to be noticed, even among their friends."

Sunday Business Post writer Garvan Grant takes Moore's criticism a step further in the next selection, "We Are Not Alone," offering sarcastic praise for a world where digital relationships have replaced real ones. "For a long time, human beings have dreamed of a way of keeping in contact with people without actually having to meet them," the author says. "The internet has now made that a reality."

The chapter concludes with "The Web Means the End of Forgetting," in which Jeffrey Rosen ponders whether society will be made more forgiving by social media. Now that information is permanent, and our transgressions, once posted on-line, haunt us for life, Rosen wonders, will we learn to look past each other's embarrassing Facebook photos? Just in case we don't, a number of scholars have begun brainstorming ways—some technical, others legal—to make information disappear from the Internet.

With Friends Like These[*]

By Jeremy McCarter
Newsweek, September 27, 2010

Fifty years before Mark Zuckerberg arrived at Harvard—back when facebooks were actually books, back when poking a friend had a whole different set of connotations—Thornton Wilder came to campus to deliver the Charles Eliot Norton Lectures. He devoted one of them to "the loneliness that accompanies independence and the uneasiness that accompanies freedom." Raising such difficult subjects made him uncomfortable, he recalled later, but he felt better knowing that all of his listeners were American. It meant that "these experiences are not foreign to anyone here."

What Wilder called "the American loneliness" ran rampant long before he talked about it in 1952. And to judge from the stories our culture has produced in the last few months, all our Skype calls and Gchat sessions haven't stopped it from running just as rampant now. The latest and most vivid example comes courtesy of *The Social Network*, and its nickname is Zuck.

David Fincher's film arrives in a cloud of gossip about its scandalous goings-on. Based on *The Accidental Billionaires*, Ben Mezrich's libidinal account of Facebook's founding in a Harvard dorm, it delivers the advertised sex and drugs amid its coding binges. On the big question—whether Zuckerberg stole the idea for the world's most popular Web site from the Olympic rowing twins Cameron and Tyler Winklevoss and their partner, Divya Narendra—the film stays agnostic, letting you decide for yourself whether he's a 10-figure American success story or a devious, thieving cheat.

Beneath the tawdry fun, though, there's a surprising undertow. The halting dorm-room conversations, the lawsuits, the recriminations: they all look like up-to-date expressions of the loneliness and unease that Wilder described. The film turns out to have less in common with other campus caper flicks than with *Freedom*, Jonathan Franzen's masterful new novel about an imploding family. Nobody comes right out and says that Zuckerberg and his associates (I almost said *friends*) don't know how to live, as someone says of the Berglunds early in Franzen's book, but the trouble appears to be the same. And the reason why both the book and the film resonate—why they stick with you afterward—is that plenty of the rest of us have that trouble too. By suggesting that a modern kind of loneliness led an obnoxious hacker (business card: 'I'm CEO, Bitch!') to start Facebook, the film helps pinpoint our own loneliness—the feelings of aimlessness and isolation that make us do things like sign up for Facebook.

Here we have to make a distinction. The "Zuckerberg" to whom I refer is not Mark Zuckerberg, the proud son of Dobbs Ferry, N.Y., the one with the well-documented longtime girlfriend and mania for flip-flops. "Zuckerberg" is a character in a movie: a groupie-screwing, friend-betraying jerk who still manages to win some sympathy in spite of himself. This Zuckerberg plainly shares some traits with his off-screen counterpart (cf. the hoodie). On the other hand, it's fair to think that Movie Mark is better spoken than Actual Mark, having been polished to a shine by the precision tools of screenwriter Aaron Sorkin. For the moment, the resemblance or lack thereof doesn't matter: the Zuckerberg under discussion is the one created by Fincher and Sorkin, not the real live boy billionaire.

It was Sorkin who, in last week's *New Yorker*, offered the capsule premise for the film: "It's a group of, in one way or another, socially dysfunctional people who created the world's great social-networking site." You don't have to wait long to see what he means. On the night the story begins, we watch Zuckerberg (Jesse Eisenberg), drunk and angry that he's just been dumped, call his ex a bitch in a blog post, hack into Harvard's servers, and create a site that lets visitors rate the looks of their female classmates. That's social dysfunction, all right. Yet Sorkin's comment implies that the people around them must function better. They don't. While Mark's prank is crashing Harvard's servers, we catch glimpses of behavior that's at least as antisocial at the choosy finals club that he wants to join: a party full of drugs, booze, and misogyny. The rest of the movie isn't a church picnic, either: Fincher and Sorkin show us a world in which all sorts of smart, successful people prove pathetically unable to form healthy adult relationships.

As if to underscore the brittleness of all these social ties, the action keeps skipping back and forth from the months around Facebook's launch in February 2004 to depositions in the lawsuits brought against Zuckerberg a few years later. In one case, the Winklevoss twins press Zuckerberg to acknowledge that the site was their idea. "If you guys were the inventors of Facebook, you would have invented Facebook," he shoots back. In the other case, the one person who has genuine affection for Zuckerberg, his onetime business partner Eduardo Saverin (Andrew Garfield), tries to win back the share of the company he claims Zuckerberg denied him. The fact that these putative friends can deal with each other only through legal counsel is one of the darkest touches in a dark film. (How dark? No less than Trent Reznor, the man behind the unremittingly dark Nine Inch Nails, recently said so. And he would know: he and Atticus Ross wrote the buzzy, menacing, excellent score, one that frequently makes you think an alien invasion is imminent—which I mean as a compliment.)

Floating above the hazy bass lines and legal squabbles is Sean Parker, the Napster cofounder played with unexpected finesse by Justin Timberlake. A dotcom Mephistopheles, he entices Zuckerberg to Silicon Valley, the promised land of venture capital and Victoria's Secret models. In fact, Parker offers so much of what Mark could want that he seems like a phantom only he can see, like Brad Pitt and Edward Norton in Fincher's *Fight Club*. (This despite the scene in which Parker seduces Mark, Eduardo, and Eduardo's girlfriend over sushi and appletinis—a sequence that's mesmerizing enough by itself to justify casting a pop star.)

Yet as the movie wears on, you wonder more and more: what *are* Zuckerberg's needs, exactly? Eduardo, who justifiably claims he was Zuckerberg's only friend, also justifiably claims that Mark didn't care about money. Groupies aside, he seems no more libidinal than most of the people around him. The most consistent answer offered by Fincher and Sorkin is that he wants distinction: specifically, he wishes he were as clubbable as a Winklevoss. "You're obsessed with finals clubs," says the girl who dumps him in the first scene. But the many recurrences of that note are the weakest and least convincing parts of the film. It's as if Orson Welles spent all of *Citizen Kane* making sledding metaphors.

The film strains in these places because it's trying to close a gap that can't really be closed. Nobody can say what Zuckerberg wants because Zuckerberg himself doesn't seem to know. Like the Berglunds, he has great abilities, but the ability to be satisfied isn't one of them. Why did Zuckerberg turn down the pile of money AOL and Microsoft offered for some music software he'd written, deciding to put it online for free? He won't say. Why, at the moment when Facebook goes live, does he react not with joy but with a knotted expression that suggests intestinal distress or prayer? Could he tell you if you asked?

Much of the credit for this enigmatic character goes to Eisenberg, whose astonishing performance goes deeper than the writing. When he clenches an eyebrow, it's like a conductor dipping a baton, soon to be followed by a series of facial twitches, darting eyes, and other gestures meant to keep the world at bay. He's defensive and vulnerable and needy and, despite his awkwardness, capable of piercing insights into what makes people tick.

His opacity leads to an irony that's not quite tragic but, in light of how many of us share it, still plenty sad. Zuckerberg and his employees spend enormous time and energy trying to make people connect to each other via their online social network, but they've got the situation backward. The route to a happy life, let alone a meaningful one, doesn't lie in escaping loneliness. As Wilder tried to tell his audience, it is an inescapable part of living in a country as big and free and unencumbered as this one. (See also the testimony of Hank Williams Sr., Billie Holiday, Edward Hopper, Bessie Smith.) The trick for us, and for the people around the world living as we do, lies in using our loneliness. Wilder stated the challenge best and for all time when he described "the typical American battle of trying to convert a loneliness into an enriched and fruitful solitude." Like the Berglunds—or another touchstone of contemporary culture, Don Draper—these characters can't get along with each other because they haven't learned to get along with, and don't even really know, themselves.

When you log into Facebook after the film—and you know you will—you might find that it feels a little different. On one hand, hanging around the site begins to seem like a bad idea. In a world that's ever noisier and more demanding, it only gets harder to develop a "fruitful solitude" when dozens or hundreds of friends are constantly a click away. This round-the-clock aspect of Facebook, the perpetual presence of somebody to distract you from your anxieties and fears, begins to feel like being stuck in college.

The bigger shift, though, lies in how poignant Facebook suddenly seems. A site that began as a response to modern loneliness looks, after the film, like a record of our own struggle with that condition. The connection comes through most vividly in the movie's trailer, of all places, which distills its virtues to three haunting minutes. To the accompaniment of a choral version of Radiohead's "Creep," we see glimpses of some Facebook profiles. These flickers of daily life add up to a panoramic view of a society's vulnerabilities and dreams, à la *Our Town*. The insistent connecting can't fix what really ails us, but we go on doing it anyway. We're all trying to figure out the rules, we're all trying to learn how to grow up, we're all hoping to avoid turning into Mark Zuckerberg.

A Cyber-House Divided[*]

The Economist, September 2, 2010

In 2007 Danah Boyd heard a white American teenager describe MySpace, the social network, as "like ghetto or whatever". At the time, Facebook was stealing members from MySpace, but most people thought it was just a fad: teenagers tired of networks, the theory went, just as they tired of shoes.

But after hearing that youngster, Ms Boyd, a social-media researcher at Microsoft Research New England, felt that something more than whimsy might be at work. "Ghetto" in American speech suggests poor, unsophisticated and black. That led to her sad conclusion: in their online life, American teenagers were recreating what they knew from the physical world—separation by class and race.

A generation of digital activists had hoped that the web would connect groups separated in the real world. The internet was supposed to transcend colour, social identity and national borders. But research suggests that the internet is not so radical. People are online what they are offline: divided, and slow to build bridges.

This summer Ms Boyd heard from a scholar in Brazil who, after reading her research, saw a parallel. Almost 80% of internet users in Brazil use Orkut, a social network owned by Google. As internet use rises in Brazil and reaches new social groups, better-off Brazilians are leaving Orkut for Facebook. That is partly because they have more friends abroad (with whom they link via Facebook) and partly snobbishness. Posh Brazilians have a new word: *orkutificação*, or becoming "orkut-ised". A place undergoing *orkutificação* is full of strangers, open to anyone. Brazilians are now the second biggest users of the micro-blogging site Twitter; but some wonder whether the dreaded o-word awaits that neighbourhood too.

Facebook's architecture makes it easy for groups to remain closed. For example, it suggests new friends using an algorithm that looks at existing ones. But simpler, more open networks also permit self-segregation. On Twitter, members can choose to "follow" anyone they like, and can form groups by embedding words and shortened phrases known as "hashtags" in their messages. In May Martin Wattenberg and Fernanda Viégas, who research the display of social information, looked at the ten most popular hashtags on Twitter and discovered that most were used almost exclusively by either black or white authors. The hashtag "#cookout" was almost entirely black; the hashtag "#oilspill" almost entirely white.

With ideology, the pair's findings were a bit more hopeful; liberals and conservatives at least communicate—by trading taunts. They do so by appropriating hashtags so as to surface in each others' searches. By now, only one keyword in American political discourse remains unaffected by such games of tag: #NPR, or National Public Radio, used only by liberals.

All this argues for a cautious response to claims that e-communications abate conflict by bringing mutually suspicious people together. Facebook has a site called "Peace on Facebook," where it describes how it can "decrease world conflict" by letting people from different backgrounds connect. (The optimism is catching; this spring a founder of Twitter described his service as "a triumph of humanity".)

Peace on Facebook keeps a ticker of friend connections made each day between people from rival places. Israelis and Palestinians, the site claims, made about 15,000 connections on July 25th, the most recent available day. That is hard to put in context; Facebook does not make public the total number of friendships in any country. But Ethan Zuckerman, a blogger and activist, used independent data to estimate that these links represent roughly 1–2% of the combined total of friendships on Israeli and Palestinian accounts. Using the same method for Greece and Turkey, his estimate was 0.1%. That understates the role of Greek-Turkish friendship groups, or groups dedicated to music or films that both countries like. Among, say, people from either country who are studying outside their homeland (and have a better-than-average chance of becoming decision-makers), the share of trans-Aegean links would be far higher. And their mere existence sends an important moral signal.

But Mr Zuckerman frets that the internet really serves to boost ties within countries, not between them. Using data from Google, he looked at the top 50 news sites in 30 countries. Almost every country reads all but 5% of its news from domestic sources. Mr Zuckerman believes that goods and services still travel much farther than ideas, and that the internet allows us to be "imaginary cosmopolitans".

Peace on Facebook offers data for India and Pakistan, too. That is even harder to put in context. Pakistan has banned Facebook in the past, and offers too few users to qualify even for independent estimates. John Kelly, founder of Morningside Analytics, a firm that analyses social networks, examined links between blogs and twitter accounts in India and Pakistan and discovered two hubs that link the two countries. South Asian expats in London who self-identify as "Desis"—people from the sub-continent—link freely to each other and to their home countries. And cricket fans in both countries link up spontaneously.

Mr Kelly believes that clusters of internet activity, when they do cross national borders, flow from pre-existing identities. Ethnic Baloch bloggers in three different countries link mainly to each other. Blogs in Afghanistan show some ties to NGOs and American service members, but a far greater number to Iranian news services and poetry blogs. That reflects old reality, not some new discovery. There is also some hope in Morningside's data. Four websites most consistently account for links between countries: YouTube, Wikipedia, the BBC and, a distant fourth, Global Voices Online. The last of these, launched at Harvard University in 2005 and mainly funded by American foundations, works to create links between bloggers in different countries, and to find what it calls "bridge bloggers": expats and cultural translators, like London's Desis, who help explain their countries to each other. (This newspaper has a loose editorial collaboration with the site.)

Onnik Krikorian, Global Voices' editor in Central Asia, is a British citizen with an Armenian name. He couldn't go to Azerbaijan and had difficulty establishing any online contact with the country until he went to a conference in Tbilisi in 2008 and met four Azeri bloggers. They gave him their cards, and he found them on Facebook. To his surprise, they agreed to be his friends. Mr Krikorian has since found Facebook to be an ideal platform to build ties. Those first four contacts made it easier for other Azeris to link up with him.

But the internet is not magic; it is a tool. Anyone who wants to use it to bring nations closer together has to show initiative, and be ready to travel physically as well as virtually. As with the telegraph before it—also hailed as a tool of peace—the internet does nothing on its own.

Do You Own Facebook?

Or Does Facebook Own You?*

By Vanessa Grigoriadis
New York Magazine, April 13, 2009

Let's begin with a typical parable of life in the era of web 2.0. On Presidents' Day, Julius Harper turned on his computer at 9 A.M. This was later than usual, but he had the day off from his job as a video-game producer in Los Angeles. He began his daily "blog check"—Digg, Reddit, "anything interesting, disasters, plane crashes"—before turning to a post on the Consumerist, a consumer-advocacy blog, about the finer points of user privacy on Facebook.com. "Facebook's new Terms of Service: 'We Can Do Anything We Want With Your Content. Forever,'" it read. "Facebook's terms of service used to say that when you closed an account on their network, any rights they claimed to the original content you uploaded would expire. Not anymore. Now, anything you upload to Facebook can be used by Facebook in any way they deem fit, forever, no matter what you do later."

Harper, a 25-year-old graduate of the University of Southern California, didn't like this too much. "I thought, *This is bull-crap*," he says. With a few clicks of his mouse, he created a protest group on Facebook, which came to be called People Against the New Terms of Service. "That's the first group like that I started," he says. "The other ones I've made are just for my friends, like Hey Guys, Let's Go See *Watchmen* This Weekend." Around 10 A.M., he drove to Wal-Mart, where he bought several Healthy Choice lunches for the upcoming workweek. By the time he arrived home, at noon, over 800 people had joined his group. Soon the membership rolls reached 20,000. The next day, *NBC Nightly News* came to his home in Valencia, California. He checked their I.D.'s at the door. "I thought they might be from *The Daily Show* or playing a joke on me," he says. "I mean, I've seen *Borat*."

Overnight, Harper had become a consumer-rights activist, and his protest was turning into a PR disaster for Facebook, a social-networking site of about 200 million members that is both based on an expansive idea of community and invested in controlling it for commercial purposes. Soon, the company's 24-year-old paterfamilias, Mark Zuckerberg, who also owns over 20 percent of the company's shares, joined the discussion. We're family, he seemed to be saying. On his blog, he protested that there was nothing to worry about because "in reality, we wouldn't share your information in a way you wouldn't want"—a version of the "Trust us" comment that Google's Eric Schmidt made to Charlie Rose last year—but, if anything, his remarks only threw fuel on the fire: Why change the terms if it didn't matter who owned what? And anyway, the issue was more a matter of a kind of pre-rational emotion than any legalistic parsing of rights. What people put up on Facebook was themselves: their personhood, their social worlds, what makes them distinctive and singular. It was a pursuit-of-happiness type of thing. No one else should be permitted to own it.

But Facebook is as sensitive as any politician to feedback from its constituents, especially on the issue of privacy. No other social-networking site provides users the kind of granular privacy settings for their profiles and applications that Facebook does. After Harper received a call from privacy experts who wanted his support in a $5 million FTC complaint—"I was like, 'Whoa, we don't care about money,'" he says, "'we're just trying to get the TOS changed'"—he heard from a Facebook spokesperson, who asked him for a memo summarizing his group's complaints. Harper put these together carefully. He thought that Facebook should allow users to decide whether their information could be used for commercial purposes, inform them of which third parties have access to their content, and delete a user's information the moment he closes his account. Furthermore, changes to the TOS should be made visibly and put to a vote before implementation. Also, it was important that Facebook write its legal documents in a straightforward way. "No Latin!" he wrote. "I'm not sure what *forum non conveniens* means, and I shouldn't have to."

But Zuckerberg made a bold move, aligned with Facebook's corporate image: He turned the site into a democracy. He decided to reinstate the former TOS, then released a new version a week later that took broad latitude to use our content while we were on the site but fell short of claiming ownership, and that Facebook revoked its rights to our content when we delete our accounts. This version was open for user comments until March 29. Facebook will release its response to the comments by April 10 and put the entire document to a vote by all users during the week of April 20.

With the vote, though, Zuckerberg set a high bar—perhaps an impossibly high bar—for user voices to be heard: It will be binding only if 30 percent of members cast a ballot. That's about 60 million people. "You can't get 60 million people to agree on anything, so the fact that Facebook is requiring it makes this all seem a little fake," says Harper, over lunch at a Hawaiian fast-food restaurant near his office in Burbank, California. Harper is stiff and proper, with a pressed shirt and a silver cross around his neck yet now he shifts his eyes downward uneasily. Facebook listened to him, and he is uncomfortable judging it. "I have to think that they are showing good faith here," he says, then nods his head. "I'm going to give them the benefit of the doubt."

If there were one word to describe what Facebook has added to my life, I would use it. It's a multidimensional pleasure: It's given me a tool for exceptionally mindless, voyeuristic, puerile procrastination; crowd-sourced pesky problems like finding a new accountant; stoked my narcissism; warmed my heart with nostalgia; and created a euphoric, irrational, irresistible belief in the good in men's hearts among the most skeptical people I know—people who should know better. As the dominant social network on the web (the Internet began, essentially, as a social network, with Usenet in the late seventies) Facebook has created a space similar to a college quad, where members can check each other out, talk about culture, gossip, and pass mash notes. Users really like Facebook; they believe in it so strongly that they want to protect it from itself. That much is clear from the anger over the redesign, released a couple of weeks ago, meant to outmaneuver Twitter in the realm of speedy exchange of information—a redesign that, ironically, created a much louder protest, at two-and-a-half-million users and counting, than Harper's protest about the security of one's personal information. As of now, Harper's group has around 148,000 users. Organizing has basically come to a standstill. "We're waiting to see what Facebook does next," he says.

This is a crucial moment for Facebook, and a delicate one, because We, the users, are what Facebook is selling. "Facebook is walking a fine line of keeping the trust of its members, and wanting to exploit them for profit," says Nicholas Carr, author of *The Big Switch*. "It's having a tough time balancing the two." In 2007, the company was valued at $15 billion, after Microsoft bought a 1.6 percent stake for $240 million, but profit has been elusive. If they can solve this problem, come up with a viable business model—one might note that if they charged $1 a month for the service and even half its users stuck around, it would take in $100 million each month—it could go public and even become the first big IPO to reinvigorate the market; if Facebook doesn't, Zuckerberg & Co. will struggle to resist a takeover by a very rich tech company (well, Microsoft) for a fire-sale price of a billion or two. After CFO Gideon Yu announced his exit last week the company claimed that it was looking for a replacement with public-company experience, but the way forward is far from clear. The history of social networks is an absurd one of missed opportunities, from Tripod to Geocities to AOL, though Facebook thus far has avoided their pitfalls. It's been unaffected by Friendster's technical glitches and its taint of uncoolness; Facebook's antiseptic design clears away the lascivious, spamified, knife-wielding clutter of MySpace, a site that was double Facebook's size in the U.S. eight months ago but whose technological innovation has been stymied by News Corp until recently.

Facebook is exceptional at public relations. Harper may think that it's impossible to get millions of people to join hands, but Facebook's particular genius has been convincing 200 million people to color within the lines, to behave a certain way without being told to. When it moved the lines a bit with the redesign, the company issued a statement that it only meant well—"Whenever we build something new or tweak something old, our motivation is the same: to help you share with the people you care about," it said—which wasn't strictly true; advertisers seemed to be more prominent on the home page, for one thing, and group pages were redesigned to look like "friends." For users, it can feel like information is rushing toward us as through a beer funnel, too much information about too many people, much as on Twitter, though that's part of why Twitter is still largely used by tech-heads, nerds, and those who work in marketing or want to market themselves (though all bets are off regarding Twitter when the war over social networks on mobile heats up).

Still, Facebook was clearly spooked by Twitter—and spooked, also, by the fact that we were spooked. Because this is how social networks collapse. Do things feel uncomfortable? Am I oversharing? Are others oversharing? Or is the company stealing my soul by mining my personal information? Wispy perceptions. A slight paranoia. And then, for no rational reason, a queasiness sets in, the comfort level drops, and people start to drift away. One day the numbers are growing exponentially, and the next they're stagnant, none of the users are actually showing up, and there's another network that's getting all the buzz. Friendster had numbers. AOL had numbers. It's like the Yogi Berra line: Nobody goes there anymore, it's too crowded. It's easy to join on the web and just as easy to leave.

I'm part of one of the fastest-growing segments on Facebook, users over 30, and I'm a late-adopter. About three years ago, a trendy 22-year-old colleague who wore T-shirts with slogans like THIS IS WHAT A FEMINIST LOOKS LIKE over her ample chest invited me to join, but I did not accept, as we were friends of no sort. Soon, my e-mail box began to fill with weekly requests from slightly more mature friends—or, at least, people I know vaguely—to "Check out my Facebook profile!" Just like the boomers who missed out on the Summer of Love finally threw on some tie-dye and flocked to EST in the seventies, Gen-Xers have eagerly embraced Facebook as a chance to join millennial culture—the Paris Hilton-posey, authority-loving, hive mind of kids today—through Facebook. Says a friend in her forties, "Facebook makes us feel very young, which feels really great. Connecting with old crushes, even younger." I'm not a joiner by nature—I have never been to a high-school or college reunion—but by last year, acquaintances at parties were no longer asking me "What's your e-mail?" the way they have for the past few years, since they stopped asking "What's your phone number?" (No one can be bothered to use phones anymore, even cell phones.) Now they were saying "I'll find you on Facebook." And if you weren't on Facebook—where were you?

Because on Facebook, people are doing things. Their "status updates" say they are at the Cardio Barre, or haggling over prices at the Range Rover dealership, or making soup from scratch at home; in fact, it seems to me that someone is always making soup. This information scrolled rapidly down my screen when I was staring at my computer at work, and maybe it wasn't quite as fast as Twitter, but the people providing the information were twice as important to me. It formed a constant reminder that there was still a real world out there with real people walking around in it, even if they had chosen to leave that world for a moment to join me in the pretend, Facebook world. On Facebook, I didn't have to talk to anyone, really, but I didn't feel alone, and I mean "alone" in the existential use of the word; everyone on Facebook wished me well, which I know not to be the case in the real world; and, most important, there was nothing messy or untoward or unpleasant—the technology controlled human interaction, keeping everyone at a perfect distance, not too close and not too far away, in a zone where I rarely felt weird or lame or like I had said the wrong thing, the way one often feels in the real world. This is the promise of Facebook, the utopian hope for it: the triumph of fellowship; the rise of a unified consciousness; peace through superconnectivity, as rapid bits of information elevate us to the Buddha mind, or at least distract us from whatever problems are at hand. In a time of deep economic, political, and intergenerational despair, social cohesion is the only chance to save the day, and online social networks like Facebook are the best method available for reflecting—or perhaps inspiring—an aesthetic of unity.

In any case, these status updates formed a pleasant collage, a kind of poetry, like first-draft scribbles in Gertrude Stein's notebook—the poetry of the mundane. *Emily is in the heavenly land of Williamsburg; Brian is tired and sweaty from a day of playing the Safety Ape and a clam and garlic pizza; Elizabeth is reading, happily, with sunshine through a windowpane*—and then got sucked into the vortex that is Facebook. This micro-knowledge of others has been termed "ambient awareness" by sociologists, a new kind of social proprioception or ethereal limb, and I learned to flex it with ease. But I thought that I would take a different angle for my first status update, something suitably ironic and a little bit outré: *Vanessa is doing cocaine and piercing her nipples.* A Facebook faux pas, I quickly realized. My fellow users pretended not to hear.

This safe and happy community is very much a product of design. The old web, the frontier world of autonomy, anarchy, fantasies, and self-made porn, is being tamed. The flaming, snarky, commenter-board culture that dips in periodically to bang heads against the floor and foster self-hate among humanity's ranks has been deemed not good for business. Facebook's relentless emphasis on literal representation—the site maintains a "blacklist" of celebrity names to discourage impersonation and reserves the right to delete anyone who claims to be someone he is not, or who creates multiple accounts—turns out to be the weapon to quell the web's chaos. Now online life is a series of Victorian drawing rooms, a well-tended garden where you bring your calling card and make polite conversation with those of your kind, a sanitized city on a hill where amity reigns, irony falls flat, and sarcasm is remarkably rare. We prepare our faces, then come and go, sharing little bits of data, like photos, haikus, snippets of conversations—the intellectual property that composes our lives.

Sharing is actually not my word. It's the most important Newspeak word in the Facebook lexicon, an infantilizing phrase whose far less cozy synonym is "uploading data." Facebook's entire business plan, insofar as it is understood by anyone, rests upon this continued practice of friends sharing with friends, and as such it is part of the company's bedrock belief, as expressed in the first line of its principles:

"People should have the freedom to share whatever information they want." "A lot of times users—well, I don't want to say they undervalue sharing, but a lot of times they don't want to share initially," said Chris Cox, Facebook's 26-year-old director of products. "And then eventually, they say, 'Okay, I'll put a profile picture up here. I'll do it.' Immediately, their friends comment on it, and there are no tacky, weird strangers around, and suddenly they start to realize, 'Hey, wait, this is different. I am on the Internet, but I am in a safe place.'"

Cox, a dropout from Stanford's graduate program in symbolic systems, is known professionally as Zuckerberg's better half and twice as handsome. We were talking at the Facebook offices in Palo Alto earlier this year, when I spent three hours in a windowless conference room meeting with executives in one of the company's ten small buildings near the campus of Stanford University (the company is moving to an office park next month). Colorful graffiti of Facebook-cap-wearing kids waving Facebook flags line the corridors, and semi-ironic signs like THANKS, SILICON VALLEY, FOR INVENTING THE INTERNET! hang on office doors. It's all very Facebook-y: intimate, twee, and above all friendly, like the research offices of a well-funded postdoctoral project.

I took a trip to visit Facebook because I was interested in the way it is remaking social groups of old friends, so I mostly wanted to talk about that, but all these executives wanted to talk about was sharing. And privacy. And control. (Although I did learn the biggest user complaint on the site: the inability to remove unflattering photos of themselves posted by friends.) They said this kind of stuff: "People have been traditionally too scared to share on the web," that from another executive, Chris Kelly, the company's chief privacy officer at the moment, though he is widely rumored to be leaving soon to run for attorney general of California. "They lost all control because they were too open with sharing information," he continued. "We give them back that control, so they will share again, and we think people will soon be much more comfortable about sharing more with more people." He cleared his throat. "Ultimately, human beings are very social," said Kelly. "They want to share. They just want to share with people that they know and trust."

For all the talk of sharing, it was a slightly tense environment, a little like being in a capsule, hurtling into the great unknown, which is the future of the web. It was all a little vertiginous. In our conversation, we marveled at Facebook's runaway growth of about a million new members a day, which Kelly called an "explosion." It's an astonishing number, but things are moving and changing incredibly fast on the web right now. They know that Facebook's massive cultural footprint could be washed away tomorrow by forces not yet understood, not least by the micro-choices and preconscious perceptions of its users.

Then again, these are smart guys who have thought deeply about the ways their little planet can perish. They're not wicked corporate invaders; they're behaviorists and lawyers, psychology majors and big thinkers. There's a moral undercurrent to their pronouncements—this is what they're selling, of course—and they talk the talk so well, it's hard to imagine they're not walking the walk, too. "I don't think of our users as customers," says Cox. "That reminds me of someone coming into a store and buying a sandwich. We're all Facebook users here, and our parents, friends, colleagues, and loved ones are Facebook users. This is a much more intimate relationship, frankly. We take it very personally."

When we first use Facebook, we're back in college, and just like the first day there, we really want to make friends. We love sharing: We'll talk to the loser girl down the hall who only listens to the Eagles, the kid who sits next to us in physics, the R.A. who doesn't seem as cool as an R.A. should be. Within a week on the service, I had 50 friend requests, many from people I did not recall from any particular time in my life, and there was a certain loss of innocence as I realized this wasn't a sign of brain freeze: I really didn't know these people. They were just nice people using the site as they thought it should be used, for social networking, though this isn't the way cool people use the site, so I quickly de-friended them. (Although one could argue that deciding who to be and not to be friends with on Facebook is the most uncool thing in the world.)

This is part of the magic of Facebook, where many actions that take on weight in the real world simply don't pack the same punch: You can reconnect with long-lost friends without a gooey, uncomfortable e-mail about why you grew apart; you can forget to return Facebook e-mail and nobody minds; you can click obsessively on someone's profile and there's no way for him to know it. "Stalking on Facebook doesn't feel like stalking," says Rachel Zabar, my friend from high school. "It feels innocent, like when you were a kid and had a crush on someone and you'd call him and hang up." At lunch with girlfriends, we talked endlessly about negotiating the boundaries of this new social world: which estranged friends had most recently come out of the woodwork; whose profile was cool and whose was too "Facebook-y"; who was a "Facebook abuser": "He tried to get all of the people on his friend list to send his mom a birthday note!" The dark art of stalking ex-boyfriends on Google began to shift over to Facebook, as many more personal details were suddenly available there. "I saw Facebook pictures of my ex with his new wife and their new baby on a private jet!" wails a friend. "That was too much for me." She sighs. "I can't believe I'm stalking people's babies on Facebook."

The deeply voyeuristic pleasure of Facebook, wherein one feels as though one were sucking the very life out of the person whose profile one is viewing, was only part of the story, and many of the conversations that I had with friends about Facebook quickly catapulted past Jane Austen and into the territory of Eckhart Tolle, as we confessed the details of deep exchanges that we'd had on the site, the healing that was going on. A friend got back together with her ex-husband, who had resettled in Norway; another reconnected with a friend who had supported her when she was experiencing sexual abuse as an adolescent. Facebook wants you to form these bonds; it wants to create "folksonomies," an academic term for what we're doing when we tag people's photos and write Facebook haikus to lovers and in general pass the network more and more information, because, by the law of network effects, the more that you parse out your relationships to other people, the stronger their networks become.

Here is another parable about web 2.0 culture: In nursery school at Bank Street on 112th and Broadway, a kid used to bite me—a lot. It was a progressive pre-school in the seventies, and crazy stuff happened there—one day, my friend's mother jumped in front of the subway after she dropped her off at school, and Bank Street chose to share this information with us in class. Gabe would bite my arm while we playing during recess; he would bite my leg when I was coloring in my book; he would bite me when we lined up by size in the hallway, where I, the runt, was always first. (He also put another kid in an empty refrigerator in the teacher's lounge, briefly.) It took six months for the school to figure out that he was biting me, because the penalty for biting was getting sent home for the rest of the day, at which point the torture abated.

Gabe ended up at Fieldston, and I'd seen him a few times on the Manhattan prep-school social circuit, but I never knew much about him. One day he friended me on Facebook. We agreed to meet for a drink, and he looked sheepish as he told me things that I never knew. He had a learning disability as a kid and suffered from severe ear infections. When we knew each other, he couldn't speak in full sentences and every day after school he had to meet with a speech therapist. "I was confused and angry as a kid," he said. "I was so traumatized by my health problems that I didn't mind fighting. I wasn't scared of anything, because it couldn't possibly hurt worse than my ear infections already did."

This is part of who I am now—somebody who knows that her nursery-school tormentor wasn't a bully without a heart. It will get logged into my profile, and that profile will become part of the "social graph," which is a map of every known human relationship in the universe. Filling it in is Facebook's big vision, a typically modest one for Silicon Valley. It's too complex for a computer scientist to build. Just as our free calls to GOOG-411 helped Google build its voice-recognition technology, we are creating the graph for Facebook, and I'm not sure that we can take ourselves out once we've put ourselves on there. We have changed the nature of the graph by our very presence, which facilitates connections between our disparate groups of friends, who now know each other. "If you leave Facebook, you can remove data objects, like photographs, but it's a complete impossibility that you can control all of your data," says Fred Stutzman, a teaching fellow studying social networks at the University of North Carolina at Chapel Hill. "Facebook can't promise it, and no one can promise it. You can't remove yourself from the site because the site has, essentially, been shaped by you."

This graph, this most intimate of databases, is so immensely valuable, and powerful—if in ways as yet impossible to comprehend—that it is hard to imagine it being held in the hands of a 24-year-old eager to make his stamp on the world. Facebook may thicken social bonds, but it was founded on the ruins of a relationship. Zuckerberg, a confident, privileged programmer and fencer from Dobbs Ferry who graduated from Exeter, started the site in 2004, as a Harvard sophomore studying computer science and psychology. After he created a stir on campus with a mean-spirited comparison of Harvard students' relative attractiveness (quick-ly shut down by university administrators), a trio of entrepreneurial classmates, including Olympian rowing twins, approached him to write code for an online Harvard Facebook that they planned to call Harvard Connection. According to the Connection guys, Zuckerberg agreed to the project, then blew them off for a couple months. Then he launched TheFacebook.com. (The three students settled with him for $65 million in June 2008; they are now suing one of their law firms for making them a questionable deal, as the sum was awarded partially in Facebook stock).

A slight five foot eight with a cocky attitude but a halting way of speaking, and a near-daily uniform of a fleece paired with a tie, Zuckerberg enjoys his position of power immensely, though a friend says that he doesn't care about money at all—except he really wants a jet. He used to have a business card that read I'M CEO . . . BITCH. Sweeping proclamations fall from his lips, as when he declared he had started a "movement" when he opened Facebook's API to developers, or that "once every hundred years, media changes," upon the release of Beacon, an ad program that he had to cancel because of user discontent (it was reintroduced as an opt-in program a few months later, and continues with a small number of participating sites today). At his core, he is a programmer—he loves the nerd widgets on the site, like (fluff)Friends—and like most programmers, he believes that more information makes a better world, and a more tolerant one. And he could be right. Your digital self could be even more sensitive, and powerful, than your real self: It could possess more information, and more information is power; it could push progressive cultural norms, like the Saudi women who organized for driving privileges with the help of Facebook; more friends on Facebook already mean more job opportunities, and will likely produce free iPods for those who are identified as influencers by marketers.

But web cognoscenti tend to think that people who worry too much about privacy are sentimentalists who should grow up, and while maintaining a sense of privacy is Facebook's core strength, it's hard to believe that Zuckerberg and the Facebook staff are all that different. Facebook does not give advertisers access to personal information, but third-party widget developers are allowed to scrape some of it with user consent (they are prevented from accessing information like e-mails and IM addresses). The U.S. government, plus criminal attorneys and divorce lawyers, don't technically have access to it either, but it's not hard to get a subpoena in this country these days. And the developers are sometimes located in foreign countries, which means that they could pass our information to foreign governments. I asked Kelly about this, too, and perhaps he found me too credulous. "So the Indian government knows that you like Bon Jovi, and that's a threat to national security?" he asked, laughing.

I get his point, but I still don't like it. Kubrick dreamed of villains like this: nerds in fleece, controlling the information, calling their cult a family. It was an image, a kind of inchoate anxiety about the future, rather than anything you could put your finger on. In many conversations with privacy experts, it was hard to see what, specifically, was upsetting them so much; part of their strategy is clearly to pressure the big dog to set good policies now, so that others follow them later. Twenty years down the road, as algorithms and filtering mechanisms are significantly stronger and we've moved from PCs to home monitors with information stored in remote locations—"the cloud"—we will entrust ever more of ourselves to large data centers, many of which are already built around the Columbia River. Facebook already has tens of thousands of servers in a few data centers throughout the country, but this pales in comparison to Microsoft's facility in Quincy, Washington: Their data center is the area of ten football fields, 1.5 metric tons of batteries for backup power, and 48 megawatts of electricity, enough to power 40,000 homes. An uncanny simulacrum of your life has been created on the web. It may not be too hyperbolic to talk about a digital self, as a fourth addition to mind, body, and spirit. It's not the kind of thing that one wants to give away.

To get to this endgame, though, Facebook has to get through the current phase, which involves keeping people interested. I enjoyed myself on Facebook until a couple of months ago, when I went to a dentist with a little dog in her office, which she put in my lap during my exam. I found this odd enough to justify writing a status update. Several of my friends commented appropriately—"Not so hygienic, I'm thinking, LOL"—but my friend Judd took offense. "And then what happened, Vanessa?" he sneered. "I mean in a moment like that, there's you, the dentist, the dog. It puts dog-lovers and dental fanatics and probably some perverts on the edge of their chairs. So go on, WHAT HAPPENED NEXT?"

"This is why you have 100 friends on Facebook and two in real life," I replied, somewhat lamely. "Oops—now you have one!"

He quickly chastised me. "Suggestion," he shot back. "Start a group called Everybody Please Hate Judd. I'll join it! Or rehabilitate me, via Facebook: Encourage me to share, with the kind of warm, dull, 12-steppish type comments that real Facebookers offer each other every day. The truth is, everyone here has gone back to high school, but now they've read some books, got some cool corporate skills, and this time, they're going to win this game. You go girl!"

This was the beginning of the end. Suddenly, Facebook began to irk me—the way friends always posted about procrastinating, being stuck in traffic, needing a nap or a vacation, or seemed to formulate their updates in declarative yet vague form, like "Michelle is upset" or "Roya is pouting," thus coming off like a needy jerk and making us take time out of our day to plead with them to answer the burning question: "Why are you pouting?" There was the day someone posted about bowel movements. There were too many days when friends, in pathetic attempts to rattle their cages, posted joke updates like "I'm gay!" or "I just got arrested!" There was the day that a friend of mine posted the passport of their newborn, because it was supercute, but I thought of the jpeg finding its way into one of Facebook's servers and it was just . . . creepy.

Friends of mine began to freak out, like a guy with intimacy issues who dropped his girlfriend after reading a list that she had posted on Facebook about her favorite memories; another woman became so addicted to the site that she appeared blank-faced and wobbly in the real world, suddenly uncomfortable with unmediated experience. Other friends started to react poorly as well. "One day, I finally sent a

Facebook message to the guy who is the love of my life, even though technically I broke his heart," says a friend, 38. "I said, 'I know you work at IAC, and I've just moved down the street from where you work—do you want to get coffee?' He wrote me back, 'I think it would hurt too much. Plus you and I were never the coffee kind of people anyway.'" Because he had responded to her message, Facebook allowed her to see the guy's profile—and, for the first time, she found out that he was married. "I had no idea, and I was so devastated," she says. "I cried for days."

Why has the number of MySpace visitors remained essentially flat in the past year? Why do social networks fail? Maybe it's claustrophobic to know this much about other people. Maybe we like the way we've been able to live over the past 50 years, the freedom to move where we want, date who we like, and insert ourselves into any number of social cliques, before we cast aside those who bore us and never look back. Independence is a gift, even if it's lonely sometimes, and solving childhood mysteries may make people happier, but it doesn't necessarily turn them into the people they dream of being. So we keep perpetuating the cycle of birthing and abandoning new online communities, drawing close and then pulling away, on a perpetual search for the perfect balance of unity and autonomy on the web.

I don't want to leave Facebook—reloading personal photos and making new friends on another site feels very junior high; it would be a drag. But it's easy to imagine a circumstance—the wrong ads, too much information about too many people, some invisible level where being commodified starts to drive me nuts—when I might stop showing up, living my life in the real world, checking the site every couple of months. Monetize that . . . bitch.

Facebook may well turn out to be some sort of democracy, or at least, as Cox says, a "democracy in spirit." "I think there's a little-*d* democratic analogy here, to the U.S. government for instance," says Chris Kelly. "You don't get to vote on every budget item: You get to vote for your representatives, and you can rise up in constitutional convention, if you want to organize one of them, but on a foundational level, there's a consent to be governed." This might be as much as we can expect on the web. If it is, then our fates are already tied together, because we can either rise up in large numbers, or remain silent—rule-followers, faceless Facebook members.

It's possible that even Harper will go back [to] being nobody, to doing as he's told. After all, it's a big victory, getting an important company to change its Terms of Service, even if it didn't take all of his suggestions. He's a busy guy, and apolitical; he didn't vote in the presidential election, but says that if he had, he would have chosen Barack Obama or Alan Keyes. Last week, Facebook called him again to ask him if he would look over a summary of user feedback before they publish the new Terms of Service on April 10, and told him that it was consulting an independent auditor for the upcoming vote. "I think they wanted some kind of comment like, 'This totally restores my faith in Facebook,'" he says. "I was like, 'Okay, I'm happy you're doing this, but I'm not going to be your mouthpiece.'" Harper may not fully understand what he's fighting, but he still wants to fight. He's not ready to blend in the crowd. Now, he's even thinking about applying to law school.

"I like that my claim to fame is something that helps people, that I'm not Omarosa from *The Apprentice*," he says, his brown eyes lighting up. "I'd like to be a person who makes decisions. That would be cool."

Curb Your Urge to Overshare[*]

By Fernanda Moore
Women's Health, January/February 2010

If you've been on Facebook for more than three years, you might remember the good old days when you logged on simply to see if your old roommate did something cool over the weekend. Back when status updates simply kept everyone, you know, up to date. "At first, updates were a more efficient way of sharing the normal stuff you'd talk about with friends—and really, only your friends were reading them," says media expert Steven Johnson, author of the best seller *Everything Bad Is Good for You: How Today's Popular Culture Is Actually Making Us Smarter*.

But then our "friend" networks mushroomed, and suddenly our news feeds were logjammed with the banal hourly banter of people we hardly knew—and they weren't just posting for their friends, but for an audience. "Paradoxically, as people's social networks have grown, they have become less cautious and more brazen," says Johnson, adding, "I think it's the shy crowd that is finding the most gleeful freedom posting on Facebook. They can say anything, stuff they've never dared talk about before! It's quite a thrill."

Behold: the birth of the Facebook overshare.

Danah Boyd, Ph.D., a social media researcher at Microsoft Research and fellow at Harvard's Berkman Center for Internet & Society, takes Johnson's theory a step further. In her mind, updates don't just broadcast information—they project your identity. "This is the digital street, where the goal is to see and be seen," she says. "People want to be noticed, even among their friends. Getting noticed is hard. So they use different tactics, most of which are well known to middle schoolers. There's the gross-out approach, the slut approach, the I'm-cooler-than-thou approach, and the help-me approach."

And that's not all. Read on as we quote actual status updates, with experts' views on what motivates these outrageous, embarrassing, and just plain perplexing TMI offerings.

---

[*] Article from *Women's Health* copyright © 2010 Rodale, Inc. All rights reserved. Reprinted with permission.

THE OH, SHUT UP-DATE

Megan* loves it when her paragraphs sing.
Jonathan is THRILLED by Time Out's favorable review of his club gig! (link)
Susan My kid just gets cuter . . . and cuter. . . and cuter every day!

Posting exciting news is one thing. You finished grad school? Got engaged? Won the Super Bowl? Good For you. Posting in a way that makes people want to throttle you is another.

Clearly, these folks take the "status" part of updating too seriously. Parents are often the worst—crowing incessantly about their unremarkable offspring and posting photo after photo. "Face-to-face, people tend to be more humble," Johnson says. "But Facebook validates indiscriminate boasting. You never see people rolling their eyes or recoiling from you in horror, and sometimes they I even write 'Congratulations!' So there's a feedback loop effectively encouraging everyone to unleash their inner braggart."

There's a delusion that comes with overposting—that the world is fascinated with our every little move!

THE EWWWPDATE

Anna My rash is better, but still oozing.
Josie Flu, day 3: Vomiting gone, but have the runs instead. And now Jack is throwing up.

Maybe these people think they're witty. (Potty humor never goes out of style. right?) Says Johnson: "One of my sons, when he was an infant, was a projectile pooper." (Thanks for sharing!) "If Facebook had existed back then, I would have rushed to post about it. Sometimes you just need to vent." Still, updates about bodily functions are TMI. You want to look away, but it's too late.

Actually, Ewwwpdaters may simply be upping their own antes. If no one comments on posts about your garden, then go for the gross-out! "The urge for attention turns ordinary folks into shock jocks," says Julie Albright, Ph.D., a sociologist at the University of Southern California. "The more revolting your updates, the more people will notice you."

THE SCHTUPDATE

Jacqueline is putty in the hands of a man who brings her coffee in bed.
Melissa just loves morning sex.

Oh, she does, does she? Well, goody for her. Some people aren't getting any, and they really don't want to hear about other people's awesome rolls in the hay! And if it's, say, a coworker's post, we really don't want the image stuck in our heads.

---

* Names have been changed.

"Way back when, you'd have this intimate conversation with your closest friend
. . . maybe," Johnson say. "But bragging about your sex life to hundreds of people
shows that people's boundaries have become ridiculously eroded." Albright thinks
it's simpler than that. "Look, sex sells," she says. "It's the most basic attention-seek-
ing device there is. Describing their sexual antics online makes people feel twice as
desirable—live, in front of a virtual audience!"

THE DON'T SAVE THE (UP)DATE

Alexandra Hey, girlfriend! Psyched for J's wedding! Want to share a room?
Charlie I land on Friday—will be great to catch up! Can't wait to see you!
Now this is what Facebook is for—networking between friends! Except . . . Alexandra's friend wasn't invited to J's wedding, and Charlie just pissed off everyone
he hasn't made plans to visit while he's in town. "This is an unfortunate side effect
of communicating in a public forum." Johnson. says. "It used to be harder to find
out you were being snubbed."

Facebook is supposed to be an inclusive environment. but this kind of oversharing—which, really, is a violation of common etiquette—makes people feel exclud-
ed. If you don't want to hurt anyone's feelings, remember that even in cyberspace,
it's important to mind your manners.

Quick: What color are your BFF's eyes? If you can't remember, it's time to hang
out face-to-face.

THE JUST SUCK IT UP-DATE

Candice 'Tis a sad, sad day when one realizes she doesn't mean a thing to anyone.
Joe Wish I could just disappear. Just the fact I exist has always hurt people.
"Rather than burdening a friend, some people leave a note out there hoping
that someone somewhere will help them," Boyd says. OK, so maybe post a "Hey,
cheer up!"-date. But if you're the sad updater and you're not really desperate, tone
it down. "I know this great guy whose posts always say things like 'I'm completely
incompetent and a bloody idiot.'" Johnson says. "The more he insists he's pathetic,
the more I believe it." So unless you want your status updates to actually lower your
status, stop whining.

THE I SCREWED UP-DATE

Sara I'm so sorry. I have a few reasons, but no excuses. Weepy sleeplessness =
complete penance.

Bill Oh, Susanna, don't you cry for me. I can't believe I said what I said. Forgive me?

To err is human. To apologize in public, when no one else has the faintest idea what you're talking about, is bizarre. Why the showy display of emotion? "There used to be the occasional guy who proposed to his girlfriend on the JumboTron at a baseball game." Johnson says. "He needed thousands of strangers to witness his intimate moment, to legitimize it. Those people used to make up a very small segment of the population. But now? It seems like they're half the world."

THE I CHEWED UP-DATE

Christine is eating toast.

Christine just made ramen.

Christine has linguine with clam sauce—yum!

What's with the people who constantly post about food? The rest of us ate toast today too, but we fought the urge to shout it from the rooftops. Let's call them DCPs—digestive-compulsive posters—and leave it at that, "If you think about it," muses Albright, dining is a social activity. The social significance of eating together goes back to our earliest roots, right?

"So if someone is at home alone, eating ramen she made for herself," Albright says, "posting on Facebook lets her break bread, virtually, with a community she apparently lacks." Says Johnson: "Aw, it's harmless. Just think. some people are still excited about this use of Facebook—saying 'Finally! I can tell everyone what kind of cereal I had . . . in real time!' "

THE RE-UP-DATE

Samantha is on the plane!

Samantha is landing!

Samantha is getting off the plane!

Samantha Here comes my suitcase!

Overposters—those whose constant stream of drivel sends sensible people lunging for the "hide" button on their news feed—compulsively chronicle their every move and alter their profile pictures, relationship status, and so on. Sheesh. It makes you wonder what they did all day before Facebook existed. Don't these people have friends?

We Are Not Alone[*]

By Garvan Grant
Sunday Business Post (Dublin, Ireland), September 5, 2010

As you may have noticed over the past few years, the internet has grown very popular indeed.

It is no longer used just to find out who sang that annoying 1980s song you can't get out of your head or for expanding your interest in different types of pornography.

These days, you can use the internet for pretty much everything, from watching television and ordering food to stalking people and taking over the world.

You must also have the internet with you 24 hours a day, seven days a week in case you miss something important. This is why people sleep beside or near the internet and why developers in Silicon Valley are working on the first waterproof internet, which can be used safely in the bath or shower or if you go for a quick swim.

It has been calculated that most people in the western world log on to the internet nine times every seven seconds. Men are believed to log on even more often than that, particularly if their wives and girlfriends are at book club meetings.

It has been reported that in Colorado in the US, the entire population of the town of Saltsville no longer bothers using their imaginations as there is much better stuff online.

"The stuff on the web is not only more interesting than our imaginations, it is also better produced, cheaper and often features real-life celebrities," said Kelley Horsmann, Mayor of Saltsville.

It is in the area of making friends and keeping in touch with people you don't like, however, that the internet has really come into its own. For a long time, human beings have dreamed of a way of keeping in contact with people without actually having to meet them. The internet has now made that a reality.

Social networking websites are by far the most popular ones, outstripping porn and short videos of pets hurting themselves in hilarious ways. If you don't use one of these websites, you are not, to put it simply, popular. It is now estimated that 96 per cent of people living on the planet are 'on' a social networking site of some description.

Even people who are so poor they have never seen a computer or heard of the internet are still probably logged on somewhere.

Facebook, which is the world's favourite website, now has more inhabitants than the entire United States. The US, which had recently been planning to invade Facebook, bringing democracy, freedom and sub-contractors to its people, backed down when it realised it was heavily outnumbered.

As an indication of how popular social networking is, think about this fact: Facebook now has well over 28 billion registered users worldwide. Staggeringly, that is about four times the actual population of the planet.

The main use for Facebook is to make friends with other people, even if they're not really your friends. If you've tried being friends with real people and have failed because you have poor personal hygiene and are extremely rude and boring, Facebook is for you. People don't care about petty stuff like that on the internet. In fact, you can be someone else entirely online, even someone interesting and popular.

Facebook is also great because you can bring it with you wherever you go. If you fancy dinner with friends, you can just head into the kitchen, get some cereal and log on. If you want to go for a drink with old mates, just grab a bottle of vodka, head back into the living room and log on.

Twitter is another extremely popular website which means you will never be alone again. It is a mix of friendship, news and interesting observations about what people eat for breakfast. If you've ever wondered what a particular celebrity thinks about rain, you will be able to find out if they're on Twitter and decide to share their opinions with the world.

It can also be used for finding out which celebrities have died in the last minute or so, which is very useful. Imagine being able to know that Michael Jackson had died even before he did. That kind of information is truly invaluable.

The latest social networking website to sweep the world is Look At Me, which has 19 billion registered users. It mixes the best parts of Twitter and Facebook with Big Brother and YouTube, allowing people to watch what other people do and say 24 hours a day. You can either 'follow' celebrities or just ordinary people, who are sort of like celebrities except, of course, that they are really ordinary.

The only bad thing about Look At Me is that it can't yet access every single thought that another human being is having, though it is to be hoped that some bright spark is working on that at the moment.

The Web Means the End of Forgetting[*]

By Jeffrey Rosen
The New York Times, July 25, 2010

Four years ago, Stacy Snyder, then a 25-year-old teacher in training at Conestoga Valley High School in Lancaster, Pa., posted a photo on her MySpace page that showed her at a party wearing a pirate hat and drinking from a plastic cup, with the caption "Drunken Pirate." After discovering the page, her supervisor at the high school told her the photo was "unprofessional," and the dean of Millersville University School of Education, where Snyder was enrolled, said she was promoting drinking in virtual view of her under-age students. As a result, days before Snyder's scheduled graduation, the university denied her a teaching degree. Snyder sued, arguing that the university had violated her First Amendment rights by penalizing her for her (perfectly legal) after-hours behavior. But in 2008, a federal district judge rejected the claim, saying that because Snyder was a public employee whose photo didn't relate to matters of public concern, her "Drunken Pirate" post was not protected speech.

When historians of the future look back on the perils of the early digital age, Stacy Snyder may well be an icon. The problem she faced is only one example of a challenge that, in big and small ways, is confronting millions of people around the globe: how best to live our lives in a world where the Internet records everything and forgets nothing—where every online photo, status update, Twitter post and blog entry by and about us can be stored forever. With Web sites like LOL Facebook Moments, which collects and shares embarrassing personal revelations from Facebook users, ill-advised photos and online chatter are coming back to haunt people months or years after the fact. Examples are proliferating daily: there was the 16-year-old British girl who was fired from her office job for complaining on Facebook, "I'm so totally bored!!"; there was the 66-year-old Canadian psychotherapist who tried to enter the United States but was turned away at the border—and barred permanently from visiting the country—after a border guard's

Internet search found that the therapist had written an article in a philosophy journal describing his experiments 30 years ago with L.S.D.

According to a recent survey by Microsoft, 75 percent of U.S. recruiters and human-resource professionals report that their companies require them to do on-line research about candidates, and many use a range of sites when scrutinizing applicants—including search engines, social-networking sites, photo- and video-sharing sites, personal Web sites and blogs, Twitter and online-gaming sites. Seventy percent of U.S. recruiters report that they have rejected candidates because of information found online, like photos and discussion-board conversations and membership in controversial groups.

Technological advances, of course, have often presented new threats to privacy. In 1890, in perhaps the most famous article on privacy ever written, Samuel Warren and Louis Brandeis complained that because of new technology—like the Kodak camera and the tabloid press—"gossip is no longer the resource of the idle and of the vicious but has become a trade." But the mild society gossip of the Gilded Age pales before the volume of revelations contained in the photos, video and chatter on social-media sites and elsewhere across the Internet. Facebook, which surpassed MySpace in 2008 as the largest social-networking site, now has nearly 500 million members, or 22 percent of all Internet users, who spend more than 500 billion minutes a month on the site. Facebook users share more than 25 billion pieces of content each month (including news stories, blog posts and photos), and the average user creates 70 pieces of content a month. There are more than 100 million registered Twitter users, and the Library of Congress recently announced that it will be acquiring—and permanently storing—the entire archive of public Twitter posts since 2006.

In Brandeis's day—and until recently, in ours—you had to be a celebrity to be gossiped about in public: today all of us are learning to expect the scrutiny that used to be reserved for the famous and the infamous. A 26-year-old Manhattan woman told The New York Times that she was afraid of being tagged in online photos because it might reveal that she wears only two outfits when out on the town—a Lynyrd Skynyrd T-shirt or a basic black dress. "You have movie-star issues," she said, "and you're just a person."

We've known for years that the Web allows for unprecedented voyeurism, exhibitionism and inadvertent indiscretion, but we are only beginning to understand the costs of an age in which so much of what we say, and of what others say about us, goes into our permanent—and public—digital files. The fact that the Internet never seems to forget is threatening, at an almost existential level, our ability to control our identities; to preserve the option of reinventing ourselves and starting anew; to overcome our checkered pasts.

In a recent book, "Delete: The Virtue of Forgetting in the Digital Age," the cyberscholar Viktor Mayer-Schönberger cites Stacy Snyder's case as a reminder of the importance of "societal forgetting." By "erasing external memories," he says in the book, "our society accepts that human beings evolve over time, that we have the capacity to learn from past experiences and adjust our behavior." In traditional societies, where missteps are observed but not necessarily recorded, the limits of human memory ensure that people's sins are eventually forgotten. By contrast, Mayer-Schönberger notes, a society in which everything is recorded "will forever tether us to all our past actions, making it impossible, in practice, to escape them." He concludes that "without some form of forgetting, forgiving becomes a difficult undertaking."

It's often said that we live in a permissive era, one with infinite second chances. But the truth is that for a great many people, the permanent memory bank of the Web increasingly means there are no second chances—no opportunities to escape a scarlet letter in your digital past. Now the worst thing you've done is often the first thing everyone knows about you.

THE CRISIS—AND THE SOLUTION

All this has created something of a collective identity crisis. For most of human history, the idea of reinventing yourself or freely shaping your identity—of presenting different selves in different contexts (at home, at work, at play)—was hard to fathom, because people's identities were fixed by their roles in a rigid social hierarchy. With little geographic or social mobility, you were defined not as an individual but by your village, your class, your job or your guild. But that started to change in the late Middle Ages and the Renaissance, with a growing individualism that came to redefine human identity. As people perceived themselves increasingly as individuals, their status became a function not of inherited categories but of their own efforts and achievements. This new conception of malleable and fluid identity found its fullest and purest expression in the American ideal of the self-made man, a term popularized by Henry Clay in 1832. From the late 18th to the early 20th century, millions of Europeans moved from the Old World to the New World and then continued to move westward across America, a development that led to what the historian Frederick Jackson Turner called "the significance of the frontier," in which the possibility of constant migration from civilization to the wilderness made Americans distrustful of hierarchy and committed to inventing and reinventing themselves.

In the 20th century, however, the ideal of the self-made man came under siege. The end of the Western frontier led to worries that Americans could no longer seek a fresh start and leave their past behind, a kind of reinvention associated with the phrase "G.T.T.," or "Gone to Texas." But the dawning of the Internet age promised to resurrect the ideal of what the psychiatrist Robert Jay Lifton has called the "protean self." If you couldn't flee to Texas, you could always seek out a new chat room and create a new screen name. For some technology enthusiasts, the Web was supposed to be the second flowering of the open frontier, and the ability to segment our identities with an endless supply of pseudonyms, avatars and categories of friendship was supposed to let people present different sides of their personalities in different contexts. What seemed within our grasp was a power that only Proteus possessed: namely, perfect control over our shifting identities.

But the hope that we could carefully control how others view us in different contexts has proved to be another myth. As social-networking sites expanded, it was no longer quite so easy to have segmented identities: now that so many people use a single platform to post constant status updates and photos about their private and public activities, the idea of a home self, a work self, a family self and a high-school-friends self has become increasingly untenable. In fact, the attempt to maintain different selves often arouses suspicion. Moreover, far from giving us a new sense of control over the face we present to the world, the Internet is shackling us to everything that we have ever said, or that anyone has said about us, making the possibility of digital self-reinvention seem like an ideal from a distant era.

Concern about these developments has intensified this year, as Facebook took steps to make the digital profiles of its users generally more public than private. Last December, the company announced that parts of user profiles that had previously been private—including every user's friends, relationship status and family relations—would become public and accessible to other users. Then in April, Facebook introduced an interactive system called Open Graph that can share your profile information and friends with the Facebook partner sites you visit.

What followed was an avalanche of criticism from users, privacy regulators and advocates around the world. Four Democratic senators—Charles Schumer of New York, Michael Bennet of Colorado, Mark Begich of Alaska and Al Franken of Minnesota—wrote to the chief executive of Facebook, Mark Zuckerberg, expressing concern about the "instant personalization" feature and the new privacy settings. The reaction to Facebook's changes was such that when four N.Y.U. students announced plans in April to build a free social-networking site called Diaspora, which wouldn't compel users to compromise their privacy, they raised more than $20,000 from more than 700 backers in a matter of weeks. In May, Facebook responded to all the criticism by introducing a new set of privacy controls that the company said would make it easier for users to understand what kind of information they were sharing in various contexts.

Facebook's partial retreat has not quieted the desire to do something about an urgent problem. All around the world, political leaders, scholars and citizens are searching for responses to the challenge of preserving control of our identities in a digital world that never forgets. Are the most promising solutions going to be technological? Legislative? Judicial? Ethical? A result of shifting social norms and cultural expectations? Or some mix of the above? Alex Türk, the French data-protection commissioner, has called for a "constitutional right to oblivion" that would allow citizens to maintain a greater degree of anonymity online and in public places. In Argentina, the writers Alejandro Tortolini and Enrique Quagliano have started a campaign to "reinvent forgetting on the Internet," exploring a range of political and technological ways of making data disappear. In February, the European Union helped finance a campaign called "Think B4 U post!" that urges young people to consider the "potential consequences" of publishing photos of themselves or their friends without "thinking carefully" and asking permission. And in the United States, a group of technologists, legal scholars and cyber-thinkers are exploring ways of recreating the possibility of digital forgetting. These approaches share the common goal of reconstructing a form of control over our identities: the ability to reinvent ourselves, to escape our pasts and to improve the selves that we present to the world.

REPUTATION BANKRUPTCY AND TWITTERGATION

A few years ago, at the giddy dawn of the Web 2.0 era—so called to mark the rise of user-generated online content—many technological theorists assumed that self-governing communities could ensure, through the self-correcting wisdom of the crowd, that all participants enjoyed the online identities they deserved. Wikipedia is one embodiment of the faith that the wisdom of the crowd can correct most mistakes—that a Wikipedia entry for a small-town mayor, for example, will reflect the reputation he deserves. And if the crowd fails—perhaps by turning into a digital mob—Wikipedia offers other forms of redress. Those who think their Wikipedia entries lack context, because they overemphasize a single personal or professional mistake, can petition a group of select editors that decides whether a particular event in someone's past has been given "undue weight." For example, if the small-town mayor had an exemplary career but then was arrested for drunken driving, which came to dominate his Wikipedia entry, he can petition to have the event put in context or made less prominent.

In practice, however, self-governing communities like Wikipedia—or algorithmically self-correcting systems like Google—often leave people feeling misrepresented and burned. Those who think that their online reputations have been unfairly tarnished by an isolated incident or two now have a practical option: consulting a firm like ReputationDefender, which promises to clean up your online image. ReputationDefender was founded by Michael Fertik, a Harvard Law School graduate who was troubled by the idea of young people being forever tainted online by their youthful indiscretions. "I was seeing articles about the 'Lord of the Flies' behavior that all of us engage in at that age," he told me, "and it felt un-American that when the conduct was online, it could have permanent effects on the speaker and the victim. The right to new beginnings and the right to self-definition have always been among the most beautiful American ideals."

ReputationDefender, which has customers in more than 100 countries, is the most successful of the handful of reputation-related start-ups that have been growing rapidly after the privacy concerns raised by Facebook and Google. (ReputationDefender recently raised $15 million in new venture capital.) For a fee, the company will monitor your online reputation, contacting Web sites individually and asking them to take down offending items. In addition, with the help of the kind of search-optimization technology that businesses use to raise their Google profiles, ReputationDefender can bombard the Web with positive or neutral information about its customers, either creating new Web pages or by multiplying links to existing ones to ensure they show up at the top of any Google search. (Services begin from $10 a month to $1,000 a year; for challenging cases, the price can rise into the tens of thousands.) By automatically raising the Google ranks of the positive links, ReputationDefender pushes the negative links to the back pages of a Google search, where they're harder to find. "We're hearing stories of employers increasingly asking candidates to open up Facebook pages in front of them during job interviews," Fertik told me. "Our customers include parents whose kids have talked about them on the Internet—'Mom didn't get the raise'; 'Dad got fired'; 'Mom and Dad are fighting a lot, and I'm worried they'll get a divorce.'"

Companies like ReputationDefender offer a promising short-term solution for those who can afford it; but tweaking your Google profile may not be enough for reputation management in the near future, as Web 2.0 swiftly gives way to Web. 3.0—a world in which user-generated content is combined with a new layer of data aggregation and analysis and live video. For example, the Facebook application Photo Finder, by Face.com, uses facial-recognition and social-connections software to allow you to locate any photo of yourself or a friend on Facebook, regardless of whether the photo was "tagged"—that is, the individual in the photo was identified by name. At the moment, Photo Finder allows you to identify only people on your contact list, but as facial-recognition technology becomes more widespread and sophisticated, it will almost certainly challenge our expectation of anonymity in public. People will be able to snap a cellphone picture (or video) of a stranger, plug the images into Google and pull up all tagged and untagged photos of that person that exist on the Web.

In the nearer future, Internet searches for images are likely to be combined with social-network aggregator search engines, like today's Spokeo and Pipl, which combine data from online sources—including political contributions, blog posts, YouTube videos, Web comments, real estate listings and photo albums. Increasingly these aggregator sites will rank people's public and private reputations, like the new Web site Unvarnished, a reputation marketplace where people can write anonymous reviews about anyone. In the Web 3.0 world, Fertik predicts, people will be rated, assessed and scored based not on their creditworthiness but on their trustworthiness as good parents, good dates, good employees, good baby sitters or good insurance risks.

Anticipating these challenges, some legal scholars have begun imagining new laws that could allow people to correct, or escape from, the reputation scores that may govern our personal and professional interactions in the future. Jonathan Zittrain, who teaches cyberlaw at Harvard Law School, supports an idea he calls "reputation bankruptcy," which would give people a chance to wipe their reputation slates clean and start over. To illustrate the problem, Zittrain showed me an iPhone app called Date Check, by Intelius, that offers a "sleaze detector" to let you investigate people you're thinking about dating—it reports their criminal histories, address histories and summaries of their social-networking profiles. Services like Date Check, Zittrain said, could soon become even more sophisticated, rating a person's social desirability based on minute social measurements—like how often he or she was approached or avoided by others at parties (a ranking that would be easy to calibrate under existing technology using cellphones and Bluetooth). Zittrain also speculated that, over time, more and more reputation queries will be processed by a handful of de facto reputation brokers—like the existing consumer-reporting agencies Experian and Equifax, for example—which will provide ratings for people based on their sociability, trustworthiness and employability.

To allow people to escape from negative scores generated by these services, Zittrain says that people should be allowed to declare "reputation bankruptcy" every 10 years or so, wiping out certain categories of ratings or sensitive information. His model is the Fair Credit Reporting Act, which requires consumer-reporting agencies to provide you with one free credit report a year—so you can dispute negative or inaccurate information—and prohibits the agencies from retaining negative information about bankruptcies, late payments or tax liens for more than 10 years. "Like personal financial bankruptcy, or the way in which a state often seals a juvenile criminal record and gives a child a 'fresh start' as an adult," Zittrain writes in his book "The Future of the Internet and How to Stop It," "we ought to consider how to implement the idea of a second or third chance into our digital spaces."

Another proposal, offered by Paul Ohm, a law professor at the University of Colorado, would make it illegal for employers to fire or refuse to hire anyone on the basis of legal off-duty conduct revealed in Facebook postings or Google profiles. "Is it really fair for employers to know what you've put in your Facebook status updates?" Ohm asks. "We could say that Facebook status updates have taken the place of water-cooler chat, which employers were never supposed to overhear, and we could pass a prohibition on the sorts of information employers can and can't consider when they hire someone."

Ohm became interested in this problem in the course of researching the ease with which we can learn the identities of people from supposedly anonymous personal data like movie preferences and health information. When Netflix, for example, released 100 million purportedly anonymous records revealing how almost 500,000 users had rated movies from 1999 to 2005, researchers were able to identify people in the database by name with a high degree of accuracy if they knew even only a little bit about their movie-watching preferences, obtained from public data posted on other ratings sites.

Ohm says he worries that employers would be able to use social-network-aggregator services to identify people's book and movie preferences and even Internet-search terms, and then fire or refuse to hire them on that basis. A handful of states—including New York, California, Colorado and North Dakota—broadly prohibit employers from discriminating against employees for legal off-duty conduct like smoking. Ohm suggests that these laws could be extended to prevent certain categories of employers from refusing to hire people based on Facebook pictures, status updates and other legal but embarrassing personal information. (In practice, these laws might be hard to enforce, since employers might not disclose the real reason for their hiring decisions, so employers, like credit-reporting agents, might also be required by law to disclose to job candidates the negative information in their digital files.)

Another legal option for responding to online setbacks to your reputation is to sue under current law. There's already a sharp rise in lawsuits known as Twittergation—that is, suits to force Web sites to remove slanderous or false posts. Last year, Courtney Love was sued for libel by the fashion designer Boudoir Queen for supposedly slanderous comments posted on Twitter, on Love's MySpace page and on the designer's online marketplace-feedback page. But even if you win a U.S. libel lawsuit, the Web site doesn't have to take the offending material down any more than a newspaper that has lost a libel suit has to remove the offending content from its archive.

Some scholars, therefore, have proposed creating new legal rights to force Web sites to remove false or slanderous statements. Cass Sunstein, the Obama administration's regulatory czar, suggests in his new book, "On Rumors," that there might be "a general right to demand retraction after a clear demonstration that a statement is both false and damaging." (If a newspaper or blogger refuses to post a retraction, they might be liable for damages.) Sunstein adds that Web sites might be required to take down false postings after receiving notice that they are false—an approach modeled on the Digital Millennium Copyright Act, which requires Web sites to remove content that supposedly infringes intellectual property rights after receiving a complaint.

As Stacy Snyder's "Drunken Pirate" photo suggests, however, many people aren't worried about false information posted by others—they're worried about true information they've posted about themselves when it is taken out of context or given undue weight. And defamation law doesn't apply to true information or statements of opinion. Some legal scholars want to expand the ability to sue over true but embarrassing violations of privacy—although it appears to be a quixotic goal.

Daniel Solove, a George Washington University law professor and author of the book "The Future of Reputation," says that laws forbidding people to breach confidences could be expanded to allow you to sue your Facebook friends if they share your embarrassing photos or posts in violation of your privacy settings. Expanding legal rights in this way, however, would run up against the First Amendment rights of others. Invoking the right to free speech, the U.S. Supreme Court has already held that the media can't be prohibited from publishing the name of a rape victim that they obtained from public records. Generally, American judges hold that if you disclose something to a few people, you can't stop them from sharing the information with the rest of the world.

That's one reason that the most promising solutions to the problem of embarrassing but true information online may be not legal but technological ones. Instead of suing after the damage is done (or hiring a firm to clean up our messes), we need to explore ways of pre-emptively making the offending words or pictures disappear.

EXPIRATION DATES

Jorge Luis Borges, in his short story "Funes, the Memorious," describes a young man who, as a result of a riding accident, has lost his ability to forget. Funes has a tremendous memory, but he is so lost in the details of everything he knows that he is unable to convert the information into knowledge and unable, as a result, to grow in wisdom. Viktor Mayer-Schönberger, in "Delete," uses the Borges story as an emblem for the personal and social costs of being so shackled by our digital past that we are unable to evolve and learn from our mistakes. After reviewing the various possible legal solutions to this problem, Mayer-Schönberger says he is more convinced by a technological fix: namely, mimicking human forgetting with built-in expiration dates for data. He imagines a world in which digital-storage devices could be programmed to delete photos or blog posts or other data that have reached their expiration dates, and he suggests that users could be prompted to select an expiration date before saving any data.

This is not an entirely fanciful vision. Google not long ago decided to render all search queries anonymous after nine months (by deleting part of each Internet protocol address), and the upstart search engine Cuil has announced that it won't keep any personally identifiable information at all, a privacy feature that distinguishes it from Google. And there are already small-scale privacy apps that offer disappearing data. An app called TigerText allows text-message senders to set a time limit from one minute to 30 days after which the text disappears from the company's servers on which it is stored and therefore from the senders' and recipients' phones. (The founder of TigerText, Jeffrey Evans, has said he chose the name before the scandal involving Tiger Woods's supposed texts to a mistress.)

Expiration dates could be implemented more broadly in various ways. Researchers at the University of Washington, for example, are developing a technology called Vanish that makes electronic data "self-destruct" after a specified period of time. Instead of relying on Google, Facebook or Hotmail to delete the data that is stored "in the cloud"—in other words, on their distributed servers—Vanish encrypts the data and then "shatters" the encryption key. To read the data, your computer has to put the pieces of the key back together, but they "erode" or "rust" as time passes, and after a certain point the document can no longer be read. Tadayoshi Kohno, a designer of Vanish, told me that the system could provide expiration dates not only for e-mail but also for any data stored in the cloud, including photos or text or anything posted on Facebook, Google or blogs. The technology doesn't promise perfect control—you can't stop someone from copying your photos or Facebook chats during the period in which they are not encrypted. But as Vanish improves, it could bring us much closer to a world where our data didn't linger forever.

Kohno told me that Facebook, if it wanted to, could implement expiration dates on its own platform, making our data disappear after, say, three days or three months unless a user specified that he wanted it to linger forever. It might be a more welcome option for Facebook to encourage the development of Vanish-style apps that would allow individual users who are concerned about privacy to make their own data disappear without imposing the default on all Facebook users.

So far, however, Zuckerberg, Facebook's C.E.O., has been moving in the opposite direction—toward transparency rather than privacy. In defending Facebook's recent decision to make the default for profile information about friends and relationship status public rather than private, Zuckerberg said in January to the founder of the publication TechCrunch that Facebook had an obligation to reflect "current social norms" that favored exposure over privacy. "People have really gotten comfortable not only sharing more information and different kinds but more openly and with more people, and that social norm is just something that has evolved over time," he said.

PRIVACY'S NEW NORMAL

But not all Facebook users agree with Zuckerberg. Plenty of anecdotal evidence suggests that young people, having been burned by Facebook (and frustrated by its privacy policy, which at more than 5,000 words is longer than the U.S. Constitution), are savvier than older users about cleaning up their tagged photos and being careful about what they post. And two recent studies challenge the conventional wisdom that young people have no qualms about having their entire lives shared and preserved online forever. A University of California, Berkeley, study released in April found that large majorities of people between 18 and 22 said there should be laws that require Web sites to delete all stored information about individuals (88 percent) and that give people the right to know all the information Web sites know about them (62 percent)—percentages that mirrored the privacy views of older adults. A recent Pew study found that 18-to-29-year-olds are actually more concerned about their online profiles than older people are, vigilantly deleting unwanted posts, removing their names from tagged photos and censoring themselves as they share personal information, because they are coming to understand the dangers of oversharing.

Still, Zuckerberg is on to something when he recognizes that the future of our online identities and reputations will ultimately be shaped not just by laws and technologies but also by changing social norms. And norms are already developing to recreate off-the-record spaces in public, with no photos, Twitter posts or blogging allowed. Milk and Honey, an exclusive bar on Manhattan's Lower East Side, requires potential members to sign an agreement promising not to blog about the bar's goings on or to post photos on social-networking sites, and other bars and nightclubs are adopting similar policies. I've been at dinners recently where someone has requested, in all seriousness, "Please don't tweet this"—a custom that is likely to spread.

But what happens when people transgress those norms, using Twitter or tagging photos in ways that cause us serious embarrassment? Can we imagine a world in which new norms develop that make it easier for people to forgive and forget one another's digital sins?

That kind of social norm may be harder to develop. Alessandro Acquisti, a scholar at Carnegie Mellon University, studies the behavioral economics of privacy—that is, the conscious and unconscious mental trade-offs we make in deciding whether to reveal or conceal information, balancing the benefits of sharing with the dangers of disclosure. He is conducting experiments about the "decay time" and the relative weight of good and bad information—in other words, whether people discount positive information about you more quickly and heavily than they discount negative information about you. His research group's preliminary results suggest that if rumors spread about something good you did 10 years ago, like winning a prize, they will be discounted; but if rumors spread about something bad that you did 10 years ago, like driving drunk, that information has staying power. Research in behavioral psychology confirms that people pay more attention to bad rather than good information, and Acquisti says he fears that "20 years from now, if all of us have a skeleton on Facebook, people may not discount it because it was an error in our youth."

On the assumption that strangers may not make it easy for us to escape our pasts, Acquisti is also studying technologies and strategies of "privacy nudges" that might prompt people to think twice before sharing sensitive photos or information in the first place. Gmail, for example, has introduced a feature that forces you to think twice before sending drunken e-mail messages. When you enable the feature, called Mail Goggles, it prompts you to solve simple math problems before sending e-mail messages at times you're likely to regret. (By default, Mail Goggles is active only late on weekend nights.) Acquisti is investigating similar strategies of "soft paternalism" that might nudge people to hesitate before posting, say, drunken photos from Cancún. "We could easily think about a system, when you are uploading certain photos, that immediately detects how sensitive the photo will be."

A silly but surprisingly effective alternative might be to have an anthropomorphic icon—a stern version of Microsoft's Clippy—that could give you a reproachful look before you hit the send button. According to M. Ryan Calo, who runs the consumer-privacy project at Stanford Law School, experimenters studying strategies of "visceral notice" have found that when people navigate a Web site in the presence of a human-looking online character who seems to be actively following the cursor, they disclose less personal information than people who browse with no character or one who appears not to be paying attention. As people continue to experience the drawbacks of living in a world that never forgets, they may well learn to hesitate before posting information, with or without humanoid Clippys.

FORGIVENESS

In addition to exposing less for the Web to forget, it might be helpful for us to explore new ways of living in a world that is slow to forgive. It's sobering, now that we live in a world misleadingly called a "global village," to think about privacy in actual, small villages long ago. In the villages described in the Babylonian Talmud, for example, any kind of gossip or tale-bearing about other people—oral or written, true or false, friendly or mean—was considered a terrible sin because small communities have long memories and every word spoken about other people was thought to ascend to the heavenly cloud. (The digital cloud has made this metaphor literal.) But the Talmudic villages were, in fact, far more humane and forgiving than our brutal global village, where much of the content on the Internet would meet the Talmudic definition of gossip: although the Talmudic sages believed that God reads our thoughts and records them in the book of life, they also believed that God erases the book for those who atone for their sins by asking forgiveness of those they have wronged. In the Talmud, people have an obligation not to remind others of their past misdeeds, on the assumption they may have atoned and grown spiritually from their mistakes. "If a man was a repentant [sinner]," the Talmud says, "one must not say to him, 'Remember your former deeds.'"

Unlike God, however, the digital cloud rarely wipes our slates clean, and the keepers of the cloud today are sometimes less forgiving than their all-powerful divine predecessor. In an interview with Charlie Rose on PBS, Eric Schmidt, the C.E.O. of Google, said that "the next generation is infinitely more social online"—and less private—"as evidenced by their Facebook pictures," which "will be around when they're running for president years from now." Schmidt added: "As long as the answer is that I chose to make a mess of myself with this picture, then it's fine. The issue is when somebody else does it." If people chose to expose themselves for 15 minutes of fame, Schmidt says, "that's their choice, and they have to live with it."

Schmidt added that the "notion of control is fundamental to the evolution of these privacy-based solutions," pointing to Google Latitude, which allows people to broadcast their locations in real time.

This idea of privacy as a form of control is echoed by many privacy scholars, but it seems too harsh to say that if people like Stacy Snyder don't use their privacy settings responsibly, they have to live forever with the consequences. Privacy protects us from being unfairly judged out of context on the basis of snippets of private information that have been exposed against our will; but we can be just as unfairly judged out of context on the basis of snippets of public information that we have unwisely chosen to reveal to the wrong audience.

Moreover, the narrow focus on privacy as a form of control misses what really worries people on the Internet today. What people seem to want is not simply control over their privacy settings; they want control over their online reputations. But the idea that any of us can control our reputations is, of course, an unrealistic fantasy. The truth is we can't possibly control what others say or know or think about us in a world of Facebook and Google, nor can we realistically demand that others give us the deference and respect to which we think we're entitled. On the Internet, it turns out, we're not entitled to demand any particular respect at all, and if others don't have the empathy necessary to forgive our missteps, or the attention spans necessary to judge us in context, there's nothing we can do about it.

But if we can't control what others think or say or view about us, we can control our own reaction to photos, videos, blogs and Twitter posts that we feel unfairly represent us. A recent study suggests that people on Facebook and other social-networking sites express their real personalities, despite the widely held assumption that people try online to express an enhanced or idealized impression of themselves. Samuel Gosling, the University of Texas, Austin, psychology professor who conducted the study, told the Facebook blog, "We found that judgments of people based on nothing but their Facebook profiles correlate pretty strongly with our measure of what that person is really like, and that measure consists of both how the profile owner sees him or herself and how that profile owner's friends see the profile owner."

By comparing the online profiles of college-aged people in the United States and Germany with their actual personalities and their idealized personalities, or how they wanted to see themselves, Gosling found that the online profiles conveyed "rather accurate images of the profile owners, either because people aren't trying to look good or because they are trying and failing to pull it off." (Personality impressions based on the online profiles were most accurate for extroverted people and least accurate for neurotic people, who cling tenaciously to an idealized self-image.)

Gosling is optimistic about the implications of his study for the possibility of digital forgiveness. He acknowledged that social technologies are forcing us to merge identities that used to be separate—we can no longer have segmented selves like "a home or family self, a friend self, a leisure self, a work self." But although he told Facebook, "I have to find a way to reconcile my professor self with my having-a-few-drinks self," he also suggested that as all of us have to merge our public and private identities, photos showing us having a few drinks on Facebook will no longer seem so scandalous. "You see your accountant going out on weekends and attending clown conventions, that no longer makes you think that he's not a good accountant. We're coming to terms and reconciling with that merging of identities."

Perhaps society will become more forgiving of drunken Facebook pictures in the way Gosling says he expects it might. And some may welcome the end of the segmented self, on the grounds that it will discourage bad behavior and hypocrisy: it's harder to have clandestine affairs when you're broadcasting your every move on Facebook, Twitter and Foursquare. But a humane society values privacy, because it allows people to cultivate different aspects of their personalities in different contexts; and at the moment, the enforced merging of identities that used to be separate is leaving many casualties in its wake. Stacy Snyder couldn't reconcile her "aspiring-teacher self" with her "having-a-few-drinks self": even the impression, correct or not, that she had a drink in a pirate hat at an off-campus party was enough to derail her teaching career.

That doesn't mean, however, that it had to derail her life. After taking down her MySpace profile, Snyder is understandably trying to maintain her privacy: her lawyer told me in a recent interview that she is now working in human resources; she did not respond to a request for comment. But her success as a human being who can change and evolve, learning from her mistakes and growing in wisdom, has nothing to do with the digital file she can never entirely escape. Our character, ultimately, can't be judged by strangers on the basis of our Facebook or Google profiles; it can be judged by only those who know us and have time to evaluate our strengths and weaknesses, face to face and in context, with insight and understanding. In the meantime, as all of us stumble over the challenges of living in a world without forgetting, we need to learn new forms of empathy, new ways of defining ourselves without reference to what others say about us and new ways of forgiving one another for the digital trails that will follow us forever.

Bibliography

Books

Awl, Dave. *Facebook Me! A Guide to Having Fun with Your Friends and Promoting Your Projects on Facebook*. Berkeley, Calif.: Peachpit Press, 2009.

Blossom, John. *Content Nation: Surviving and Thriving as Social Media Changes Our Work, Our Lives, and Our Future*. Indianapolis, Ind.: Wiley Publishing, Inc., 2009.

Brogan, Chris. *Social Media 101: Tactics and Tips to Develop Your Business Online*. Hoboken, N.J.: John Wiley & Sons, Inc., 2010.

Christakis, Nicholas A., and James H. Fowler. *Connected: The Surprising Power of Our Social Networks and How They Shape Our Lives*. New York: Little, Brown and Company, 2009.

Comm, Joel. *Twitter Power 2.0: How to Dominate Your Market One Tweet at a Time*. Hoboken, N.J.: John Wiley & Sons, Inc., 2010.

Harfoush, Rahaf. *Yes We Did! An Inside Look at How Social Media Built the Obama Brand*. Berkeley, Calif.: New Riders, 2009.

Kirkpatrick, David. *The Facebook Effect: The Inside Story of the Company That Is Connecting the World*. New York: Simon & Schuster, 2010.

Mezrich, Ben. *The Accidental Billionaires: The Founding of Facebook: A Tale of Sex, Money, Genius and Betrayal*. New York: Doubleday, 2009.

O'Reilly, Tim, and Sarah Milstein. *The Twitter Book*. Sebastopol, Calif.: O'Reilly Media, Inc., 2009.

Osuagwu, Nnamdi Godson. *Facebook Addiction: The Life & Times of Social Networking Addicts*. Ice Cream Melts Publishing, 2009.

Penenberg, Adam L. *Viral Loop: From Facebook to Twitter, How Today's Smartest Businesses Grow Themselves*. New York: Hyperion, 2009.

Qualman, Erik. *Socialnomics: How Social Media Transforms the Way We Live and Do Business*. Hoboken, N.J.: John Wiley & Sons, Inc., 2009.

Rice, Jesse. *The Church of Facebook: How the Hyperconnected Are Redefining Community*. Colorado Springs, Colo.: David C. Cook, 2009.

Rutledge, Patrice-Anne. *The Truth About Profiting from Social Networking*. Upper Saddle River, N.J.: FT Press, 2008.

Safko, Lon. *The Social Media Bible: Tactics, Tools, and Strategies for Business Success*. Hoboken, N.J.: John Wiley & Sons, Inc., 2010.

Sagolla, Dom. *140 Characters: A Style Guide for the Short Form*. Hoboken, N.J.: John Wiley & Sons, Inc., 2009.

Shih, Clara. *The Facebook Era: Tapping Online Social Networks to Build Better Products, Reach New Audiences, and Sell More Stuff*. Boston: Pearson, 2009.

Silver, David. *The Social Network Business Plan: 18 Strategies That Will Create Great Wealth*. Hoboken, N.J.: John Wiley & Sons, Inc., 2009.

Web Sites

Readers seeking additional information on social networking and related subjects may wish to consult the following Web sites, all of which were operational as of this writing.

Facebook

www.facebook.com

Launched in 2004 by Harvard undergrad Mark Zuckerberg, Facebook has grown into the world's largest social-networking platform. The site allows its 500 million-plus users to share information in a variety of ways, including uploading photos; posting "status updates," or quick descriptions of what they're doing or thinking; sending private messages; and leaving comments on each other's "walls." Facebook members also play interactive games, swap surveys and personal questionnaires, and indicate their approval for certain things—consumer goods, films, albums, articles, etc.—by clicking a "Like" button now ubiquitous on outside Web sites.

Foursquare

www.foursquare.com

Created in 2009, Foursquare has emerged as the most popular of the location-based social-networking sites. Using smart-phone apps, users can "check in" from bars, restaurants, airports—just about any place they visit. Members become "mayors" by checking in from a given location more often than anyone else, and they earn other types of "badges" based on the types of places they frequent. Those who hit the gym ten times in 30 days, for example, get the "gym rat" badge, while checking in from an airplane earns one the "mile high" badge.

Mashable

www.mashable.com

Established in 2005, Mashable bills itself as "the top source for news in social and digital media, technology and web culture." The site covers all the major platforms—Facebook, Twitter, Foursquare, etc.—and the ways in which they overlap with business, technology, popular culture, and current events.

MySpace

www.myspace.com

Although it's been overtaken by Facebook as the world's leading social-media site, MySpace remains popular, particularly among artists, filmmakers, celebrities, and musicians seeking an easy way to share their work with the public. In 2010, amid dwindling membership and plummeting ad revenues, MySpace rebranded itself a "social entertainment" platform—a move parent company News Corp. hopes will revitalize the site. Despite its emphasis on shared content, the redesigned MySpace features traditional user profiles and messaging features, enabling friends to interact much as they do on Facebook.

Twitter

www.twitter.com

As of October 2010, the microblogging site Twitter boasted 175 million members—70 million more than it had a mere six months earlier. Founded in 2006, the site allows users to read and write "Tweets," or short postings of 140 characters or less. Celebrities and politicians are among those who have embraced the site and attracted large numbers of "followers," or regular readers of their Tweets. While Twitter has been used to break major news stories and, according to some, galvanize protestors in the wake of Iran's 2009 national elections, it's also a way for friends to keep in touch and update each other on their day-to-day activities.

Additional Periodical Articles with Abstracts

More information about social networking can be found in the following articles. Readers interested in additional material may consult the *Readers' Guide to Periodical Literature* and other H.W. Wilson publications.

What Happens When Facebook Trumps Your Brand Site? Jack Neff. *Advertising Age* v.81 pp 2–3+ August 23, 2010.

Facebook has quietly become the largest relationship-marketing provider for many brands, Neff writes, explaining that many marketers have seen their Facebook fan bases become their biggest Web presence, outstripping brand sites or e-mail programs, either because their brand's traditional Web presence is atrophying or because more consumers are moving to social media. Increased marketer dependence on Facebook for CRM programs and parallel declines in brand sites' traffic could offer a valuable revenue opportunity for Facebook, Neff adds.

Stepping Up. Rebecca Cullers. *Adweek* v.51 pp24–25 September 13, 2010.

With a small budget, Geoff Cottrill has resuscitated Converse through a quirky and imaginative focus on digital and social media, Cullers observes. As an indication of Cottrill's success, the Converse brand has 8.8 million fans on its two Facebook pages, about four times more than Converse owner Nike. Cullers discusses Cottrill's work for Converse.

The Variables of Like. Brian Morrissey. *Adweek* v.51 p8 September 13, 2010.

Brands that are only beginning to establish themselves on Facebook are pulling out all the stops to garner what Facebook now calls "Likes"—social actions by which consumers express interest in a brand, Morrissey reports. In order to obtain these Likes, brands are going beyond ads and bartering for friendship through offers of exclusive content, discounts, and special offers.

MySpace: Still Here. Brian Morrissey. *Adweek* v.51 p4 September 6, 2010.

Once-dominant social network MySpace is now fighting for relevance, Morrissey observes. MySpace is seeking to escape from the shadow of Facebook by enhancing its usability, focusing on its core audience of youth, and emphasizing the sharing of music and entertainment, while reminding people that it still matters, the writer explains. Several brands have found success on MySpace, particularly with integrated programs combining advertising and entertainment content, Morrissey adds.

Ping Them Bells. Antony Bruno. *Billboard* v.122 p8 September 11, 2010.

Apple's Ping, a music-focused social network for iTunes, is unlikely to threaten other efforts to combine music appreciation and social networking, Bruno writes. In contrast to the emerging digital-media player market that the iPod quickly came to dominate, social networking already involves entrenched giants such as Facebook, Twitter, and MySpace, and music is already a focal point of interaction, the writer adds. Bruno asserts that MySpace, a popular channel for artists to communicate with fans, has most to be concerned about but still has some factors in its favor.

Direct Connect. Mariel Concepcion and Mitchell Peters. *Billboard* v.122 p5 September 4, 2010.

Social media channels are playing a bigger role in recording artists' album promotion campaigns, Concepcion and Peters write. Although many recording artists have long used social-media services like Facebook and Twitter, these platforms have become a much more important part of album promotion campaigns than they have been in the past, the writers insist. Fueling these trends are the continued increase in the number of consumers using social networks, the emergence of newer services like Ustream and location-based networking site Foursquare, and the growing popularity of the Apple iPhone and other smart phones, which allow consumers to access the Web from anywhere.

Winging It Does Not Equal a Social Media Strategy. Gannon Hall. *Brandweek* v.51 p56 September 13, 2010.

A recent study from marketing firm Digital Brand Expressions, published in July 2010, states that nearly half of the companies that employ social media for advertising, marketing, or public relations do not possess strategic plans in place to help guide those activities. In addition to this lack of a cohesive strategy, marketers often assume that all they need to be ready is to set up a Facebook and Twitter account, Hall reports. The writer also discusses the need for marketers to have social-media strategies.

Social Media Is Murky Area For Marketers of Alcohol. Todd Wasserman. *Brandweek* v.51 p6 August 9–16, 2010.

Although, for some time now, alcohol brands have self-policed their Web sites by forcing visitors to enter their dates of birth in order to get past the outer wall, Facebook and Twitter especially seem to leave more doors open, enabling minors to wander into the drinking realms and leave inappropriate messages, Wasserman reports. Not surprisingly, the writer adds, both the Federal Trade Commission (FTC) and consumer watchdog groups are also closely examining how marketers of alcohol brands are behaving on social media.

Friends with Benefits. Jon Lafayette. *Broadcasting & Cable* v.140 pp8–9 October 11, 2010.

Sponsors are taking an increased interest in TV networks' social-media connections, Lafayette reports. In addition to enabling networks to communicate with viewers and build bigger, more engaged audiences for their shows, networks' ventures into social media accumulate enough followers to attract their advertising clients' interest. Lafayette cites examples of how networks are monetizing their social-media communities and advertisers are adding social-media components to TV campaigns.

You've Been Tagged! (Then Again, Maybe Not): Employers and Facebook. William P. Smith and Deborah L. Kidder. *Business Horizons* v.53 pp491–99 September/October 2010.

This article offers a discussion on the way that some firms use social-networking sites to gather information regarding job applicants. As an employer, checking out an applicant's Facebook page is tempting, the authors write, since Facebook pages can offer plenty of information beyond, or even contradicting, an applicant's submitted documents. Although it may seem like a potentially useful tool, there are a number of reasons for caution, Smith and Kidder insist. Facebook's own policies imply that an organization may face legal challenges if it considers an applicant's Facebook page in its selection process. The authors assert that organizations should develop guidelines regarding the use of social networking sites in the application process, based on practical, legal, and ethical issues.

Companies Often Unprepared for Risk Social Media Pose. Louise Esola. *Business Insurance* v.44 pp12–13 September 13, 2010.

According to experts, companies that use social media to market their brand may not be prepared for the risks that come with such communications, Esola writes. They warn that the greatest risks fall into two categories: information technology and reputation. They recommend that companies establish alerts notifying them when their brands are mentioned on-line.

How Nonprofit Groups Need to Adjust to a 'Networked' World. Allison Fine and Beth Kanter. *The Chronicle of Philanthropy* v.22 pp43–44 June 17, 2010.

With the growing use of social media, power will move away from institutions and toward individuals, and nonprofit leaders can thrive in this new world by migrating from stand-alone entities to networked organizations, Fine and Kanter write. Nonprofit fortresses—organizations that work hard to keep their communities and constituents at a distance—are losing ground today because they spend a huge amount of time fearing what will happen if they open up to the world, the authors observe, adding that that trajectory changes when organizations learn to engage in social media and actually become their own social networks.

Give and Go. Patrick J. Sauer. *Fast Company* pp64+ November 2010.

According to Web site Sports Fan Graph, the National Basketball Association (NBA) has over 6.7 million combined Facebook fans and Twitter followers, much higher than the National Football League (NFL)'s 2.5 million or Major League Baseball (MLB)'s 1.1 million, Sauer reports. Melissa Rosenthal Brenner, the NBA's vice president of marketing, says that the league has been so active in social media because sports are communal experiences. Sauer provides further details on the NBA's social-media initiatives.

Yes We Can, Too. Austin Carr. *Fast Company* p68 October 2010.

Some candidates in the 2010 midterm elections used then-new location-based social-networking tool Gowalla to connect with constituents, Carr reports, one month in advance of the election. Gowalla released a tool kit that enables campaigns to schedule events such as town hall meetings or fundraisers and reward supporters who attend and check in with candidate-branded badges. Governors Charlie Crist of Florida and Rick Perry of Texas and Arizona congressional hopeful and Gowalla board member Jim Ward were among those using the service, according to Carr.

Tweet Patrol. Patrick Tucker. *The Futurist* v.44 pp8–9 November/December 2010.

A group of researchers in Britain are using the power of social networks and location broadcasting to make cities safer, Tucker observes. The program, Voice Your View, enables pedestrians to record their opinions about their surroundings into a database via their cell phones or strategically situated kiosks. The information is then shared with both city planners and the public through Web sites and at the public spaces themselves. Voice Your View slightly resembles the popular location-based marketing service Foursquare, which rewards users with points and coupons for "checking in" with their phones at different venues and commercial establishments around the city, Tucker explains, but the Voice Your View program solicits real-time data from residents and visitors about areas that require improvement.

Social Networks Go to Work. Steve Towns. *Governing* v.23 p48 August 2010.

Although flashy creations such as Facebook "virtual town halls" tend to draw the most attention, some of the biggest Web 2.0 advantages for state and local governments may be accruing behind the scenes, Towns writes. One example comes from Oregon, where the state CIO's office employs social-networking tools to boost collaboration and reduce the time it takes to complete complex technology deployments. Two years ago, Towns reports, Oregon launched a small test project to give state workers an internal social-networking platform, kind of a private Facebook site, where they could rapidly build on-line communities around projects, issues, or agency business functions. The concept was to promote interaction among state agencies and with local governments and contractors, among other stakeholders. Oregon signed a deal for 200 user licenses with Silicon Valley, California-based Jive Software, a firm that bills itself as the world's largest provider of "social business software."

Court: Social Networking Comments Private, in Part. *Information Management Journal* v.44 p19 September/October 2010.

A U.S. district court has found that private messages sent via social-networking sites are protected under the Stored Communications Act (SCA) but more public wall and comment posts may not be, the author of this article reports. In *Crispin v. Christian Audigier Inc.*, defendants in a copyright-infringement case had sought disclosure of wall postings and private messages from Crispin's Facebook and My-Space accounts, the writer explains. The court found that the sites were covered by the SCA but that the act did not cover material readily available to the public.

Cyberbullying: How to Make it Stop. Caralee Adams. *Instructor* v.120 pp44–49 Fall 2010.

Teachers need to take steps to address the new phenomenon of cyberbullying, or persistent harassment of individuals through the use of Web technology, Adams writes. Cyberbullying occurs most frequently on social-networking sites, and most commonly between middle-school students. Schools faced with the after-effects of cyberbullying need to educate students about the harm it can cause, Adams asserts, rather than simply banning the technology. Moreover, she writes, teachers need to familiarize themselves with current trends in social media and help educate students on strategies to avoid being victimized. Adams also discusses the importance of recognizing the signs of cyberbullying, requiring students to report incidents, responding quickly and correctly, and getting parents involved in tackling this problem.

Measuring Rules of Engagement. Chris Daniels. *Marketing Magazine* v.115 pp19–20+ September 13, 2010.

The exploding popularity of social media is transforming engagement marketing and how marketers measure success, Daniels writes. Agencies have typically helped clients measure engagement and experiential programs through such metrics as person-to-person interactions, media clippings, and brand awareness, Daniels explains, but with the introduction of new tools, namely social media, another layer has been created that, although providing new data, can complicate the matter for a lot of marketers. Daniels discusses the role of social media in measuring the success of engagement marketing programs.

Social Media Meets Insurance Regulation: Where Are We Headed? Susan T. Stead. *National Underwriter (Property & Casualty/Risk & Benefits Management Edition)* v.114 p14+ June 7, 2010.

As the insurance industry's use of social networking grows, Stead writes, insurance firms and agents need to be aware of risks that are unique to the insurance sector. The level of insurance regulation and the industry's dependence upon agency distribution channels combine to present special regulatory and legal risks for both insurance firms and agents, the writer explains. Moreover, Stead reports, old issues concerning disclosure and inducements are reemerging in social media. Stead also discusses the outlook for insurance regulation of social media use and insurer risks relating to advertising requirements and errors and omissions.

Potential of Social Networking Sites for Distance Education Student Engagement. Jaime Lester and Michael Perini. *New Directions for Community Colleges* pp67–77 Summer 2010.

This chapter explores the potential of social-networking sites for increasing student engagement for distance-education learners. The authors present a modified student-engagement model with a focus on the integration of technology, specifically social-networking sites for community college distance-education learners. The chapter concludes with challenges and implications for integrating social-networking sites in the classroom and on the college level.

Defacebook. Emily Nussbaum. *New York* v.43 pp130–32+ October 4, 2010.

Maxwell Salzberg, Ilya Zhitomirskiy, Daniel Grippi, and Raphael Sofaer have founded a new social-networking system called Diaspora* that is designed to be an escape route from Facebook for those who have come to fear the dark side of the social network, Nussbaum reports. Diaspora* would function in the same way as Facebook, but data would belong to the users. The aim is to create something that is so cool to use that it does not feel like something radical. Nussbaum profiles Diaspora*'s founders and discusses their work.

Governing Without a Net. Daniel Lyons. *Newsweek* v.156 p22 November 15, 2010.

In 2008, Lyons writes, it seemed credible that the on-line activists who helped to elect Barack Obama would stick around and support him as he pushed through a sweeping list of progressive measures, but those idealistic young people have disappeared. The pro-Obama Netroots movement has collapsed, he insists, while Tea Partiers have used Facebook, Twitter, and other social media to lead a backlash. In October 2008, BarackObama.com attracted 8.5 million unique visitors in the United States, but by last September, traffic had dived to just 664,000, says Internet researcher ComScore. According to Don Tapscott, an Internet pundit and author of *Macrowikinomics: Rebooting Business and the World,* Obama changed the way a candidate gets elected but not the way one governs.

Privacy Is Dead. Jessica Bennett. *Newsweek* v.156 pp40–41 November 1, 2010.

Tech experts say that people's on-line profiles will become the credit score of the future, a kind of ranking for every aspect of their lives, Bennett reports. According to Nicholas Carr, author of *The Shallows: What the Internet Is Doing to Our Brains,* most people are still under the illusion that they are anonymous when they go on-line, but the reality is that every move they make is being amassed in a database. All kinds of personal information can be surmised by anybody with a Web connection and little background data who wants to compile it all. Indeed, credit card companies and data aggregators are already selling personal information to advertisers, and third parties receive personal information when users download certain apps on Facebook, according to a recent report in the *Wall Street Journal.*

Digg This. Daniel Lyons. *Newsweek* v.156 p16 November 1, 2010.

The decline of Digg, a Web site where people can vote for news stories they like so that popular stories rise to the top, has become a cautionary tale for so-called Web 2.0 companies in Silicon Valley, Lyons writes. When Digg was established by Kevin Rose in 2006, it was hailed as a superstar, but it struggled for a few years, swooned, and is now in free fall. The problem, Lyon insists, with new-media companies such as Digg, Facebook, and Twitter is that they do not really have customers as much as audiences. Starting one of these companies is less like building a traditional tech company and more like launching a TV show, Lyons writes, pondering whether, like TV shows, these companies are ephemeral in nature, in that their popularity is short-lived.

Can You Really Trust Facebook? Erik Larkin. *PC World* v.28 p40 August 2010.

In answer to yet another user uproar, Facebook recently took steps to simplify its privacy controls and introduce some other welcome changes, Larkin writes. They are good steps to take, the writer says, but it indicates a grave disconnect in how the social network and its users view privacy. Larkin considers whether Facebook is doing enough to guard users' data.

Pee-Wee's Tricks with Tweets. Gordon Cox. *Variety* v.420 p35 September 13–19, 2010.

As Broadway producers seek ways of transforming new-media initiatives into ticket sales, Cox reports, the producers of *The Pee-wee Herman Show* have uncovered some interesting options. A strong early seller of the fall season, the show, which began performances on October 26, 2010, made use of social networking prior to the more traditional television, outdoor, and print advertising. Cox discusses the use of social marketing in promoting *The Pee-wee Herman Show*.

Tweet Heat Elusive. Lisa Engelbrektson. *Variety* v.419 p28 June 7–13, 2010.

Although microblogging site Twitter has given media-savvy celebrities the ability to quickly and cheaply bond with their fans, it has proved problematic for media companies, Engelbrektson reports. Twitter seems to work in a "one-to-many" format, sometimes with the "many" talking back, but when the company sending out the messages has no identifiable face or personality, Twitter is less successful, the writer adds. In addition, Engelbrektson notes, whereas Twitter helps to generate buzz and "mindshare," there is no clear connection between that buzz and the revenue that media companies desire.

Socially Evolved. Susan Ladika. *Workforce Management* v.89 pp18–20+ September 2010.

In light of the huge popularity of Facebook, Twitter, and other social media, an increasing number of companies are developing or buying their own social networks, Ladika writes. The internal networks might feature employee blogs, wikis to help streamline project collaboration, profiles of staff members highlighting fields of expertise, training courses, or discussion groups centering on both business and personal issues, the writer explains. Ladika discusses the growing use of corporate social networks and the internal social networking strategies of a number of companies.

Index

Abrams, Jonathan, 8
Acquisti, Alessandro, 194
Adams, Paul, 23
Albright, Julie, 179–181
Allen, George, 91
Amos, Denise Smith, 121–124
Anderson, April, 147–149
Anderson, Chris, 33
Anderson, Holden, 148
Anderson, Steven W., 114
Anderson, Tom, 8, 33–34
Angle, Sharron, 95

Bachmann, Michele, 88–89
Bacon, Kevin, 76
Balasubramanian, Srinivas, 53
Barger, Christopher, 49, 54
Barrett, Phil, 47–48
Begich, Mark, 187
Bennet, Michael, 187
Berra, Yogi, 169
Bilchik, Nadia, 55–56, 58
Binhammer, Richard, 78
Birch, Michael, 9–10, 40
Blake, Brad, 99
Blumenthal, Richard, 93–94
Boehner, John, 95
Bollier, David, 29–30
Borges, Jorge Luis, 192
Bough, Bonin, 76
Bourgon, Lyndsie, 47–48
Boyd, Danah, 30, 163, 178, 180
Brand, Stewart, 6
Brandeis, Louis, 185
Brees, Drew, 76
Brisbourne, Nic, 38, 41
Bush, George W., 86
Bykkkten, Orkut, 10

Calacanis, Jason, 22, 134

Calo, M. Ryan, 194
Campos-Duffy, Rachel, 88
Carr, Nicholas, 168
Chandlee, Blake, 37, 39–41
Cheney, Liz, 89–90
Christensen, Ward, 5–6
Clement, Celia, 151–153
Clinton, Hillary, 86, 91
Clooney, Nick, 124
Cody, Chris, 153
Comm, Joel, 51
Connelly, Phoebe, 28–31
Conner, Adam, 96
Conrads, Randal, 7
Cook, Peter, 38
Coons, Chris, 97
Cowan, James, 129–136
Cox, Chris, 171–172, 176
Coyle, Jack, 95–97
Crenshaw, Dorothy, 59

David, Nour, 56–57
Davis, Michelle R., 111–116
Dean, Howard, 96
Dell, Michael, 76
DeWolfe, Chris, 8, 32–34
Dickson, Tom, 66
Dorsch, Meagan, 98–102
Dorsey, Jack, 37

Eisenberg, Jesse, 160–161
Eliason, Frank, 51
Erickson, Tom, 51
Evangelista, Benny, 22–24
Evans, Jeffrey, 192

Faber, John, 53
Fertik, Michael, 188–189
Fewer, David, 129, 131, 135
50 Cent, 92
Fincher, David, 91, 159–161

Finn, Mindy, 96–97
Fiorina, Carly, 91
Fodor, Marek, 62–71
Fox, Russell, 122
Franken, Al, 187
Franzen, Jonathan, 159
Frost, David, 38
Frost, Debbie, 131–132
Fry, Stephen, 37
Fuller, Steve, 59–60

Garfield, Andrew, 160
Gartenbeg, Michael, 131
Gates, Bill, 130
Gavales, Lisa, 60
Gesemer, Thomas, 86
Gibb, Brandon, 152
Gladwell, Malcolm, 89–90, 92–93
Gosling, Samuel, 196
Grant, Garvan, 182–183
Greenberg, Pam, 98–102
Greene, Alvin, 94
Grigoriadis, Vanessa, 166–177
Gross, Shawn, 113
Grove, Steve, 95

Hargadon, Steve, 112
Harper, Julius, 166–168, 176–177
Harrelson, Steve, 100
Hoberman, Brent, 40–41
Hoffman, Donna L., 62–71
Hoffman, Reid, 34
Hoole, Christina, 39
Horowitz, Andreessen, 48
Hrywna, Mark, 103–106
Hughes, Chris, 9, 86–87

Jacobson, Jennifer, 147–148
Jarvis, Jeff, 67
Jay, Robin, 57–58
Jobs, Steve, 130
Johnson, Eileen Morgan, 137–146
Johnson, Paddy, 26–27
Johnson, Steven, 178–181

Judge, Barry, 60

Kelly, Chris, 171, 174, 176
Kelly, John, 164
Kerbs, Scott, 147–150
Keyes, Alan, 176
Kirk, Mark, 93–94
Kirkpatrick, David, 130
Kohno, Tadayoshi, 192
Krikorian, Onnik, 165
Krizelman, Todd, 7
Kutcher, Ashton, 37

Lacter, Mark, 32–35
Learmonth, Michael, 85–87
Lifton, Robert Jay, 186
Lightman, Ari, 53, 54
Liias, Marko, 99
Lippert, Barbara, 59–61
Loesch, Dana, 88–89
Love, Courtney, 191
Ludlow, Peter, 29

Madden, Mary, 134–135
Malone, Noreen, 88–90
Marwick, Alice, 29, 31
Mayer-Schönberger, Viktor, 185–186, 192
McCaffrey, Mary, 122
McCain, John, 92
McCarter, Jeremy, 159–162
McDonald, Barbara, 50, 52
Mehta, Manish, 77, 78
Mehta, Nihal, 20
Mezrich, Ben, 159
Miller, Jonathan, 33
Miller, Montana, 115
MonCrief, Anita, 89
Moore, Demi, 76
Moore, Fernanda, 178–181
Moran, Ed, 50, 52–53, 54
Morissey, Brian, 75–79
Moskovitz, Dustin, 9
Mueller, David, 121

Murdoch, Rupert, 8, 14–15, 32–33, 35, 38
Murdock, Michael, 24
Muscari, Mary, 153

Narendra, Divya, 159
Nazar, Jason, 34
Neely, Dan, 75
Neumann, Roger, 151–154
Norton, Edward, 161

Obama, Barack, 55, 85–87, 89, 91–92, 97, 176
O'Donnell, Christine, 93–94, 97
Ohm, Paul, 190
Opsahl, Kurt, 23
Orsini, Anthony, 115

Palin, Sarah, 90, 92, 95
Parker, Sean, 13, 161
Paternot, Stephan, 7
Patrick, Dan, 99
Patrick, Deval, 99
Patrick, Jeff, 104–106
Paul, Ron, 92
Penna, Albert, 153
Pennington, Enos, 122
Phillips, Paul, 104
Pinelo, Greg, 87
Pitt, Brad, 161
Pitts, Chip, 135
Popkin, Helen A.S., 25–27
Prince, Phoebe, 151

Quagliano, Enrique, 187
Quayle, Ben, 93–94

Rainie, Lee, 95, 97
Ramig, Renee, 117–120
Raskin, Jef, 5
Ratchaga, Ezer, 9
Redstone, Sumner, 32
Reid, Harry, 95
Reinhardt, Susan, 122

Reznor, Trent, 160
Rich, Frank, 91–94
Richardson, Will, 122–123
Richter, Chris, 53
Rojas, Peter, 134
Rosch, Mark, 96
Rose, Charlie, 167, 195
Rosen, Jeffrey, 184–197
Rosin, Hanna, 89
Rospars, Joe, 85–86
Ross, Atticus, 160
Rove, Karl, 93
Rubin, Ted, 60

Sala, André, 27
Salzman, Marian, 59
Sanford, Mark, 92
Saunders, Andrew, 36–41
Saverin, Eduardo, 9, 160–161
Schmidt, Eric, 167, 195
Schrage, Elliot, 134
Schumer, Charles, 187
Scott, A.O., 92
Scott, Jason, 29–30
Seacrest, Ryan, 61
Shakespeare, William, 124
Shank, Chris, 99
Shappell, Brian, 55–58
Shaw, Aaron, 148–150
Sheninger, Eric C., 111, 113, 115
Shust, Dan, 50, 54
Simon, Michael, 5–10
Sloan, Glen, 47
Snyder, Pete, 86
Snyder, Stacy, 184, 191, 195–197
Soat, John, 49–54
Solove, Daniel, 191
Sorkin, Aaron, 91, 160–161
Spears, Britney, 92
Sterling, Bruce, 31
Stewart, Morgan, 75–76
Stiller, Ben, 61
Stoddart, Jennifer, 135
Stone, Biz, 37

Strom, Aaron, 77
Stutzman, Fred, 173
Suess, Randy, 5–6
Sullenger, Wes, 101
Sunstein, Cass, 191
Suster, Mark, 11–21

Tenby, Susan, 105–106
Terrell, Shelly, 114–116
Timberlake, Justin, 161
Tolisano, Silvia Rosenthal, 112
Toplansky, Marshall, 54
Tortolini, Alejandro, 187
Trump, Donald, 93
Türk, Alex, 187
Turner, Frederick Jackson, 186

Valdes, Ray, 22–24
Viégas, Fernanda, 163
Vondracek, Sara, 152–153

Walker, Hazel, 55–57
Ward, Peter, 39–40

Warren, Samuel, 185
Wattenberg, Martin, 163
Weintraub, Megan, 104–105
Weist, Zena, 78–79
Welles, Orson, 161
Whitby, Thomas, 113–114
Widmer, Kathy, 72
Wilder, Thornton, 159, 161
Williams, Ev, 37
Winklevoss, Cameron, 159–161
Winklevoss, Tyler, 159–161
Wolff, Michael, 36, 38–40

Yu, Gideon, 168

Zabar, Rachel, 172
Zittrain, Jonathan, 189–190
Zuckerberg, Mark, 9, 13, 15, 22–24,
    33–34, 36–38, 91, 129–136, 159–
    162, 167–168, 171, 173–174, 187,
    193
Zuckerman, Ethan, 164

About the Editor

Writer and editor KENNETH PARTRIDGE has been with the HW Wilson Company since 2007—back when Facebook had yet to sign up its 100 millionth user, and My-Space was still the go-to spot for sharing embarrassing photos and subjecting friends to rambling blog posts about the trivialities of life. A Connecticut native and Boston University graduate, Partridge mostly uses social media to keep up with new music. He moonlights as a freelance rock journalist, and his work has appeared in the *Village Voice, USA Today*, the *Hartford Courant, M Magazine*, and AOL Music's Spinner site, among other publications. He lives with his wife and record collection—his two favorite things in the world—in Brooklyn, New York.